AGEING
Indian Perspective

Edited by
L. Thara Bhai

Decent Books
New Delhi

Published and printed by:
Decent Books
D-36/A-1, Mohan Garden
Najafgarh Road
New Delhi - 110 059

Distributed by:
D.K. Printworld (P) Ltd.
Regd. office : '*Sri Kunj*', F-52, Bali Nagar
New Delhi - 110 015
Phones : (011) 545-3975, 546-6019; *Fax* : (011) 546-5926
E-mail: dkprintworld@vsnl.net

ISBN 81-86921-19-2

First Published in India in 2002

Acknowledgements

WITH great pleasure I present this book to you as it gives me mixed feelings. One of my goals was to do an academic contribution to the old as they are today one of the crucial demographic and social category. Ageing and the aged are a concern of our country because they are unproductive, unhealthy, at the same time they are a vital demographic component.

I am indebted to many people especially Indian Council of Social Science Research and Madurai Kamaraj University who gave me financial support to conduct the seminar. Prof. M. Salihu the Vice-Chancellor gave me confidence and support to organise this seminar and later for publishing this work.

The authors of the various papers, without any pressure modified the paper twice to suit the publishers standard. I thank all the authors for giving the paper in time. The papers were scrutinised and retyped and the proofs were read by Ms. Suba Priya, Mr. L. Ganesan, Ms. L. Packiam, Mr. R. Sridhar, Ms. Sangeeth Ratha, Ms. B. Geetha, and Mr. Franklin. I sincerely place on record the services of these people. However the role of Ms. Suba Priya need a special mention for the time and energy spend by her to materialise this book.

I take this opportunity to thank the publisher who has done a good work in spite of the delay on my part to submit the manuscript in time.

I have great appreciation to my family members who encouraged me to take up these types of works.

30-11-2001 **L.Thara Bhai**

Contents

Section II
Problems and Prospects of the Old

Section III
Institutional Care of the Old

Introduction

P.K.B. Nair

THIS book is the outcome of a National Seminar on current issues in Ageing organised by Madurai Kamaraj University in late 1999 and contains selected papers presented there. Prof. L. Thara Bhai who organised the seminar is also the editor of this timely publication. The book is divided into five sections: Society and the Old, Problems and Prospects of the Old, Institutional Care of the Old, Gender Perspective and Ageing and Old Age Policies, spread over 26 well-arranged papers. The authors of the papers are known for their contributions to Gerontology. The papers are scholarly, well-researched and well-written.

The book opens up with a paper by the editor — Intergenerational Problems of the Old. In this paper, the author describes the traditional family support system extending over three generations and the threats faced by it from modernisation. The old are the worst victims of this change. This paper serves as a good prelude to the problem of ageing in its different dimensions.

In many cases, the problems of the old arise out of the lack of adjustment between generations, an aspect of generation gap involving old persons. This is brought out in the second paper by M. Thavamani who also offers a few solutions. T. Karunakaran describes the influence of environment on the elderly while D. Selvaraju and A. Murugan examine two critical aspects of the ageing, Interface: ageing expectations and society's responses. The authors point out that the growing demands of the ageing population need greater provision of social infrastructure. R. Sridharan points to the importance of religion in older years as a relief from old age stresses and strains. Kalarani Rengaswami stresses the importance of a comprehensive national policy for the old in the context of an increasing elderly population in the country. C.R.W. David's theme is whether old age is a calamity. He feels that it is not and given facilities for graceful living, old age could be made quite satisfying. D. Sivakumar points to the importance of people's participation in empowering families for the care of their elders. Many of the needs of older persons cannot be met by their families by themselves, but these have to be provided by the community and the state. Altogether this section of the book gives an overall picture of ageing in its various facets.

In Section II the problems and prospects of the old are portrayed in more specific terms. The need for an integrated approach to old age care is pointed out by B. Suguna and G. Sandhya Rani. Old age care should be the responsibility not only of the family but also of the community and the State. The leadership and integrative role has to be provided by the Government, the author's argue. This point is further endorsed by another author, R. Murthy, who feels that family support, counselling, community-oriented programmes and Government initiative are very important in old age care. R. Sankar in his analysis of the future of gerontology in India sees good prospect for the development of this branch of knowledge in India which has already produced a large body of research in social gerentology. Padma Mohanan in her study of 200 urban elders found that almost all of them experienced one or other form of neglect and 56 per cent were most frustrated due to lack of care. Usha Johns's paper has attempted to relate age with usual sociological variables and has come out with the following priority areas among ageing problems; health, nutrition, family, social welfare and living environment. Godse Jayasree reports the findings of a nutrition education programme. She found that lack of awareness regarding nutrition and health among the elderly and argues for a good nutrition education programme for healthy ageing. Joni C. Joseph analysed the three basic needs of a group of elderly persons living in slums and found that deprivation of psychological need was more severe than physical and social needs. The last paper in this section by C. Karuppiah focusses on the health problems and need of the elderly in a rural community and offers a few suggestions for solving them.

Institutionalisation is a growing area in elderly care and naturally, assumes importance in studies on ageing. For the destitute old, for those who have no care givers at home and for those with adjustment problems institutionalisation has been found to be a fairly good solution. The present volume devoted four paper for examining the different aspects of institutionalisation of the elderly. S. Irudayarajan reports the findings of a survey of old age homes in Kerala and throws light on the background and network systems of the inmates of old age homes and the factors behind their entry into the homes. L. Pakiam's paper on emerging alternate in caring for the aged gives some suggestions for improving the services in old age homes. I. Sobha, Vijaya Lakshmi Ramamohan and M.S.N. Reddy reporting about institutional care for the old addresses the question of the feasibility of old age homes as a substitute for traditional family old age security. J.J. Kattakayam's comparative study of elderly care by families and institutions in Kerala brings out many plus and minus points of old age homes. The common point that emerges from these papers is that old age homes are very useful in the changingcontext though they are only second best in elderly care.

Section IV of the book deals with the special problems of the old women. Their problems are not the same as those of old men. Gender discrimination, widowhood, poverty and longer period of misery due to longer life span make old age worse for women. Analysing these factors, N. Audinarayana, J. Sheela and N. Kavitha conclude that elderly women are the most deprived among the deprived. The paper also suggests some policy interventions. G. Sandhya Rani and B. Suguna follow similar lines, attempting to highlights the problems of aged women and suggest certain strategies to enable women to lead peaceful and comfortable life during their last years. The problems of old widows especially the several constraints on their autonomy by the family and society are brought to light by B. Dharmalingam and K.R. Murugan. Altogether this section points to the need for special attention by policy planners and welfare workers in the case of old women.

The fifth and final section of the book is devoted to old age policies. The paper by R. Mangayarkarasu deals with the old age policies and programmes in India and another paper by N. Saraswathy deals with a national policy for the welfare of the aged in India. Both papers give a general picture of old age policies and programmes in India, while the second paper additionally gives a few suggestions for inclusion in the national policy. M.S. Kitchlu's paper gives a description of old age programmes and policies in the Indian Railways. The good thing about this section of the book is that it points to the inadequacies in the existing programmes for the welfare of the old in India and the needed additional programmes which will contribute to the well-being of the rapidly growing ageing population of India.

Altogether the book promises to be a very good addition to the literature on ageing in India already expanded considerably by the stimulus received from the international year of older persons 1999. Though much of the primary data used in the different papers relate to south India, the finding of the empirical studies as well as other studies are quite relevant and pertinent to the whole country. This has been achieved largely by an imaginative and thoughtful selection of papers of macro level significance, their careful editing to ensure refinement and clarity and above all, the piecing together of the papers in a meaningful sequence. Prof. Thara Bhai, the editor deserves to be complemented for the happy blending of these virtues. I am sure that a perusal of the chapters of the book will give the reader delight and satisfaction. I have no doubt that the book will be quite useful to the academic community of gerontologists and to the general readers as well as planners and social workers.

Section I
Society and the Old

1

Intergenerational Problems of the Old

L. Thara Bhai

ELDERLY people are becoming one of the significant group in the society. The presence of elderly people in the demographic structure is not blended properly with the result that the elderly are becoming an isolated group requiring lot of attention from the general society. The number of 'elderly' or 'aged' or 'old' are increasing day by day in our population and their dependency on society are also increasing giving problems to the old as well as to the society. Most of the societies are not geared enough to welcome the old and therefore the aged are not given a permanent position either by the society or by the institutions which are caring them.

The aged in the society are the people who have given their resources to the society and when their resources are eroded they are pushed back by the society to the periphery. This problem of the old are realised by the old whereas it is not understood properly by the society. Usually the care givers do not realise the services rendered by the old to the society and to the family and treat them as people who are of no use in the present-day society.

There is lot of communication problem between the old and the young that interdependence between the generations are becoming a undesired, purposeful relationship. The young and the old do not conceive the idea that they belong to the same system. The intergenerational bond is missing in almost all the communities which is necessary for the continuity of life (Friedan 1993). The interrelationship between the generations are necessary for a balanced society. The roles of the old and the young are complementary to each other and the equilibrium of the society depends very much on recognising the various roles played by the respective actors (Parsons 1968). The various generations who form the kinship structures of the society is a system by its own and the mutual adaptation between the elements of this system is essential for the well-being of the society. Though total adaptation is not possible, partial adaptation is essential for the stability and continuity of the social system. Interrelationship between the kin groups vertically and horizontally affect the people in different ways, but interrelationship between the vertical kin groups should be keenly observed in order to avoid the imbalances in the society. Radcliff Brown observes that most the relationships are institutionalised according to the normative system of the respective societies (Radcliff Brown 1964, 1952). In kinship groups, the relationship is based on supports the people get from one another. Social relationships and interactions are largely based on support systems derived from the society especially from the primary group relations.

Support system is the major criteria of individual relationship in all the social institutions. During the younger days individuals support each other as the resources are plenty with them and as the age increases the support will be withdrawn as the resources are diminished during this time. The old age see withdrawal of supports from many directions which will tilt the balance of the person and tend to change their attitudes towards the various pivotal elements of the family.

The systems which were giving the supports also changes their attitude and hence the whole support system get a reshaping and remoulding during the old age. Though Betty Friedan repeatedly warned that grey power should be used to solve the issues of the young, most of the societies discard the gray power thinking that their wisdom is not suitable to solve the modern problems (Kuhn, 1993). Though this is the common feature of every society, the relationship between the old and the young is largely depending upon the support they mutually extend to each other. In this type of support system a consensus approach is required whereas it is not seen in many of the societies.

The intergeneration problems are common in all the societies and this will be the number one problem in the world in the coming years (Kalache 1994). The old and the young do not participate simultaneously in the societies which will create problems which neither the old nor the young nor the society can solve easily. The support which are given and taken are to be well balanced and should be recognised by each other so that the care giving and care providing will become meaningful. M.S. Gore says that care giving largely depends upon the support system as caring is inspired by the material or the non-material support the young derived from the old (Gore 1992).

Gore rightly pointed out that one of the fundamental needs of old age is to find a meaningful social role so that people who are near the elderly get a kind of support from these people which will enhance the status of the old from the perspective of the young. The support system of the young and the old have various dimensions as 'support' is a general term used to understand the relationship between the young and the old.

Support can be broadly understood as the resources available to the young and the old which are used by both in the day-to-day activities or otherwise for the physical and the mental satisfaction of the young as well as the old. There are two types of supports for elderly. One is the material and the other one is the non-material. The material support is largely depending upon the financial contribution of the old towards the young and vice versa whereas the non-material support is the support the young and the old derive from each other for their physical and the social comforts like companionship, visiting, spending leisure, health, etc.

It is generally observed that both the young and the old seek support from each other but the amount and nature of the support derived were not known as most of these support are unaccountable in nature.

In India, old age was not a problem till recently as there were institutionalised norms to look after the old. The intergenerational conflicts are a new phenomenon in India as the normative system of India has undergone lot of changes in the recent times. Changes in social structure, preponderance of individualistic and materialistic values, attitudes of younger generations towards the old are some of the contributory factors for the intergenerational problems (Misra 1991). In the present-day society old has changed their attitude completely and the world-view has accordingly changed but these changes are not well taken by the younger generations. The consequences of these changes are the changing support systems of the young and the old. Support system which were prevailing in the traditional Indian society were mostly confined to the family, village and caste. But today the support system have a wider network extending from the financial support to the peer group and the neighbourhood support. The various supports of the old and the young are in a hierarchy and hence it is termed as support system. Support system vary from one society to another depending upon the culture and therefore one can say that support system is culturally maintained and culturally emerged. The aged in rural and urban India have an entirely different support system. Shabeen Ara investigated the friendship nature of the aged persons and observed that the male and the female are having different types of friendship network in the urban areas (Ara 1994). Likewise support system also changes depending upon the socio-economic background of the old people. The support system of the old is a continuation of the youth, the adult and the later adult life and this continues in the old age also. The elderly population is a continuation of the youth and the middle age and therefore his or her support system is also a continuation of the younger years (Sen 1994).

Social changes in the society affects elderly population also. Traditionally Indian aged is not an isolated group. As they grew old, the support system of the old shrink down giving very little opportunity for the elderly population to maintain their already developed personality. In one way, we can say that social ageing is always associated with disengagement (Cumings and Henry 1961). During this time, there will be a restructuring of the support system to suit the new environment. In India disengagement and 'thinking out' of the old population is of special interest because the dominant theological system of Hinduism contains a culturally prescribed model of disengagement for the older people. However, the old builds their own support system taking into account their needs or requirements, mental and social make up, socio-economic background, etc. *In this context it is worth analysing the support system of elderly which reveal their interests, preferences and requirements.* With this main objective this study was initiated. The study covers the following points also:

1. To identify the major support systems of the old within and outside the family.
2. To find out the criteria of choosing the support system by the elderly.
3. To find out the reciprocal relations in terms of support systems.
4. To study the hierarchy of support system of the elderly.
5. To find out the differential support systems of male and the female elderly.

Methodology

Pluralistic characteristics of Indian society is seen in all spheres and categories of society including the old. As the studies covering whole India is impossible, one state is taken for the present study, viz., Kerala.

The State of Kerala lies in the southern tip of Indian penisula with all the features of the Indian subcontinent with little variations. Social structure of Kerala is a little different from rest of the country with the presence of the dominant caste (Srinivas 1962) and their influence on the other layers of the population. Influence of Westernisation especially English education quickened the process of social change in the State giving a new shape to the various social institutions like family, religion, economy, polity, etc. Changes in the family brought out the changes in the structural and functional relationships within the family. One of the important social relationship that affected due to these changes is the position of the old in the family and their network and the support system. In fact, they lost their upper position in the family because their status in the family is determined by their contributory power in the family. In most of the families of Kerala, the care giver-care receiver relationship have taken a new turn in the context of increased migration of people from Kerala to other parts of the country or world, women going for work and a new outlook towards life (Nayar 1987). These changes forced the aged to switch over to new support system which are available in societies. This phenomenon is very true in the cities and therefore it is decided to study the aged in the city in terms of their support system.

Thiruvananthapuram city is taken as the universe of the study from where four residential areas were selected for the study. From each residential area a sample household of 100 were selected on the basis of the aged in the household. The old population were selected in such a way that sample included at least two generations of the old population. Though the concentration of the study is the old population their caretakers are also studied as the support system should be viewed in a holistic way. Support system is mutually functional and therefore the aged and their care givers were taken for the study.

As the support system was a new terminology in social gerontology, this study conceptualised the term from the existing literature. Support system contains within it the structural and functional elements required for the person to adapt to the environment in the best possible manner. For this study the system analysis of Radcliff Brown and Parsons in the context of social roles were taken which goes very well in the studies of this kind. Cummings and Henry's disengagement and thinning out theories are also taken to analyse the support system of the old people.

Three classes of the old people are taken for analysis, the young old (60-70 years), middle old (70-80 years) and the old old (80 years and above) on the basis of this socio-economic status. Data were mainly collected through an interview schedule, though many times it changed itself to in-depth interviews. The data were analysed on the basis of age and sex. In order to find out the preference of various support system ranking is done giving single score for a single response. This method enabled to find out the positions of the various support systems according to the individual preferences.

Major support system of the elderly

Aged are an increasing dependent group and the correlation between support system and the aged determines the social and physical well-being of them. Most of the aged have to face loss of their spouse during the old age which is a shock for them because that was the main support they had during their life. This study show that only 36.0 per cent of the sample have their spouse living. Interestingly in the sample population 82 per cent of the old-old are living with the spouse, whereas only 23 per cent of the middle old and 44 per cent of the young old live with their respective spouses. 90 per cent of the respondents said that the death of the husbands or wives was a major shock in their life as they were too much dependent on them for physical needs are as well as for emotional needs. The socio-economic background of the respondents reveal that 59.67 per cent of the old people had self-employment during their younger years.

In Kerala, the dominant caste namely the Nairs were following the matriarchal culture till recently. The impact of the matriarchal culture is seen in the present-day society also. Unlike other parts of India, aged in Kerala prefers to stay with their daughters and not with their sons. Majority of the respondents (49 per cent) stay with their daughters rather than their sons. 58 per cent of the old, 51 per cent of the middle old and 45 per cent of the young old live with their daughters whereas only 26 per cent of the old and 23 per cent of the middle old and 10.67 per cent of the young old live with their sons. There are many aged who are either living alone or live with other kinship relations. In this sample itself there are 16 per cent of the old people who are above 80 years live with other kinship relatives such as brothers, grandsons, granddaughters, etc. Given an option, majority of the old people prefers to stay with their daughters rather then with their sons.

Table 1: Respondents preference of stay

Respondents	*Sons*	*Daughters*	*Others*	*Total*
60-70	32 (10.67%)	67 (22.33%)	51 (17%)	150 (50%)
70-80	23 (7.67%)	51 (17.0%)	26 (8.67%)	100 (33.33%)
80 +	113 (4.33%)	29 (9.67%)	8 (2.67%)	50 (16.67%)
Total	68 (22.66%)	147 (49%)	85 (28.33%)	300 (100.06%)

It is interesting to note that the data reveal that both the male and female aged depend on their daughters or daughters-in-law for receiving their care. Major care givers in the family are the women members and the aged prefers women members for the care giving (Kattakayam 1997). At the same time for 'emergencies' the aged depend on their sons or close male consanguinal kins. All the respondents, both male and the female said for financial crisis, health crisis or other such family crisis, in spite of the fact that they are staying with their daughters or other female consanguineous kin, they call their sons or other male consanguine kin. From this one can feel that the attitude of the old towards the male and the female are different. Females are considered as care givers whereas the males are considered as 'providers'.

The importance of family as the care giving institution continues even in the present-day society. In India, family is the main institution where everybody prefers to live in families rather than the other institutions. 94.66 per cent of the young old, 89 per cent of the middle old and 76 per cent of the old-old preferes to live in families rather than outside agencies. On the whole, 90 per cent of the old say that they prefer in family because they like to stay with their relatives and in a culture which is known to them. Though they prefer to live with the families, for moral support they go to neighbourhood or to their relatives. It is found that 34 per cent of the old who falls in the age group of 60-70 depends upon their neighbours for consultation and to build-up their confidence. 19 per cent of the old-old in the same age group go to their relatives for moral support. Quite a few of the old of this group depend upon their friends for moral support. 38 per cent of the people, who fall between 70-80 years believe in their immediate families for moral support, but 26 per cent of the old of this group have confidence on their neighbours and 19 per cent have confidence on their relatives. For confidential talks old people mainly depend upon their neighbours. It is found that the confidential talks are very little among the old and whatever they want to talk, they go to their neighbours or to their friend. Only 12 per cent of the young old 9 per cent of the middle old and 7 per cent of the old-old depends on their family members for confidential talks. 17.67 per cent of the young old go to their neighbourhood for confidential talks for spending leisure, and many old find companions in the neighbourhood. Observations during interviews showed that the old people get friendship easily from their neighbourhood. Their friends include not only the old people, but the young and even the children. 54.67 per cent of the old-old people spend their leisure with neighbours and 40 per cent of the young old, 18 per cent of the middle old and 2 per cent of the old-old spend their leisure with the friends. As mentioned earlier, neighbours and friends are only peripheral support system and the main support system for the elders are their family. This is inferred from the fact that for emergencies the aged believe only their immediate families. 69 per cent of the respondents said that they go to their immediate families when there is a crisis for them. This is true with old people irrespective of their socio-economic background. 69 per cent of the old between 60-70 years, 73 per cent of the old between 70-80 years and 74 per cent of the old above 80 years are of the same opinion. For medical support also they confined themselves to their familial members.

From the analysis in Table 2, it is clearly known that the main support system of the aged in India is the family. The scores of the present study is highest for the family followed by neighbourhood, relatives and friends. Indian society is still family oriented society and therefore the aged prefers family rather than any other institutions.

Table 2 : Pivotal support system

Situations	*Support Systems*					
	Immediate Family			*Neighbourhood*		
	60-70	70-80	80+	60-70	70-80	80+
Living	142 (47.33%)	89 (29.67%)	38 (12.67%)	1 (0.33%)	3 (1.0%)	2 (0.66%)
Moral Support	40 (13.33%)	38 (12.67%)	29 (9.67%)	51 (17.0%)	26 (8.67%)	21 (17.0%)
Confidential	36 (12.0%)	27 (9.0%)	21 (7.0%)	53 (17.67%)	23 (7.67%)	18 (6.0%)
Spending Leisure	21 (7.0%)	22 (7.33%)	5 (1.67%)	49 (16.33%)	40 (13.33%)	35 (11.67%)
Emergencies	97 (32.33%)	73 (24.33%)	37 (12.33%)	22 (7.33%)	20 (6.67%)	7 (2.33%)
Physical Concepts	63 (21.0%)	36 (12.0%)	24 (6.0%)	57 (19.0%)	42 (14.0%)	26 (8.67%)
Medical Support	111 (37.0%)	78 (26.0%)	38 (12.67%)	21 (7.0%)	10 (3.33%)	12 (4.0%)
Total Score	510	363	192	254	164	121
		1065			539	

Factors determining support system

Major factors determining the support system are affinity, care giving, prestige, etc. Social network of the old people depends upon the roles they play in their living environment. Support system of the old people changes according to the social relationship they develop during that time. Usually family support system, kinship support system, friendship support system and neighbourhood support system are seen among the old people among which the old people consider one or two very close to them as they depend on them mostly. The aged select the support system mainly on the basis of care giving and care providing basis. The criteria for the male and the female differs as their approach to life differs from one and another. Female consider affinity or affection as the most important criteria for choosing the support system as family is the main support system here. Affection plays an important role to live.

34 per cent of the women say that affection is the main criteria in choosing the main support system namely the family whereas 19 per cent of the women say that it is the companionship which attracted them to the family in which they live. 30 per cent of the women choose the present living because they like care giving in those families. For the old male population, more than affection and companionship there are other factors like prestige, rights and care giving for choosing the present living environment. However, it is found that 29 per cent of the old male choose the present support system because of the care giving system whereas 22.6 per cent choose the present families due to prestige. A keen observation show that old male feel that going elsewhere is below their dignity and therefore they stay along with their daughters or sons. For both male and the female, tradition and money are not important for choosing their support system. From the above, one can understand that as a person become old, they require affection and care giving than anything else. When affinity was one of the important criteria for old women, care giving is an important criteria for both men and women. 29.41 per cent of the male and 30 per cent of the female say that care giving is the main criteria for choosing the present residence. Money was one of the least criteria for respondents in choosing their residence.

It is determined that family is the main support system in the present study. In the family the old mainly depend upon women for their requirements.

It is found that 77.76 per cent of the respondents depend upon women for their everyday living. Though many respondents said that they depend upon their sons as care giver in emergency they prefer women in the family. Various studies have proved that women are the main structural component of the family support system.

Table 3 : Important individual of main support system

Respondent	Women	Men	Children	Others	Total
60-70	111 (37%)	25 (8.33%)	4 (1.33%)	10 (3.33%)	150 (50%)
70-80	89 (29.67%)	8 (2.67%)	— —	3 (1.00%)	100 (33.33%)
80+	33 (11.00%)	11 (3.67%)	2 (0.66%)	4 (1.33%)	50 (16.67%)
Total	233 (77.67%)	44 (14.67%)	6 (2.0%)	17 (5.67%)	300 (100%)

Other support systems

Apart from the main support system, there are the other support systems for the elders namely peer group, neighbourhood, institutionalised religion, kins other than families or relatives. It is already mentioned (Table 2) that neighbourhood, relatives and friends forms the other support systems of the elderly people. Among these, neighbourhood, religion and relatives form other important support systems. Peer groups are also one of the support systems of the elderly. Though there is little contradiction in the responses of the old people regarding other support systems, they agree that neighbourhood and religion form two important support systems of the old people. Regarding the relatives, they give different answers. In the first instance, they did not give much importance to relatives whereas later when relatives were combined with neighbourhood, religion and peer group relatives were placed at high esteem. This may be due to the reason that in the first instance when the relatives were combined with family, they have not considered relatives as important as family members.

One can infer that other support systems of the elderly people are relatives, neighbourhood, religion and peer group. Peer group are ranked last in both the instances by the old. Peer group are a rare phenomena as they shift their residence from their younger days to the older days. Now coming to the male and the female option of the support system, for the females, it is the relatives who give the main support. Religion is the second support for the females and the relatives become second for the males. The following table gives a clear picture of the relationship between the elderly and the supporting system.

Supporting system and the elderly of Kerala

Main Support System ——→ Family

Other Support Systems

Male	Female
1. Peer Group	1. Relatives
2. Relatives	2. Religion
3. Neighbourhood	3. Neighbourhood
4. Religion	4. Peer Group

Alternative support systems

In India, alternative support system for the elderly are not a common feature. State care, insitutional care or community care are not a common feature. Therefore the old do not respond much as far as alternative support systems are concerned. Even after repeated insights the old people were not able to give completely various dimensions of alternative support systems. State care is not well understood by the elders so also the community care. The respondents of this study feel that the state care and the community care are for the poorer section of population and therefore only 7.67 per cent of the old prefers state care and 13.33 per cent do not have any hesitation for community care. 3.66 per cent of the old say that if they don't have immediate family members, they prefer staying with people who are related to them in one way or the other. There is no difference between the male and the female regarding the alternative support system.

Conclusion

Support system of the elderly is the boundary of social relationship.

Aged are not to be considered as an isolated group or as a marginal group because it is during the old age they need considerable support from the family as well as from the society. Radcliffe Brown and Parsons specifically say that social roles determine the personality of the individual and as the social role expands there is chances of developing the personality whereas shrinking of social roles marginalise the individual. Cummings and Henry developed the disengagement and the thinking out theory from the shrinking of the social roles. The present study confirms that the old have very few social roles as their position is marginalised in most of the families. The present study show that main support system of the aged in Kerala is either the family or the family members. The kinship bond is so strong and the residence the old people chose is mainly on the basis of affection and love. The other support systems which the aged consider important are relatives, religion and neighbourhood. As far as these support systems are concerned, it is not the affection which is the main criteria but the emotional satisfaction or these systems are considered as a let out for their anger, jealousy, authority, wisdom, intelligence, etc. Religion is considered as one of the supporting systems as the old meets their spiritual satisfaction there.

The aged accepts various supporting systems but state care and the community care are not acceptable for them. Institutional care is also not preferred by the elderly of Kerala. The first and the foremost preference is the family.

Reference

Ara, Shabeen, 1994, *Old Age among Slum Dwellers*, New Delhi, South Asian Publishers.

Cummings, E. and W.E. Henry, 1961, *Youngster and Old, The Process of Disengagement*, New York: Basic Books.

Friedan, Betty, 1993, *The Fountain Age*, Vintage.

Gore, M.S., 1992, 'Ageing and the Future of the human being', *Indian Journal of Social Work*, vol. LIII,2.

Kalache, Alex, 1994, From Kasthuri Sen, *Ageing — Debates on Demographic Transition and Social Policy*, Zaid Press.

Kattakayam, John, 1997, 'Care giving' — New challenge to the Indian families', Paper presented at the XXIVth All India Sociological Conference, Hyderabad,

Kuhn Maggy From Friedan Betty, *op. cit.*

Misra, Saraswathi, 1991, 'Emergence and Solution of the old age problem' in *Proceedings and Recommendation of National Workshop* in Pitha Maha Sava Rawa, Chinmaya Seva Trust.

Nair, P.K.B., 1987, 'Ageing and sociology, the care of the Developing Countries', *Social Welfare'*, 34 (2), May 2.3.38; 34(2) of use: 28-31.

Parsons, Talcott, 1968, *The Structure of Social Action*, vol.1. Free Press.

RadCliffe, Brown A.R., 1964, *A Natural Science of Society*, Free Press.

———, 1952, *Structure and Functions in Primitive Society*, Cohen and West.

Sen, Kasthuri, 1994, *Ageing — Debates on Demographic Transition and Social Policy*, Zaid Press.

Srinivas, M.N., 1962, *Caste in Modern India*.

2

Adjustment Problem of the Old with Younger Generation

M. Thavamani

Introduction

INDIAN society attains social progress in terms of health and increase in the life span of people. As a result the proportion of aged is increasing and witnessing new social problems. In spite of the improvements in health, retirement benefits and old age pension, the aged has separate world-view, and problems in adjusting with younger generation. This paper highlights a few of them. Very often we come across with the cases of aged that are neglected by the younger generation. They seek refuge in old age home or live alone by employing servants and in some cases taking care of themselves. In any case a human being living alone without the help of relatives is very painful and the degree of pain will be more for those who already lived productively, but now an idle life.

Studies on aged

1. Rao and Parthasarathi highlighted eight factors influencing the adjustment after retirement. They are type of job, health, income, family, purpose in life, attitude towards work, social interaction and activity. They have mentioned 'eight essential for good adjustment'. They are:

   (a) Living within physical limitations.

   (b) Adjusting to a lower income level.

(c) Achieving security in medical care without sacrificing economic security.

(d) Expressing one's self-creativity.

(e) Extending family love to the brotherhood of man.

(f) Retaining personal dignity in society.

(g) Maintaining self-interest.

(h) Passing on torch to next generation. (Rao and Parthasarathy October 1999).

2. Durairaj and Kala Rani Rengaswamy have identified the following remedies:

(a) An action plan by the Government.

(b) Documentation of gender and age groups in rural and urban areas.

(c) Retraining of the elderly for gainful employment, voluntary activities and leisure.

(e) Government subsidies for NGOs to look after the old.

(f) Establishment of family counselling centres.

(g) Sensitisation of younger generation through mass media.

(h) Midday meal scheme. (Durairaj and Kala Rani Rengaswamy October 1999).

3. Asim Bardhan very boldly proposes a few ideas to cope up with retirement life. He is of the opinion that in life it is the quality that is all important and we should look at capabilities and not count the wrinkles. Boredom should have no place in retirement and he suggests that one should involve in hobbies and other creative activities which are enjoyable by themselves. For him life begins at sixty! It is type of life-style! (Bardhan', Asim October 1999).

4. Professor M.Z. Khan admits the fact that the aged in rural areas continue to engage in economically gainful work. For

this, he identifies two basic causes. One is work habit and the other is economic compulsion. He also compares the western concept of health with that of Indian and concludes that the concept of health is culturally determined. Leisure time activities and group activities are encouraged in West as part of their culture. Indian society is bound with illness with stoicism. Similarly malnutrition is not recognised as a problem in India (M.Z. Khan 1996).

Conflict of world -views

WORLD-VIEWS OF DIFFERENT AGE GROUPS

Conflict between old and young is not a conflict of individuals but of two different world-views. This world-view can be equated with ideas, style of living, working pattern, habits and peer group influence. Accordingly each group believes what they do is right and maintains the same. Thus world-view is associated with specific age group. In other words the world-view of college-going students is liberal, flexible, enjoyment oriented which is not the same of middle-age group. One may find a few middle-aged individuals having the similarity of college-going students but these do not form the middle-aged syndrome. They either share the values with the youngsters or prepared to live in the same world-view. However, the judgement cannot be given either as a less matured or more matured because that depends how do they contribute towards the harmony or disharmony of the society.

Following this, the changes in the family correspondingly affect the balance of world-views. The main bread winner of a family usually dominate the other world-views of the family. Sometimes the numerical preponderous of a particular age group will establish its world-view and therefore there are conflict of world-views.

The world-view of one age group always differ from the other. A meaningful life for an adult is to undertake a job for the purpose of feeding himself and dependent if any. In the present-day world employment opportunities are not readily available on the one hand and it is also competitive in nature. As a result those who achieve it are treated with a higher respect than those who could not achieve. There is no social mechanism which encourages the affected. Therefore, any job that fetches him or her a huge salary or power or at least job satisfaction guarantees the specific world-view for the individual adult.

A meaningful life for middle age person is to bring up responsible children and get them settled properly in their life. At this point of time the goal is not fetching a job but to establish himself/herself as a responsible parent. Therefore his primordial loyalties differ from the previous stage. Now he is immediately tied with his offspring. many a time the world-view revolves around with the individual's spouse and children, immediate neighbours rather than the first relatives. Thus the world-view has a change from an adult to a middle aged person.

A meaningful life for an older person is the social recognition and getting respect from the younger generation. At this point of time he/she looses the control and contact on the things which are already explained namely job, children, etc. More precisely when they lead a retired life their mind is totally free to operate, and therefore whatever they expect may not exactly correlate with the existing reality which is dominated by other individuals and world-views. The problem starts here. The world-view differs. More often the manifestation of the form of respect, and the form of recognition are not the same for younger generation. Again the world-view is not the same for all classes of aged.

WORLD-VIEW OF AGED

An aged agriculturalist expects the younger generation, to seek for his/her approval for any action in life. The world-view of the aged agriculturists revolves around the system of joint endeavours, unity among individuals, absence of disparity among the family members, irrespective of education (qualification), job, earnings, savings, power, etc. The prime importance is always to be given to the aged — their health, their food, their hobbies, their friends, their philosophy of household goods and living. But the mismatchings occurs when the younger generation shifts from agricultural background to non-agricultural set-up, say for example: an officer be it a lady of gentleman his/her role as an officer may not fit into the world-view of an older person who is still living in agricultural background. The necessities arouse out of the new set-up and the corresponding world-view about the health, food, household goods, living and friendship are different and therefore it comes into conflict within the family. If the older person is already accustomed to the official set-up then he may partially understand the role of the younger generation. But still there would be some areas which may not exactly correlate and fit the mental framework of the older person. These misfiting areas are associated with the changing working conditions, the changing human relations in official settings and the changing type of work as well. For example: the role of a computer programmer is beyond the imagination of an agriculturalist or businessman who does not have any idea about computer. These mismatchings also have its repercussions among all age groups, but will have more effect between the older and younger generation rather than within generation. Unless this conflict in world-views is tackled, the aged will have psychological problems.

Normative conflicts

ECONOMIC DIMENSION

The aged expect a share of time and money from younger generation as a matter of right. There is no accepted framework or rules in this aspect. In some families the aged take care of the total budget whereas in some other families a stipulated amount is given to the expenditure of the old. However, there is no clear-cut picture is available. Their claim is they are responsible for the creation of younger generation. The counterargument from the younger generation is the aged should help them for the youngsters in their career development. Building a career is not so simple as in the past because it necessitates help from many individuals (social), expenditure — deposit, bribe, subscription, gift, (economic), influence/recommendation (power). The youngsters totally depend on their elders to play the role of godfather — social, economic and political manipulations. Since the life in the external world is competitive and they need extra energy and extra time to be contributed by the elders. Thus, there is a conflict of expectations. This problem is to be solved amenably.

ENJOYING THE LIFE

The aged wants to be always in rest as they are physically weak and worn out. They say the youngsters do not help them to enjoy their remaining days. But the counterargument is the youngsters are in their productive life and therefore need more time for their self-enjoyment, in married and family (with children) life. Here comes the conflict of who has more right to enjoy the life. This is very meticulous and complicated issue. There is no written law or established value system which says who has more right to be idle and enjoy and who has a lesser right. More often this has to be understood in terms of the necessity of the concerned individuals. The moment when it becomes a point of argument/debate then it is an endless war (of course there will be an end only when either of them die). An adjustment problem of an aged with middle-aged, middle-aged with children and aged with grandchildren occurs. This aspect is to be analysed carefully and a new social order may be evolved. This social order should pick-up the situations and accordingly present a set of solutions which may be encompassed both by law and by custom.

FAMILY POLITICS

The third aspect is a crucial one which involves more decision-making, policy oriented, involving 'family politics'. Family politics here means the politics within the family and not family in the politics. This refers to the historical syndromes of mother-in-law and daughter-in-law exerting influence on the son-cum-husband; between sisters-in-law, between brothers, between sisters, etc. Here it essentially means the politics between different age groups. The aged expect that others do not have much wisdom in planning their life and therefore oblige the wishes of aged and thus all policy decisions are to be made by them, therefore, what they think right is the ideal one. According to them, the youngster are too sensitive to luxury, attracted by worldly things and may commit a mistake emotionally. The counterargument by the younger generation is they are denied to have what is modern and therefore judged inferior by the fellow workers. If they follow the norms and wisdom of aged, then they become helpless and restless. The result is might is right' i.e., youngster succeed in ejecting the elders from the family set-up. In other words, it is a survival of the youngest (the fittest) and the failure of elders. This politics is to be broken through scientific analysis of various situations, events, sentiments and harmony oriented actions.

CULTURAL DIMENSION

It is also abstract but crucial this dimension deals with the ethics, morality, etiquette and as a whole we may call it as cultural dimension. This dimension always irritate the elders of any given period due to the changes in the dressing style, food pattern, making use of modern gadgets (like scooter, washing machine, grinder, mixie, vacuum cleaner), self-test of health, self-medication, moving with other people, entertaining visitors, cleanliness of the home, religious affairs, caring for children, etc. Very often we find the informal chatting between elders revolve around the 'culture-less-ness' of the youngsters; similarly the burning issues of youngsters always related to the 'cultural over sensitiveness of elders'. This is another form of 'cultural lag' perhaps.

Supremacy of whom

The following controversial questions are often posed either by aged or by youngsters, and end with conflict:

(a) *Who has more right to live in this world? — Young or old:* Every time when there is a conflict between old and young in sharing the scarce resources of the family, the emerging questions are who does contribute and who has the right to consume? As a result each establishes the right of living in this world by knocking out the other.

(b) *Who has more right to enjoy the existing facilities? — Young or old*: Once again if the facilities are available in plenty then there is no question of exercising the right. Otherwise conflict emerge in making use of the various facilities (cot, table fan, use of electricity, bathroom, nutritious food, costly medicine, new dresses, transportation and communication, etc).

(c) *Who is to be given importance? — Old men or women*: This reflects the typical *'innocent husband syndrome'* in which the young wife claims more attention than the parents of the husband. The husband always in a critical condition (coma) of solving the problem between old men and women.

(d) *Who is to be more powerful? — Mother of the husband or wife*: This is also a typical syndrome existing in all families. Who has the power of deciding the purchase, attending functions, savings, dealing with property, caring for household goods, pets and children.

Experiments may be conducted to ease these situations by applying various strategies. However, the spirit of equality may be culturally injected so that nobody would claim for supremacy.

Expectations and honouring contracts

Human relations are to be carefully established by giving importance to the desires, ambitions and expectations. It is very difficult to understand the momentary feelings of individuals but it is possible to create a favourable attitude about a particular phenomenon. Usually the old and the children have stubborn stand in their aspirations and it is the duty of the middle-aged to respond them according to their expectations. There are psychological contracts which are untold and unwritten. The wife not only depends the husband but also accommodate the strength and weakness of the husband and is expected to keep them in safe custody. Similarly the husband is the custodian of his wife's ideas, strength and weakness. Therefore, both of them has to honour each other for the psychological contract. In case, if this contract is broken knowingly or unknowingly then that damages the relationship between them. The same logic is also extended to various psychological contracts between age old parents and middle-aged offspring's, middle-aged parents and young offsprings. Some of the reported psychological contracts are as follows:

(a) Young offspring's being afraid of examinations and seek the help of parents to come to their protection as if the children are sick or showing some other reasons without hurting by way of disclosing the truth to the teachers.

(b) The aged parents in spite of the prohibition from sweets, tend to consume without the knowledge of those who are concerned with their health (doctor, daughter-in-law, son, etc.).

(c) Monetary helps within the siblings without the knowledge of their spouses.

(d) Middle-aged offsprings hide the secrecy of the weakness of their parents (drinking, etc.), from the outside world.

Cultural movements can be initiated to accept each others expectations and honour the unwritten social and psychological contracts mutually.

Self-esteem

Old age is said to be second childhood. They need to be recognised very often, their special needs are to be attended and above all their self-esteem is to be maintained. Human civilisation has developed in many dimensions such as education, science and technology but yet to achieve a major dimension namely *'respecting other human beings'* even if they are children. The importance of an individual should not diminish at any cost. In the real world, retired people are often neglected, their self-esteem is ignored and their presence is insulted. This also need a social backing to establish the modern human values of accommodating senior as well as junior citizens to be held in high esteem. There is no room for hierarchy among individuals of a family. The self-esteem of any individual should have a limit to that extent of not affecting the self-esteem of other individual.

Leisure time activities

With the increasing specialisation and mechanisation people are isolated and therefore the senior citizens are left alone. This enables them to live in the past, indulge in nostalgic remembrances. Because of their non-productive living, they feel bored which leads to psychological depression. Feeling of boredom can be met with creative and easy leisure time activities. Social events should be arranged periodically for meeting others and enjoying through getting together. These may be social as well as technical like handicrafts, computer, computer designing, etc. Institutional co-ordination may be extended to these activities in arranging all facilities. Apart from the regular activities the educational institutions may engage in conducting functions in praise of senior citizens — senior farmers, retired officials, members of old age home, couples without children — periodically. Similarly institutional arrangements are necessary for aged to live with some others in the form of paying- guests. The Government can also think of designing employment programmes to suit the aged. The rich experience of the aged should be channallised for maximising the welfare and minimising failure/damage.

Attitudinal change

The society must develop some of the following attitudes:

(a) *It is sweet to become old*: Older persons need not be morose. They only can mend the misdeeds of youngsters. They only have the power of endurance. They need not be guilty for unwanted happenings and they need not worry for anything except enjoying the life. Their motto should be, being sweet and making others happy.

(b) *It is fortunate to associate with an aged*: Very often aged consider to be burden but it is not so. One should learn to enjoy the company of aged. Whether it is travel (bus or train), sharing the neighbourhood, organising a function and so on, the association with the aged will definitely be useful, and enjoyable. This value system is yet to be developed and popularised.

(c) *Adjustment is the best virtue*: This is applicable not only for the theme of this paper but also to be kept as general for all human situations. Both groups — aged and young — should learn to adjust within the framework so that the aggregate result should be positive for both groups. Otherwise smaller breaches will end up in bigger gaps and thus lead to irreparable damages.

(d) *Living with different age group is the charm of life*: Heterogenity need to be habitualised as it has varieties. A homogeneous group can no doubt share the similar attitudes and behaviours within its members, but a hetrogeneous group will have more to share because that is the challenge of life. Therefore, living with different age group is to be encouraged, patronised, institutionalised. The charm of moving with different age group is entirely different because it doesn't have jealous, sabotage, betrayal and revenge. Instead it would be more protective, promotive, efficient and enjoyable.

New research

(a) How do adjustment problem differ in various settings — urban, semi-urban, rural and family in general.

(b) Training modules for aged to cope up with changes in life. New strategies.

(c) Case studies and monographs on aged.

Conclusion

The dawn of new millennium will definitely have many social problems like organised terrorism, AIDS, and problem of aged. Capitalist oriented values may increase and human relations may become commercial as Alvin Toffeler names 'Pro-father' and 'Pro-child'. In spite of these changes, social scientists should make their effort to fill up this vacum and set the society in order.

References

Bardhan, Asim, 'Life Begins At Sixty', Social Welfare, vol. 46, No. 7, October 1999.

Durairaj, N. and Kala Rani, Rengaswamy, The Aged: Need love and Protection Social Welfare, vol. 46, No. 7, October,1999.

Khan, M.Z., *Voluntary Welfare Services for the Aged*, New Delhi: Anmol Publications Pvt. Ltd., 1996.

Rao, V.N. and R. Parthasarathy, 'Coping with retired life Needs new Attitude', Social Welfare, vol. 46, No. 7, October1999.

Toffler, Alvin, *Future Shock*.

3

The Influence of Environment on Later Life

T. Karunakaran

THE impact of environment on animals and humans is quite obvious. As far as human beings are concerned environment is found to affect the health, psychological well-being and even the behaviour. The notion of environmental impact is neither new nor novel. Sociologists who engage in the field of environment conducted researches pertaining to environmental effect on human health. All the living being in this planet interact with their environment. Because of their interaction a reciprocal influence takes place between the individual and the environment. The individual is influenced by the environment and in the same way the environment influences the individual. Though the other living beings also influence the environment, only the human beings are capable to create a substantial environment. They also have the power to refurnish the environment. The refurnishing of environment is for the benefit of providing a satisfactory living condition.

The environmental problems we face nowaday are caused by effluents which are released into the natural setting. The consequence of the unplanned growth of industries is environmental pollution. When people become predominantly urban creatures, the quality of the environment also will be affected. The urban environment can be distinguished from the rural environment as it is the product of nature. Urban environment is created by the people and it involves the physical, social, economical, political and institutional features of life support systems.

The high birth rate and the flow of rural poor into metropolitan areas are reasons for the swelling of urban population. The staggering growth of urban population puts unbearable pressure on civic services. The big cities are becoming a symbol of poverty, social deprivation, pollution, unhealthiness, congestion, etc. Cities are facing many problems like traffic congestion, limited water supply, lack of sanitation, inadequate social services, poor land management, manifestation of poverty, etc.

Inadequate household ventilation is a problem that does not receive the attention accorded. Auto or factory emissions, is another grave international problem. The traditional materials that millions of poor urban dwellers around the world burn for cooking have also caused problems (Bhim Sain 1995). Though the International Drinking Water Supply and Sanitation Decade (1981-90) made arrangement to supply safe water, most of the poor people and the slum dwellers still drink contaminated water. Drinking and use for other purpose of this unsafe water leads to health problem.

When the physical environment deteriorates the health of the dwellers is affected. People are not able to protect themselves from the waste generated by them since their living environment is of a substandard level. Because of the rapid growth of the cities and towns, urban planning, urban management and improvement of condition of environment — become a problem. The increasing population size is also a threat to the urban areas. In the case of rural areas the population size remains constant. As mentioned by Bhim Sain (1995) large parts of urban areas are covered by slums, squalter settlements and unplanned, unorganised developments that impose deplorable living and working conditions on their inhabitants. Sain continues further that often the majority of an urban population lacks basic services, such as water, sanitation and adequate waste disposal and consequently faces a high rate of exposure to infections and infestations. Often, too, these unorganised developments are centres of crime and disorder.

As far as the rural areas are concerned, they are small in size, scattered and large in number. These characters lead to a special problem in terms of infrastructural facilities and services. The lack of employment opportunities exhibit the low income level among the people which leads to the problems like housing, sanitation, health, etc.

Another important consequence of bad environmental condition is diseases especially communicable diseases. In developing countries communicable diseases are major causes of the high rates of sickness, death and disability in developing countries. Diorrhea, vector borne parasitic diseases like malaria, schistosomiasis, filariasis and trypanosomiasis and vector borne viral diseases like exceptualities, dengue, zoonotic and other food borne diseases are classified under communicable disease category. Good sanitation of the surrounding, good housing and hygienic food are the only solution to escape from these diseases.

Environmental studies is one of the crucial fields in recent years. The relationship between man and his environment is the substance of and the justification for the environment programme. Quality of environment and human health and well-being are interdependent. The result of environmental degradation is the diminishing of human health and well-being. Even the animals and the plants are very much affected by the environmental degradation.

The people with a vision on environment do their best to study the relationship between the humans and the environment. Social scientists especially the sociologists view the environment with the sociological knowledge, and the special field in which they concentrate to study the environment is called as environmental sociology. This new field of inquiry emerged in 1970s. It was the American Sociological Association's section on environmental sociology which was the cause for the new sociology. It explains the role of physical-biological factors in shaping social structures and behaviours. In turn it gives knowledge about the impact of social organisation and social change on natural environment. According to Dunlop and Cotton (1979), environmental sociology is a specific category of inquiry focussing on the way in which factors in the physical environment shape and are shaped by social organisation and social behaviour.

In a nutshell environmental sociology concentrates on the following themes:

1. Various elements of the physical environment.
2. Different social organisations and social behaviour.
3. The influence of factors in the physical environment on social organisation.
4. The influence of environment on social behaviour.
5. The influence of social behaviour and social organisation on physical environment.

Using the sociological inquiry in the field of environment, environmental sociologists study the impact of the environment on the life of man. Since the old age is different from the other stages of human development, sociologists are also interested to analyse the influence of environment on the old people. The problem faced by these age groups is not only from one aspect, but it is a multidimensional one. Environment is also one of the dimensions through which they suggest some remedial measures.

Ageing is a toilsome treadmill grinding to a tragic halt as years pass by. It is a life spanning process of growth and development running from infancy to old age through childhood, adulthood and gets an end with the death of an individual (Gopalji Mishra 1997). Ageing is a process in human life and it is inevitable unless one dies earlier, i.e., in youth. Here the structure and the functioning of the body undergoes change. So ageing according to Birren (1996) is

> the regular changes that occur in mature genetically representative organism living under representative environmental conditions as they advanced in chronological age.

The present paper aims at establishing the relationship and the effect of environment on the old people. Environment is an important factor, which influences the human and even the animal life from the day one onwards. In human life all the stages, viz., infancy, childhood, adolescence, adulthood and old age is a marked one. In the old age, the old people become helpless like children so they expect assistance in all walks of their life. Both physical and mental health is to be given utmost care. The responsibility falls not only on the children of the old people or on the other members of the family but also in the hands of the environment as well.

The environment is said to cover the state, city, community service centres, units of residency, quality of housing, housing satisfaction, institution like nursing homes, retirement residence, etc. These environments affect the old people in a drastic way. If the environment of the old people both at the macro and micro level is good then a healthy old age will prevail.

With regard to the physical consideration environment of the aged people may be divided into macro-environment and micro-environment. Apart from the physical considerations a different description can be attributed to the term environment. They are focussed as group environment, personal environment, supra-personal environment and social environment. For a better understanding of these classification the meaning of these terms are explained below.

Group environment

Group environment according to Altman & Lett (1970) is the behaviour of the individuals who act as groups in any given structural relationship to a given person.

Personal environment

The personal environment refers to the interactions that a person has with significant others.

Supra-personal environment

Lawton (1980) extends supra-personal environment to be 'the characteristics of the aggregate of individuals in physical proximity usually expressed as the average or the mode'.

Social environment

In this category the phenomena like social movements, political movements, social institutions, political institutions, cultural values, legal tradition, economic cycle, etc., are identified.

Effect of environment

The effects of environment on the behaviour of the elderly are identified in the following manner.

The environment may be a source of stress and mental ill health. The stress and ill health happens when an elderly person attempts to function in a setting which is not suitable to the persons or desired lifestyle.

The environment may affect the behaviour of the elderly people. So they have to adopt to the existing environment or we must provide them an appropriate environment which would fit them in a suitable way. The environment may affect the physical health and well-being of the older people.

The environment may not be ideal for all the old people. A particular environment may be suitable for one individual whereas the same may not be suitable for another individual.

Different environments with varying degrees of focus, emphasis and details are found to affect the personality of the elderly.

With the above explanation about the environment we move further to discuss the two major types of environments macro-and micro-environment. These environments have a direct influence on the life of the old people.

Macro-envrionment

The cities, communities and neighbourhood settings are the larger scale environments classified under macro-environment.

It is clear from many studies that some cities have the higher concentration of older people. Kart and Manard (1976) explained their results of a research conducted by them which revealed that Florida had the highest concentration of persons aged 65 and above. This concentration is because of the inclination for a warm climate.

Human body cannot tolerate too hot or too cold tempereture.

The old people face such problems which are caused by the unfavourable climate. In some cities during summer death cases are reported and in most of these cases the diseased persons have crossed 50 years of age. Old age also leads to the problems in the hearing system. The cold climate in certain regions also adds to their already disabled hearing capacity.

Studies explained that concentration of elderly persons in the urban centres are constantly increasing. This concentration is because of easy accessibility and availability of facilities. Urban centres are centre points of facilities like market, medicine, hospitals, housing, transport, etc. These facilities attract the old people to settle in these places so that they need not face problems in availing these facilities.

Many old people in the modern industrial world live separately without anyone's help. Either the children leave them or the old people leave their children. In some cases these people do not have children or any relatives. In the case of old people who have relatives, it is evident that the relatives also do not want to have these people with them because they consider them as an additional burden with other burdens in their urban way of life. When no one is there to take care of these people they are forced to do their work themselves. Market, medical shop, hospital and means of transportation are important facilities which are often utilised by the old people. If these facilities are very close to their home they need not have much problem. They need not walk for a long distance or they need not wait in a bus stop for a long time and even they need not pay much for other means of transportation to get something from the market, medical shop, etc. Hospitals and nursing homes are playing an important role in providing health services to the old people. Geriatric ward is a special ward meant for the old people and most of the modern hospitals contain these services. Since these people often face some type of health problems it is easy to avail the medical service if the health centres are very close to their residence.

As far as the community is concerned Blake, Lawton and Law (1978) conducted a study to evaluate the components of an ideal community. The results of their study revealed that both old and young adults saw high quality medical care and schools, availability of good jobs and a wide variety of stores and business as most important in an ideal community. This type of ideal community will be suitable for the old people.

The neighbourhood and services are other important aspects of the elderly who are living alone without any family members with them, then it is the neighbours who would take care of them. So, the elderly people must have good neighbours who would be kind to them, who would entertain them, talk to them, share experience and their feelings with them and this indeed would enable a healthy old age.

Good neighbourhood relations not only fulfil the psychological needs of the elderly but also the other needs. When they are not able to prepare their food, when they face problem in going out for provision, market, medical shop, etc., the neighbours help these people to get the necessary things.

The elderly people expect physical proximity to the services. They expect the bus-stop, grocery or super market, church, post office, drug store, department or variety store, physicians office, hospital, senior centre, public park, library and laundromat to be close to their residence.

Apart from the distance between the home and service centres the topography of the surrounding environment also play a role in the life of the elderly people. Steep hills, traffic congested streets, high crime prone area are not congenial for the elderly people. Safe and quiet neighbourhood is ideal for the comfortable life of the elderly people.

Hilly area is not good for the old people. To walk in the plain road itself is a problem for the old people. Walking in steep street or road causes more problems. Orthopaedic problem is one of the common health problems for the elderly people. They will get pain in the joints or they will face problem because of swelling in legs when they walk in these areas. Population increase and increasing number of vehicle are another problem for the elderly. In some countries where there is no proper regulations for the pedestrians and vehicles, the old population face problem to walk in the street or to cross the roads. In a country like India a big queue or a big crowd can be seen in public places like markets, cinemas, temples and even in the street and roads. A man who already faces a problem in a normal walk will face additional problems because of overcrowding of the population and vehicles. If the residential area is highly crime prone in nature the elderly will be the victims for the criminals. The target group for the criminals is old people. Most of the old people are victimised in public places especially in markets and banks and other places where transaction of money is involved with old people.

Micro-environment

The micro-environment of the older people are small units of residency, housing quality, housing satisfaction, institutions, etc. It is found that the micro-environment directly influences the life of the elderly people.

According to Proshansky (1973)

> the environmental crisis in human dignity not just lies in the overuse, misuse and the decay of physical settings but far more significantly in how we conceive of the individual in relation to any such setting.

Proshansky brands this situation a crisis because spaces and places are improperly designed in physical terms and also human needs for privacy, territoriality and freedom of choice being overlooked. The actual settings may bring unintended consequence and they are often ignored. So it is evident that the old people will adjust to the actual situation.

When the elderly people own their own homes they become more secure and satisfied to adjust and live as they please in their own homes regardless of condition or location.

Building a house is one of the prime aims of low-class and middle- class people. In a country, like India, people live with their own tradition and culture. Taking care and giving a good life to the children in the form of education, occupation, good property, marriage and setting the family are the important responsibilities of the parents.

After fulfilling all these family and social responsibilities the people have no savings in any form for their later life. Living in a rental house is not giving any mental satisfaction. Moreover the owners of the house put forth a number of conditions which are not favourable for the elderly persons. Even if they are satisfied with these conditions it is difficult to get a house in a good location.

The quality of housing depends on income, the housing deficiency like lack of complete kitchen or plumbing facilities, broken plaster, peeling paint, leaking roofs, holes in floors, etc., will lead to dissatisfaction among the older people. The dissatisfaction on housing deficiency is more among elderly renters than among elder owners (Lawton 1980). The satisfaction on the housing status will be an added comfort for a happy life. Own house for the elderly will lead to mental satisfaction though they will not be even of good quality.

More than residence it is clear that various institutional settings forms a major classification of micro-environment for older persons and this has a bearing on these old people. These institutions are generally categorised into nursing homes, personal care units and retirement residences. Nursing homes are approved by the government which provide twenty-four hour skilled nursing, medical and other health services under the supervision of a registered nurse. Personal care units provide intermediate care facilities.

Though these institutions provide little solution for a part of their problems, there also are environmental limitations on the elderly. These people find their normal interactions seriously impaired by the institutional micro-environment limitations. Environment limitations are social in nature. It imposes constraints upon the activities of the institutionalised elderly by other people like family members, physicians, staff members, by the institution itself or by the socio-cultural context in which the institutionalised older persons lives. They do not allow normal interactions with objects and events, they allow watching T.V. but prohibit smoking, chewing tobacco and drinking. Further it can be noted that the elderly institutionalised residents are treated in a demeaning and low way;

in other words with lack of dignity, respect and support.

Privacy and self-esteem appears to be part of a complex interaction between individual and environment. Old people love to have privacy. Further there is no particular time for them to sleep, to read books, to go for a chat with peer members, meditation, etc. If no one interferes with them or no one disturbs them they can do their daily routine without any disruption.

Privacy at the institutions (hospitals, nursing homes, etc.) is, however, less because these institutions frame rules and all activities are to be performed within that frame. This endangers the institutionalised persons will to self-determination. This, however, affects their mental condition. Loss of independence may lead to overwhelming negative perception of helplessness and they are precursors of premature death. All these constraints and limitations directly affects their self-esteem which is again a negative impact on the individual's health.

Conclusion

With an individual becoming old, his functioning capacities are impaired or minimised thus bringing about the infantilisation of the elderly. It is clear that environment affects the life of the older people. The states, cities, communities, neighbourhoods, housing quality, satisfaction with housing, institutions of the elderly, service centres, etc., are found to affect the mental and physical condition of the people. So we conclude that for a comfortable and peaceful later life they must be provided a good environment. The responsibility of this rests on the children of the old people and other family members, the government, NGOs, etc.

References

Altman, L. and Lett, E., 'The ecology of personal relationships: A classification system and conceptual model', In I. Mc Grath (ed.), *Social and Psychological Factors in Stress*, New York: Holi, Rinehart & Winston 1970.

Blake, B. F., Lawton, M.P. and Lau, S., Community Resources and Need Satisfaction — An Age Comparison, Pa: Philadelphia Geriatric Centre, 1976.

Gopalji Mishra, 'Ageing: The people's concern', In Manak (ed.), *Changing Indian Society and Status of Aged*, Delhi: Husain, M.G, 1976.

Kart, C.S., and Manard, B.B., 'Ageing regions of the United States: 1970', In C.S. Kart and B.B. Manard (eds.), *Ageing in American: Readings in Social Gerontology*, Port Washington N.Y. Alfred Publishing, 1976.

Lawton, M.P., *Environment and Ageing*, Cal: Brooks' Cole (Wadsworth), 1980.

Proshansky, H., 1973, 'The environmental crisis in human dignity', *Journal of Social Issues*, 29(4) : 1-20.

4

Linking Ageing and Society Response

D. Selvaraju
A. Murugan

Introduction

AGAINST this backdrop the present paper focusses attention on the role of the family in the care of the aged both in developed and developing countries with special reference to India. An attempt has been made in this paper to sociologically examine and analyse how the changing functions of the family and its structural change have resulted in various problems of adjustment of the aged within and outside the family. With the help of one theoretical model, i.e., 'Alienation', the researcher explores various stresses and strains faced by the aged and at the same time suggests some remedical measures to overcome such problems.

Current interest in ageing and gerontology all over the globe has been stimulated by the growing proportion of the aged both in developed and developing countries and by public concern with the aged as a social problem.

At the same time the care of the aged is also assuming greater importance with general increase in longevity, particularly in the developed countries, where the old are at least measurably protected through social insurance or public assistance schemes and receive institutional care on a very large scale. The developed countries have organised systems that include pension schemes, old age assistance, institutional care, clubs for senior citizens, homes for the aged, 'meals on wheels' (mobile canteens for visiting from house to house), friendly visiting, home helps, etc. In developing countries, the pattern of the joint or extended family had traditionally provided a built-in system of care of the aged within the family itself. Where there is no separation of the workplace from residence, the aged are still able to retain social functioning in the family and the neighbourhood even after their economic productivity has ceased. This familial situation, however, is changing in developing countries; the old system does not provide sufficient protection to the age in the changing socio-economic circumstances but the developing countries lack the funds and resources to meet these new needs (Sachdeva 1995).

Profile of the aged in India

The U.N. has declared 1999 as the International Year of older persons. Aged People's Day (October 1) is celebrated every year, but very little is actually done to alleviate condition of the aged. Fundamental virtues of family life such as caring and sharing, giving and forgiving respect and love are on the decline and so are all moral and spiritual values. This is primarly responsible for the neglect of the aged.

The ageing process itself is often the major cause of problems in old age. The effects of disease and the social problems of growing old are often much more important.

For the world as a whole, the 60 years and over population was 304 million in 1970. This would increase to 581 milliion by the year AD 2000 — increase of 91 per cent. But, for South Asia an increase of 154.5 per cent is predicted. By the year AD 2000, two-third of the aged population will be in the developing world, with quite a high percentage in India and ESCAP region.

The population of those who are 60 and above constituted 5.66 per cent of the total population in 1951 in the case of India. India had 25 million persons over 60 years in 1961 and 33 million in 1971. The figure rose to 40 million in 1981. In 1991, the figure further increased to 56 million constituting 6.5 per cent of the total population. The population of the aged may become 76 million by

AD 2001 forming 7.6 per cent of population of nearly one-seventh of the world elderly. By AD 2020, the number may rise to 124 million which means 11 per cent of the population will be over 60 and only 25 per cent of the population will be under 15.

India currently ranks fourth among the countries of the world in terms of the population of the aged. By the turn of the century, it is likely to be second only to China.

The aged feel a sense of social isolation because of disjunction from work relationships, demise of relatives and friends and ability of children to far-off places for jobs. The situation worsens when there is physical incapacity and financial stringency. Financial problems add to the misery of the aged. Having spent all their hard earned money on children's education and marriage, they are generally demoralised when their offspring refuse to give them shelter. No doubt, economic security is vital for the elderly. However, very often this gets undue attention at the expense of psychological social, occupational and cultural needs. Consequently, the real solution to the problem of elderly is to organise them to fight for their rights to our strategies to solve their problems and thereby relieve from them loneliness.

Ageing is more difficult in a rapidly changing materialistic society. Modernisation, urbanisation and consequent mobility play a vital role in the ageing process of an individual. Further by the year 2025, the percentage of population in the age group of 50 to 70 years is likely to reach 25 per cent.

Elderly suffer from desires, psychological problem of usefulness and abandonment. Elderly people react in different ways to this diminishing role. Those who have not occupied positions previously welled little authority or influence perhaps feel it the least, those who occupied positions of authority have considerable difficulty in coping. It should be noted that problems of the old age are highly individualistic in nature.

To worsen matters, the older women will greatly out number the older men. Today, with 55 per cent women above 60 years of age being widows, widowhood remains a major problem with the aged population. Coupled with the tendency of men to marry women younger than them, widowhood for women is much more likely. It also means women losing their rights to the marital home. Apart from physical problems old people have mental problems also. They suffer from mental tension because of ill health of self or their life partners and feel their loneliness very strongly. They are disturbed by the feeling that they are helpless and not useful to their house and society. Thus, the emotional insecurity of the aged is a serious problem. Mostly they are abandoned by their love ones in the twilight years and reduced to being nobody within the confines of their own homes.

Traditional model

The family has generally been considered the traditional primary source of social, economic, psychological and physical support for the elderly. It is crucial even today. Recent studies confirm the continuing importance of the family in elderly care. In developed countries, where has State has assumed responsibility for the welfare of the aged, there is growing evidence of family being called to assume responsibility. Johnson (1993: 42-5) observes, 'even in a country with such extensive provisions for care of the elderly as Sweden, the bulk of their support is provided by the family'. Lizhong and Guiyun (1993) point out, 'In China, the family has a 2000 year history as care giver dating from the Spring and Autumn Period, 722 BC to 481 BC' Cattell (1993) observes, 'African values constitute an important resource in regard to family support and long-term care of the elderly'.

In developing countries, even today the aged rely almost exclusively on familial resources for survival. For families, in these countries the capacity for care of the aged is shaped not only by values and kinship structures but also by demographic conditions producing an adequate number of potential care givers. In Nigeria, 'when elderly are no longer able to continue work, the primary resources on which they rely is their family'. In Costa Rica 'most older persons reside with family members'. In India, for example, 'The elderly typically live with a son and his family for their economic necessities and emotional support'.

Thus the family occupies a central place in the care of its aged members. It will continue to play a very important role in the caring process for several reasons. Firstly, there is a widely held belief that family responsibility for the care of the elderly is a moral imperative. Supporting parents and the aged is considered a moral obligation. According to Hindu philosophy and traditions, it is enjoined upon the younger members to look after the elderly and provide care for them. Secondly, respect, love and support for the aged have been advanced in religious writings and scriptures and are propagated in the teachings of philosophers, saints and seers.

Types of care provided by the family to the aged

Help and services which are provided to the aged consists of a number of activities — from personal care to emotional support. Generally there are two types of services. The first type of services is classified as 'primary services' which include personal care and home health care. The second type is known as 'secondary services' which encompasses social and recreational acitivities and emotional support. Antonucci (1990) distinguishes three main types of informal support given to the elderly people. First, emotional support involves the provision of moral and psychological support through sympathetic and caring relationships. Second, informational support which assists the elderly with problem solving and decision-making. And lastly, instrumental support which takes the form of help with the practical tasks of everyday life.

Caring for elderly people, unlike caring for a normal child, involves increasing dependency. In dealing with increasing dependency, Braithwaite (1922) has identified five cares which encounter the aged and contrast sharply with the demands made during child rearing: awareness of degeneration, unpredictability, time constraints, the care giver-receiver relationship and lack of choice.

Examining these five crisis, it can be seen that, first, degeneration is a much feared outcome compared with the much valued development of a child. Second, the course of degeneration is unpredictable compared with the well-known stages of childhood.

Third, elder care imposes time contraints since the burden is not shared as a rule, contrasting sharply with child-rearing, which is shared with kindergartens, play groups, school, baby-sitters and by children visiting a friend's house to play or stay overnight.

The fourth crisis concerns relationships. While the relationship between parents and young children is well defined with love being reciprocal and authority residing in the parent, no such norms govern care for an older adult. Old norms may need to be reversed in adult care giving and no assurance can be given about whether the care-receiver will get along in their new dependency relationship.

Finally, in case of caring the aged, there is usually no choice. Child-rearing can be avoided or postponed while care giving to the aged must be done at once when needed, forcing care givers to put aside acitivities, plans and personal development, in matters of attending to their ill-health and financial problems. Meeting care giving demands of the aged may deprive the care givers of satisfying their own basic physiological needs. But this humanitarian task should be realised and understood in the right perspective.

Family and aged model

Types of support provided by Family

Causes of family disintegration

Disintegration of family leads to various stresses and strains

(Urbanisation, industrialisation, migration, social mobility, modern values and individualistic outlook)

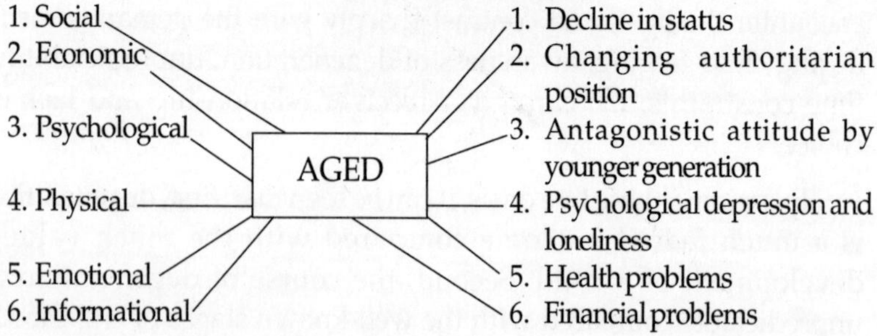

The above model shows that family provides different types of support for the aged, at the same time change in the family structure leads to various problems for the aged in contemporary society.

Hebsons choice

Given the burden of care giving in itself and the increase in the numbers of the very old, three options emerge: (a) Women will have to continue to carry the evermounting care giving burden; because women generally live longer than men and are younger than their husbands. Takako Sodei (1993) observes, 'in Japan as well as other countries, including the United States, elder care is traditionally the role of women'. Nearly 19 per cent of care givers are women; (b) Sons and other male relatives should co-operate in physical care giving; (c) Government should provide adequate instrumental supports.

Changing trends

In India old men living in traditional joint families had a say in their household affairs and they also had a role in the home and the wider community. They were consulted for guidance by the younger generation because of their experience and maturity in providing appropriate decisions. The patriarchal family norm entrusting the eldest male as family head (*karta*) is no longer rigidly followed. The breakdown of the joint family system has been one of the most important factors responsible for the changing authoritarian position of the aged male in the family. Again with the advent of industrialisation and urbanisation the joint family system has been losing its importance and gradually disintegrating in India. This has resulted in an increased rate of mobility of the rural people to the urban/ industrial sector in search of employment, higher education, etc. People, particularly the educated ones prefer to take up salaried jobs in urban and semi-urban areas mainly for job security and assured income.

But mostly the elder members do not prefer to move out of their ancestral homes and villages because of agricultural occupations on which they have been depending for generations. They have an emotional attachment towards their ancestral landed property and home. Further, there are apprehensions in their mind that the emotional support and security derived by them in the joint family and the village community would not be given to them in the urban sectors by their married sons. The power exercised by the elders in the family decision-making process and community affairs of the recent past is not enjoyed by them in the modern nuclear families and also in the urban community because of changed attitudes and values. The position enjoyed by the elders in the performance of religious and social rituals in the rural families and communities are no longer seen today as they have become outdated due to the secular and modern outlook of the younger generation. It was the popularly acceptable morals which imposed norms for care to the aged in the family and in the community. But such a moral force has weakened in the urban family system because of various modern forces. Violation of such a norm, i.e., negligence in the care of the aged was also not approved by the caste, communities and the village panchayats.

In modern Indian family system we often come across differential treatment being provided to the older members by the family head. This has resulted in the development of antagonistic attitude of the younger generation towards the elders. The comfortable living enjoyed by widows, orphans and dependants including the aged is not possible in the modern Indian family system. The spontaneous respect and regard accorded to the aged out of sincerity and emotional attachment are absent.

The knowledge and expertise gained by the senior citizen by virtue of their long experience could be of much use and would be beneficial for the younger generation and society as a whole. These qualities of the aged are not being utilised by the younger generation who consider themselves to be more knowledgeable.

Feeding of alienation and loneliness

With rapid change in the family, the aged who live in old age homes feel alienated. This happens due to lack of supportive relationship from their children, non-belonging, exclusion from social and cultural participation in the family, lack of identification with other's views and dissatisfaction in social relations.

The burden of dependency

With the growth of pensions and early retirement schemes, it has been argued that the elderly constitute an economic burden on the community and family, loss of a regular occupation and total or partial economic dependence after retirement may mean for the retire a depletion of authority and the fear of being taken for granted. He may feel that instead of being the decision-maker, decisions are now being made for him. The 'burden of dependency' as a ratio is calculated as those not eligible for employment (those past the age of retirement) over the working population. As this dependency ratio increases, it is thought that by the end of the century the elderly will constitute a considerable brake on economic growth for advanced societies.

Ageing and society response have always been inextricably intertwined. The influence is felt in both directions. Ageing influencing the nature of society and society response in turn result in modifications of the attitude towards the aged people. Attractive measures and special incentives may attract old peoples', needs and although often not directly, a vital component of the product of the life.

At the same time, it is inevitable that the old people and the society they are associated with their disability will modify the environments that they use. Change is inevitable but the evaluation of the significance of changes in ageing will vary greatly with the values to the old peoples and their relationships to that society.

Young people may have different attitudes to old people and old people may vary among themselves depending upon their backgrounds and interests and may differ from representations of the society. However, convergence in the values ascribed to ageing change is desirable if the various stake holders are not to undermine each others interests.

Old people expectations

Ageing has increased at a steady rate since the end of the Second

World War with 500 millions old people each year, due to the progress made in the field of technology (biological, engineering and more effective vaccines and drugs) economic development (better level of education, nutrition and better standard of living) and public health (better immunisation techniques, sanitation's and health education).

Ageing process has proven surprising events to changing society. While it reacts immediately to extreme event if not properly cared, and for example, global ageing declined during the medical progress, and it can recover quite rapidly so that the annual rate of ageing growth as per U.N. projection is that the proportion of elderly (65 years are above) persons in the world population will increases from 5.9 per cent in 1980 to 9.7 per cent in 2025 in the Asian region. By 2000, the population of the aged in Asia will be above 49 per cent of the less developed countries. While the ageing problem still dominates the scene, the disability is becoming increased, specialised and fragmented. Even the ageing terminology has become increasingly diverse with the list of types of disability growing at exponential rate to encompass as old, ageing, old age homes, senior citizens, responsible persons, elderly people, 'ground old age' and a host of variations on similar themes.

The old people are becoming increasingly experienced, having often several thoughts and has high expectations regarding service quality and value for life. However thought of dependency conjures up images of being powerless, of becoming a burden on others and of being kept alive by artificial means. This is especially true of the senior citizens which is growing the size, living longer, remaining less activity and which controls a great deals of the developed countries.

Ageing is becoming more universally aware and have higher expectations with respect to the society of the setting where old people live. Ageing persons when they see themselves are not aware of the full implication of their activities.

It can be known that the elderly are increasing in number and that their ratio to the total population is also rapidly increasing. This trend is getting more serious in Western countries. The problem is not only an individual problem, but also a collective social and economic problem. An important direction towards solving these problems lie in mutual efforts to provide the elderly with suitable living environments thus minimising other problems the elderly face.

Likewise old age also constitutes one of the major social problems in developing countries. This is because the number of old is increasing and social welfare measures for the support care and treatment are inadequate. In the past, ageing also posed serious problems but the traditional joint family was able to provide support and protection to the aged within the family framework. There are persons who belong to the category that is euphemistically said to die of old age and may in reality be dying in starvation. The weaker sections belonging to scheduled castes, scheduled tribes and other backward classes are worst affected.

Expectations to assist the ageing can be achieved through:

- Co-operation from the family with its ageing members.
- Counselling from the society with senior citizens centres offering guidance on all matters.
- Help from governments, special amenities and concessions.
- The aged helping themselves.

Finally old people expectations can be expressed under humanitarian issues relate to specific needs of the elderly people such as: health and nutrition; housing and environment; social welfare; income security and employment; education and the family.

The humanitarianism of elderly demand special attention, especially in the care of older women. Developmental issues relates to the socio-economic implication of the ageing population as an increasing proportion of the total population is ageing. This issue include the effects of ageing on production, consumption, savings and investments; and the impact of these changes on social and economic conditions and policies.

In looking at both humanitarian and developmental aspects of ageing populations, the question arises as how best to put to use the experience and wisdom of old persons.

Society responses

THE GROWTH IN COMMUNITY SUPPORT

Until recently welfare activities in the field of the age used to be undertaken for the poor and destitutes by religious and charitable institutions.

Out of 229 agencies, only about one-third functioned under secular auspices, the rest of them were run by religious organisations of which over 85 per cent were old age homes.

Quoting from different sources, Fernandes observes that apart from poverty which is rampart in all developing countries there are serious disparities between the poor and the rich. Society responses may isolate by above disparities. A review of academic literature, articles in newspapers and popular journals, and advertisements in nauralists publications gives the impression that ageing, is a burgeoning problem. This is an over simplification. It is true that there is growth in ageing rate but nevertheless, it constitutes a small part of the total population. To develop a proper perspective of the problems of aged *vis-a-vis* the dwindling support of the family, one has to understand the mentality of the aged, their attitudes, expectations, aspirations, fulfilled/unfulfilled ambitions, aspirations, frustration tolerance and coping with difficulties. Both the young and the old ones have their share in creating conflicts in the family. The problems faced by the care givers need to be studied and properly documented.

There will always be an economic constraint to increasing size of aged persons. The private sector usually supplies the caring homes and supporting infrastructure which are an essential part of the carrying but often do not support the resources, either financially or politically, on which their long-term welfare is ultimately based. Clearly there is a need for close consultation and co-operation between the public and private sector in such situations but this seldan occurs. Thus, it has been argued that the private sector has yet to take a leaderships role in catering to the growing demand for ageing problems and disability benign opportunities. The nature of the situation is such that it may be difficult for it to do so and collaborative ventures may offer a greater likelihood of financial and caring success.

In developed countries, the main problem is not providing economic security to the ageing, but their social marginalisation after their retirement and the need of reintegrating them in the political and cultural life of the country and helping them to get over loneliness caused by the loosening of the parent child bond and the consequent distance between generations. Further in developed countries, the older population is itself ageing. The proportion of the aged (80 plus group) is growing and is expected to continue rising. A striking feature of the senior population is the imbalance between males and females. In the years to come, care of the elderly women will be a more serious problem. It has been argued that the relationships between ageing and society response are complex. An increasingly aware society and experienced old persons is more complicated problem who request to carry quality. This has implications for all volunteers and voluntary organisations if they wish to remain in the services of old persons. More generally, the activities of a number of voluntary organisations show that cost savings can sometime be made through the adaptation of more ageing persons. However, society response is not fixed and both old persons growth and the demand for society are changing. Unless the community support is vigilant there may be an expanding tension between growing demand for caring old persons with quality and greater challenge in providing special caring experiences.

The dependency ratio which till now had rested largely on the age group below 15 or 18 will now shift its focus to the aged people thereby creating problems for the aged, and the young.

Suggestions

In the light of the above discussions, the following suggestions could be relevant in easing the problems of the aged in the developed and developing countries of the world:

(a) As societies change, systematic research and study is needed on how values are formed in the family, and how these influences the life-course development of men and women and adequate steps should be taken to mitigate problems that arise.

(b) Expected roles and relationships of older persons towards their family and community members need to be continually redefined as new groups reach the age of 60.

(c) In view of the demographic and role changes occurring in our family and society at large, measures are recommended like more goverment and community support services for family care giving; more co-operative family care giving, with training for all family members and more flexible employment practice, including care facilities adjacent to the workplace, to enable men and women to care for older family members.

(d) Older persons who have the advantage of life-long experiences should be encouraged and trained in the art of consultation and should be engaged in different workplaces.

(e) Psychologists should come forward to study the personality variables that may account for the emergence of particular problems of the aged.

(f) Social support mechanism should be provided to the aged in order to reduce physical and emotional strains to help them lead a healthy and happy old age.

(g) Another community-building device that might draw retired people into fresh contact with the young, and vice versa is that older people in every community could be appointed 'adjunct teachers' or 'mentors', invited to teach some of their skills in local schools on a part-time or volunteer basis.

(h) Need-based approach is essential. Besides covering basic and physical needs like food, shelter, clothing, necessary atmosphere should be created to fulfil other needs of the aged like, the need for companionship, recognition, the need for love and to belong, the need for esteem, and finally the need for self-actualisation in the family.

Finally, aged should be considered as a valuable cultural resource and role models for the younger generation. Therefore, governmental and non-governmental organisations should come forward to motivate and create awareness among the youth to take the care of the aged in the family. Thus, to conclude in the words of Addison, Joseph who said,

> He who would pass his declining years with honour and comfort, should, when young consider that he may one day become old, and remember when he is old, that he has once been young.

References

Antonucci, T., 1990, 'Personal characteristics, social support and social behaviour', In Binstock, R. and George, L. (ed.), *Handbook of Ageing and the Social Sciences*, 3rd edn., U.S.A., Academic Press., pp. 205-16.

Bali, A.P., 1995, 'Role of the Family in Elderly Care', *Research and Development Journal*, vol. 2, no.1, New Delhi, Help Age India.

Cattelle, Maria G., 1993, 'Caring for the elderly in sub-Saharan Africa', *Ageing International* 20(2): pp. 13.19

Gore, M.S., 1997, 'Studying problems of Ageing', *Sociological Bulletin*, vol. 46, no. 1.

Johnson, Lennarth, 1993, 'Swedes test new strategies', *Ageing International*, 20 (2): pp. 42-5.

Lizhong, Ren and Gyiyun, Liv, 1993, 'Providing for older People in China', *Ageing International*, 20 (1): pp. 27-8.

Mishra, S., 1989, 'Studying Problems of Ageing', *Sociological Bulletin*, vol. 46, no.1.

Sodei, Takako, 1993, 'Tradition impedes empowerment in Japan', *Ageing International*, 20(1), pp. 22-6.

Valleries, Braithwaite, 1992, 'Caregiving burdern', *Research on Ageing*, vol. 14, no.1.

5

Religion as a Solace to the Old

R. Sridharan

THE United Nations has declared 1999 as International Year of the old persons. India declared the year 2000 as National Year for old. We observe that there is a growing awareness and simultaneously a change of attitudes on the part of every generation, the young people, adults and older people.

Ageing is a universal phenomenon and old age is inevitable in the life of every individual. The span of human life, though theoretically fixed as 100 years, half of it is spent in sleep, twenty years in childhood and adolescence and the rest is divided into adulthood and old age. Crucial years of one's lifetime was dedicated to family life. He enjoyed and suffered from attachment, worldly pleasures and infatuation. The last years of an individual is miserable because he would have turned infirm, his faculties would not function well and he would be of no use to anyone. The attachment to worldly enjoyments bonded with powerful chords of affection are unable to make the old realise and liberate themselves to the phase of old age. The mind is the main problem for the old. The bitter feeling of social isolation could be lessened by devotional services which are envisaged by the institution of religion, within the framework of family system. The adjustment between the old and young is the perennial problem. This has been nowadays fastly widened by rapid Industrialisation, Computerisation and fast developing Information Technology along with already existing Westernisation process.

The functional sociologists and psychologists emphasis the manifest and latent functions of institution of religion. According to Emile Durkheim, religion brings solidarity among its members, however in the present day the solidarity between the generations is doubtful. Old people often feel that they are being discriminated and alienated in today's social system. Religion in the pre-British period played a vital role for keeping society healthy, particularly the old people both in body and mind. Religion had established always a right way of life to give peace for the old and it is a sure way to get rid of old day's stress and strain. Since happiness and peace would be the ultimate aim for all the old, religion acts accordingly, and carefully introspect them to be peaceful. The influence of religion makes the old do their duties and also abide the values which in turn give a respectful position for him in the society as per his position. The law of nature, control over the senses are illuminated through the examples in the religious scriptures has fascinated the minds of million of the old in the past and a proper understanding of it could help the old to lead a life in an ideal manner even in the midst of tension and strain. The sacred texts had tremendous influence at times of rigorous period in life for the old. Now the modern way of lifestyle has disturbed the old. Old are being expected to depend on sagacity and surrender. Fearlessness, unmindful of outcome of old age are essential for the old now to meet the challenges. They need the absolute confidence with tenacity of mind to meet various types of hurdles. They should not be upset by the mounting pressure whatever be its magnitude for which they need to depend upon the religious values. The entire Indian atmosphere has always been suffused with the aroma of spirituality. The concept of religion pervades everywhere.

Human kind on the brink of the new millennium has come to the realisation that the holistic approach to life especially for the old would prove more beneficial without complexity. The divine consciousness and spiritual directive help the old under all circumstances. Religious training to the young people in home, followed by school, play central role in inspiring values on old. The old are being relieved from the responsibilities and their hold on household affairs as well as outdoor activities are being shunned.

This kind of situation happens to them from 60 years onwards and this gradual loss of hold on everything in the family makes an impact on the social and psychological aspects of their personality. The emotional pain of the old becomes a pathological experience to call for a psychiatrist for counselling and guiding. A sudden change especially among the previously employed old creates anomie when they looses their profession and the consequent economy, status and power. A change that was insisted upon them as a social norm brings change of attitude on the part of young, adults and old.

After retirement, the old wishes to be economically independent and therefore they try to do some job. But the employers view that older people cost more than young as pay is to be fixed on the basis of seniority. So, naturally employers prefer to invest young rather than old forgetting their experiences and loyalties to the institutions. Hence it is not easy and possible for all the old to place themselves in the economic acitivities after they reach 60 and above.

While old age homes are evolving like mushrooms in the European countries and also in our country they do not find room in Islamic Society. It is mainly because of the Islamic culture adhere strictly to religion. Kerala is having highest number of old homes in India. This is because of the political, economic and attitude change due to increased foreign contacts and culture. Westernisation political thought, increased value for materialism, foreign opportunities have diminished the role of religious values particularly in caring the old. Few old age homes are successful. They are run by religions mutts, missionaries or *tapovanam* or Hindu *ashrama*. So we understand that religion helps in many ways to make old lead a better life.

The role of religion, henceforth is to be highlighted. More stress on religious values and doctrines which implies the regard and respect for the old should be depicted well by the present social system in solving old age problems in India. In every religion there are different type of 'tools' to help the old at the time of distress to steer through problems. When old, faculties fail then there is a need for devotion and service. No one should feel dejected when he/she is subjected to religious ideals and doctrines as pain and pleasure to be viewed as divine dispensation. Imperfect co-ordination of the organised set of normative values of the young and old may be lessened by the time honoured religious values.

Instead of providing a continuous social recognition and care for the old within the family system with the help of religious values we attempt to provide them 'homes'. These homes are not a salvation for them but it gives companionship, comfort, and peace in their everyday social relationship. This understanding is now gaining momentum in Western countries too. Today safeguarding the interests of senior citizens, promoting a positive image for old people in cultural, social, economic and political terms is a top priority for action in the European countries. The concession given to them in travelling by train has boosted a litte. Greater flexibility and humanness are required to enable the old to participate fully in the socio-economic cultural life of today and tomorrow. This is instantly possible without much revenue by administering the usage of existing institution of religion.

The challenge we must meet in the coming century is to develop humanness which would function in the long-term. A failure to comprehend the working of the latent social and economic system between the old and young may be dysfunctional and it may be hindrance for social development.

The fast development in information technology and wide-spread employment and education opportunities for women also indirectly affect the morale of the old. The role of TV channels, increasing number of creche have also affected directly the social position of the old. The model role and social role formerly played by the old in formulating the personality of the young grandchildren at home has been slowly replaced by products of science and technology such as TV, video games, etc. The attention towards new set of creation and recreation through modern science and technology left the old socially isolated. Thus, grandfather/grandmother's influence upon grandchildren are becoming less and almost a remote chance in certain section of the urban population. So the level of deprivation is greater in urban industrialised areas. The moral values backed by the religion for the respect of old are almost not favoured and found in the budding generations. There is no time and interest for the younger generation to look after the old, sincerely. The interest is to be stimulated with religious dogmas and doctrines. Values are abundant in epic and religious literature. The story of Shravana is a good example. So, the values for humanity to be reconsidered now, in betterment and uplift of the old. The concept of 'old is gold' is to be reviewed, and the service rendered by them for establishment and progress of the society is to be duly regarded and honoured by every part of the society. The advice of the medical doctors regarding the health of the old are nowadays religiously oriented. Hospitals too now have meditation halls, *yoga* centres, counselling centres, etc., to have a desired result in their treatment. Future also depends upon the past. The society needs the past experiences in the form of human resource to build-up new pattern and structure. Religious acts as a bridge between old and young would be a solace to the old. Humanness is the need of the hour in instigating the time honoured religious values.

References

Betty 'Heimann, *Facets of India Thought*, Allan and Unwin, 1964.

David, L. Gasing, *Science and Indian Religion*, CISR Publications, Bangalore, 1998, Religion and Society, vol. 4.

Emma, Petron, *'DIGNITY'*, The Magazine for the Ageing, Caminyter Road Mumbai, 1999.

Kimball, Young and Raymond, Mack, *Principles of Sociology*, Ecnasia Publishing House, New Delhi, 1973.

Robert, K. Merton, *Social Theory and Structure*, Aravind Publishing Co. Ltd., New Delhi.

Yogiraj Vedathiri Muharishi Mind, Vedathiri Publications, Erode, 1999.

The Hindu speaks on religious values, 1999, Kasthuri and Sons Madras.

6

A Society for Old Ages

Kala Rani Rengasamy

A SOCIETY where its population is engaged in preparing for old age and where its old and young alike co-operate to create a just and equitable social order is being aimed at the United Nations.

The year 1999 objective is to promote the United Nation's principles for older persons which is categorised under the following heads, (1) independence, (2) participation, (3) care, (4) self-fulfilment, and dignity.

The immortal Shakespeare in his famous play 'As you like it' described man's act, his big menly voice, turning again toward childish trouble pipes and whistles in his sound last scene of all that ends this strange eventful history. In second childish and more oblivion sans teeth, san eyes, san taste, sans everything.

This is the situation of population of the 70 million aged in India, mostly uncared for, unnourished, unattended, not honoured and neglected. In India the situation of population ageing has reached alarming properties. From 25.6 million in 1961 to number of those over sixty years is expected to touch 340 million in 2061. Between 1961 and 2061 while the total population would claim 5 times, the number of the olderly would show 13 times.

No wonder, global increase in human longevity and consequent greying of nation is a story of man's triumph and other attainments in social and economic progress. But this success carried along with it the problem of old age.

It is useful to analyse the percentage distribution of India's population by age groups.

Percentage distribution of India's population by age groups, 1911-81

Year	*0-14*	*15-60*	*60 and above*
1911	38.8	60.2	1.0
1921	39.2	59.6	1.2
1931	38.3	60.2	1.5
1951	37.4	57.1	5.5
1961	41.0	53.3	5.7
1971	41.9	53.4	5.2
1981	39.5	59.1	6.9

These old people draw everyone's attention due to their weak and problematic living conditions. These are problems of health, housing and economic dependence.

Types of problems

HEALTH

Good health is the pre-requisite of 'good quality' and adequate nutrition is to good health.

But changes are bound to happened in the ageing body and certain diseases are unavoidable the sense of taste and smell diminish with advancing age. Decline in taste and smell results is lessening of appetite and reduction in the quantity of food consumed. The most apparent change in the mouth with increasing age is loss of the natural teeth caused by two main diseases, namely tooth decay and gum diseases. Both if untreated are likely to cause pain and result in tooth loss and may affect the nutrient intake and also leads to difficulty in swallowing.

INCOME INSECURITY

In most developing countries the formal income security systems that is social insurance, social assistance, provident funds, etc., are not applicable to all and family care is still the main source of social protection for the elderly.

In most countries, while there are national co-ordinating bodies for social services, generally these have no specific mandate related to the elderly nor are there specific co-ordinating bodies specifically addressing the needs of the elderly.

The situation of the elderly in rural areas is in many ways distinct from that in urban areas. The situation of the rural elderly was worsened by migration of the young to urban centres and the deterioration in the rural farming economy. For the elderly who have migrated to urban areas and lost their support network, there is often a problem of loneliness.

No wonder elders render a great contribution to the family. One important contribution is taking care of children so that parents can work or stay away from home. Another important contribution is the labour that many older persons provide to family, farms, shops and income producing activities.

But it is felt that due recognition for their services is not being given either in the family nor by the government. Most policy-makers and officials are not sufficiently concerned about the income security needs of the elderly, because they have not yet been sensitised by reliable data and statistics on the real living circumstances of the elderly.

So it is felt that apart from physical problems of elders like health hazards they have mental problems also. They suffer from mental tension because of ill health of self or their life partners, economic dependence on others, difficulty in passing time, etc. It is noteworthy that old people, without their life partner feels their loneliness much strongly. They are disturbed by the feeling that they are helpless and not of any use to their house and society.

Thus, the emotional insecurity of the aged is serious problem. Mostly they are abandoned by their loved ones in the twilight years and reduced to nobody within the confines of their own houses.

Reason for problem

The circumstances that make the problems of aged serious are industrialisation, urbanisation, changing values, urban atmosphere and lifestyle, social change, explosion of population and increase in life span.

The effect of industrialisation and urbanisation have not left families untouched. The changes appear to be shocking as the roles and functions of the family has started getting weakened like education, economy, recreation, care of rich and aged.

These are more of structural changes like nucleation of families, individuals, education of female reflecting a decreasing trend of togetherness in the family.

According to Simmons (1958) there are recurrent basic interests which manifest themselves in old people in all soieties.

1. To preserve life as long as possible.
2. To seek release from wearisome exertion and get protection from physical hazards.
3. To maintain active participation in group affairs.
4. To meet death honourably and comfortably.

However in present generation, these interests of the senior citizens are challenged because of the break-up in the traditional values and due to the boom in the industrialisation and plagiarism in the Western lifestyle.

Expectation of the old age people

The aged expect not only the economic support from the younger generation but more of social and emotional support.

Family being the sub-system of society which takes care of aged, traditionally the task of caring for the elders has fallen on woman. Woman are main source of social, emotional and physical support for the aged and happened to be the first to be looked towards for physical care.

However as the roles of woman are changing fast to meet the demands of the present society and the family, it is generally argued that their attention towards the aged is decreasing. Old people do not expect a bombastic way of life but a kind of enquiry from their wards, a consoling voice from their family members, and a comfortable, tension-free life.

The Government of India though is trying to improve the situation by the welfare measures for the aged, there remains a basic question that how long and how well these welfare measures could solve the problem. The best option could be to strengthen the family and try to motivate the family members to take care of the aged. This would not only help to improved the situation of the aged but also to keep intact our traditional and cultural values. This is very much essential as in many of the developed countries, the problem related to the provision of welfare measures of the aged by the government is prominent.

Suggestions

1. An action plan that would ultimately lead to the formulation of a national policy is to be evolved for the older people which would seek *inter alia* better support and encouragement of care giving relationships with the old by providing for more and proper concessions, incentives and social recognition schemes. It should also focus on retarding the pace of ageing and reducing the disease spectrum through practices of health and hygiene, appropriate nutrition and exercise besides strengthening the infrastructural support of old age homes.
2. Data seggregated by gender, age group and according to rural and urban residence is needed for policy planning. Principle sources for providing data on the elderly should be explored.
3. Plans for meeting the needs of elderly people should be formulated and the ways to organise and support their needs are concretised.
4. The national budget should be formulated so that the commitment to income security of the elderly can be understood and assessed easily.

5. Personal funds and provident funds should be monitered in order to ensure that there is a sound financial management of the pension funds.

6. Programmes such as retraining of the elderly for gainful employment as well as voluntary activities and leisure could be practised which may provide new environment for the aged for development of self-management skills.

7. The state government can give subsidies to non-government organisations to enable them to look after the old and the payments and admission procedure could be made flexible irrespective of caste, gender, community.

8. Sarvodaya can be made universal principle in providing welfare measures for the old persons.

9. Realisation of the relationship of culture, community and the state in formulating policies for the old.

10. Family counselling centres could be established.

11. Mass media could be used to its maximum way to sensitise younger generation towards care of the aged.

12. Midday meal scheme could be given to village panchayat for the old.

Though most countries are having national co-ordinating bodies for social services and NGOs are doing laudable services caring for the old people, family care is still considered to be the main source of social protection for the elderly, because the aged expect not only the economic support from the younger generation but more of social and emotional support.

When such a conducive situation prevails, the mental disorders brought about by the fear of death and feelings of dependency, anxiety, boredom, loneliness and helplessness of the elderly will get vanished. So the family members should be made to know about the old people's mental problems.

The feeling of the old that 'I am good for nothing', 'I am not useful to the society' should be removed from their minds. For that one must find out that the possible work that the old people can do and engage them in some productive activities. These should not always be associated with commercial, business or monetary benefits. These could be in the form of social and developmental activities also. This will keep the elders healthy both mentally and physically and by doing so the society will be for old ages also.

7

Is Old Age a Calamity?

C.R.W. David

OLD people today seem to be convinced that it is. Longevity has begun to look like a curse to them. They feel that they are ignored and insulted and at best marginalised by the younger generations. Of course, there are elders who hold enormous powers in their hands because of circumstances as leaders and patriarchs but by and large ageing signals for most elders a quick slide down the slope.

Even for old people who retire from substantial positions, retirement signals the lose of at least a part of the glory hitherto enjoyed. Even more damaging than the financial loss that retirement normally entails is the loss that the retires feel of a loss of prestige all round. One old gentleman described himself as a widower Tithonus. Tithonus is the protagonist of a poem by Tennyson. The Goddess of Dawn, Aurora, falls in love with him and marries him, getting for him the 'blessing' of immortality. But unfortunately immortality does not free him from ageing, and the lovers suffer the insufferable pangs of ageing of one of the party. Tennyson dramatises the poor immortal praying for death. One can imagine the bitterness of feeling of this 'Widower Tithonus'. He has lost his companion for ever so long, and retirement means not only the loss of or the lessening of income and the loss of prestige outside home and within the family. It means the loss of companionship, the dissolution of many ancient and beloved ties. The loneliness aggravates the other 'privations' and ten to one the younger generation, however close to them in every possible way, is not able to quite fully understand that feeling of privation and of loneliness. Ageing is accelerated by this psychological emaciation.

But the perception of the old people is not endorsed (naturally!) by the younger people. To them, the older generation appears a liability in terms of responsibilities imposed on their children even more than in terms of finances. The attention that the old require increases with the years. The responsibilities are aggravated by the very rapid changes taking place in social and other mores in our society. Every aspect of modernisation emphasises the gap between the emerging generation and the elder generations.

Even in families in which old people are looked after without any manifestation of tension and distancing, there are widening gaps between generations. As a matter of fact, today's world of technology forces too many attitudinal differences among age-groups. May be 'age-groups-gap' is a better term to describe contemporary difficulties than the common term 'generation gap'. Attitudinal changes in familial, social, workplace, political and other fields contribute to these changes. When a person comes to that stage in his life when he is no longer a full-fledged earning member of the family, and slowly becomes a dependent in certain respects, requiring special physical and emotional care, others begin to see him as an 'old person' even if he does not think himself an aged person. This is at the root of most of the old-age complexes. In other words, the problem seems to start as a difference in perception of the person involved by the person himself and by others involved with him.

One does not have to put in too much of explanation here. There was, not long ago, a feeling in many families that women going out to work had better be avoided. In middle class families especially the feeling was quite strong. It took a world war or two, and the acute shortage of qualified male workers, for even the 'progressive' West to get used to the idea of women working with men in public places. Even in higher circles it was so. When the lady Florence Nightingale decided to take the career which made her eventually a name to conjure with her family, and her society, were non-plussed. A career for a woman! With that idea go ever so many other social conventions, about the segregation of the sexes, the status of woman as a helpmate of man and not as a bread winner, the idea of a woman's essential dependence on her family, etc. A whole way of looking at life and society characterises a generation. In subtle ways every generation builds its own distinct ethos and it is these differences that make the relationship between the generations that makes for incompatibility between them.

Our tradition — Hindu, Christian or otherwise — has been one of great, even exaggerated, respect for the elderly. In this tradition, age is associated with wisdom and with unbounded compassion, capacity for imaginative understanding and for self-effacement. Because of these assumptions, the elderly have been seen traditionally as the emotional buffers between the practical ruling generation and the growing and emotionally vulnerable growing generation. So aged grandparents and uncles and aunts have been greatly valued in family circles.

Today, children are as much in need of the emotional support of elders as children of earlier generations were. And indeed the older generation is willing and eager to give it to them. But unfortunately they live in different worlds. The sheer pace of life has changed so very radically in the last few years. The jugernaut of modernity emphasises the isolation of generations ruthlessly. The very ways in which a doting grandpa could entertain his grandchildren have lost their credibility today for the younger ones. The younger ones are exposed to and choicelessly brought up with toys and shows that the grandpa never dreamt of in his time. The slow-motioned grandpa is not a good companion to the grandchildren even on the road where the movement of life today is far faster and crowded than a few years ago. The way in which the younger generation responds to others is different. In short, what is not different for the two generations? The differences go deep into the unconscious of every generation, and so the conflicts are seen only on the surface mostly and not understood at the deeper and the real level.

Every civilised society has its own organised solution for its social problems. Ancient Indian society had developed a system that made old age capable of winning respect from the younger generation, not only from the members of one's family but from society as a whole. It divided man's life cycle into four. It began with *brahmacharyam*, the celebrate state when a person spent his time in learning, normally what his family and clan pursued, but in extraordinary circumstances taking to pursuits that suited his temper and aptitude better. After this came the phase of the *grihastha ashrama* when he was a householder, raising a family of his own, to continue the line of his race. This led him on to the phase of *vanaprastha ashrama* which meant retirement from the active secular and familial concerns and an initiation into austere living in a different environment. This prepared him and his lifemate to the final stage, *samnyasa* or renunciation. This part of life was devoted to purely spiritual pursuits, to the winning of salvation.

All the four phases were basically religiously and spiritually inclined. But the plan give judicious weightage to the material and sensual pulls, and provided them a proper channel. A person who could pass through the first two phases with detachment was glorified as a *jivan mukta*. This was a system that used the changing tendencies of the human life span at different stages. There was realism in the system, but it was shot through with a possible or feasible idealism.

There were indeed those who did not develop or evolve in themselves the values and tendencies that were appropriate to their stage in life. They suffered, and brought suffering for others. The great Dasharatha brought humiliation and sorrow upon himself because he could not retire with grace to all sides. Another symbolic figure was Yayati who with persistent penance borrowed the youth of his own youngest son so that he could prolong his indulgence. Such characters were obviously supposed to be exceptional cases.

Today's society enforces the last two phases of the ancient mode of life without providing people with the background to evolve into them. No social method is just a prescription. It is a solution a community evolves as a spontaneous response to its problems.

But changes in social perceptions have slowly undermined this deferential, idealised attitude. Though one may not agree with

Bertrand Russell that traditional concepts of the great respect due to the parents are merely a self-perpetuating and self-preserving conspiracy by the elder generations, one does not probably subscribe in full measure to the traditional vision of a self-effacing, sagely elder. It is not as though it was only the twentieth century which thus unkindly interpreted the motives of the elder generation. Lear and his daughters present a factionalising of emotional distances between generations. All the piety surrounding the elder-younger relationship is impossible to uphold at least in the modern circumstances, because they over dramatise the traditional expectations. Individualism is much more of an ingredient in today's personality than it ever was in the past. When the departure from the traditional perception becomes pronounced, there is the inevitable development of a sense of alienation between the two groups often necessitating a parting of the ways. The parting is formalised in institutions for the older people, and it is unofficial though no less real in other cases.

I agree that this is a drastic presentation. There could be elders who enter institutions for the aged voluntarily, without any resentment against anybody. Graceful ageing is possible, and the spirit behind the radical perception is not hostile; it merely shows the anxiety to see how best the difficulties could be smoothed to help more old people to age gracefully. That should be the spirit behind any deliberation of this nature. As social workers, we claim to be people who can understand both sides and so we must devise means to keep them in good working relationship.

By and large, in our society, institutions for the aged are perceived as formalised, rigid structures where elders who are to be ideally cushioned up in emotionally protective, supportive atmosphere are given up to impersonal and formal attention. In institutions where the inmates pay their way, it is seen as a mere commercial relationship; where the inmates are fully dependent, it is seen as a compromising dependence. The ideal of loving personal tending is not perceived even as a distant reality. It is quite possible that the popular perception is too dismissive, but it seems that one is not far wrong when one sees this as the prevailing popular perception. As this year has been declared as the International Year of the Aged, many popular journals in vernacular and in English have carried articles on the aged and the arrangements made to help them live a life of dignity and contentment. Reading these effusions, mostly based on isolated, cursory studies, a student of sociology is forced to the conclusion that the concern voiced by the writers is not genuine in human terms; that, if one may say so, it is only typical journalistic-concern.

It is hope that it is not out of place to mention here that gerontology as a subject should be part of the training of doctors, nurses, sociologists and such technically qualified attendants on people. The younger generation is practically in a more advantageous position than the older generations, and it behaves them to develop their sensitivity to the older people. If such institutions as are available today to take care of elders are managed by such trained people, the ventures would soon lose their tag of being human binjrapoles. They would cease to be considered more or less expensive sheds where older people could be 'quarantined' so that they wouldn't intrude upon the younger generations.

Institutionalisation and the aged

In a recent issue of a Tamil periodical (*Nakkeeran*, 15 October 1999, 12-51, 16-17), there was the story of a 107-year-old woman called Malaiyammal who is now an inmate of the Inba Illam in Pasumalai near Madurai city. The story says that the old lady, born in a village near Ettayapuram in Tirunelveli district, had taken the decision that she would be a spinster and had stuck to her decision in spite of pressure from the family. When her elder sister died giving birth to a son, she adopted him and brought him up with great care, firmly turning down the request of the widowed brother-in-law to become his wife. She ran a business and brought up the child. He was very devoted to her until he got married, and then began to ill-treat the old lady and to ask for her savings for his own use. The lady tried suicide and finally landed up at this place.

We might respond to this story in two ways. One could ask if this is just a sob-story to fill in space, written with no effort to go into details and the Other Party's version. Strictly speaking, this is not a sociologically valid contribution. It makes no effort to be objective, and generalises on the basis of this one case that old people are driven to such institutions by the heartlessness of the younger generation. But at the same time, one has also to realise that this is at least the model of cases one comes across in real life.

Yet another article in a Tamil Daily Perukivarum Mudiyore Kaappakangal', City Beat Supplement, Dinamalar 25 October 1999, 14M) squarely blames the younger generation for its selfishness in banishing its elders to the mushrooming old age homes. The article quotes the organiser of a home for the aged in Annanagar, Madurai, citing various reasons for the growing isolation of the older generation, but is of the firm conviction that the younger generation is selfish.

But a worker interested in understanding social problems and planning social relief must go into this phenomenon with more patience and imaginative understanding. There are many factors in today's society against which the younger generation is helpless: it did not initiate these processes; it is as much a victim of the processes as the elder generation because quite evidently so many of them pay an emotional price for the plight of their elders. It must also be remembered that the problem is not something that has sprung up overnight. It has been growing with us for sometime, and it has begun to attract popular attention only now.

In an official paper presented at the Vienna Conference on the aged, the Social Welfare Department of the Government of India listed several reasons for the unenviable plight of elders in this country. This paper is now seventeen years old.

The age old joint family system is now breaking down. Any student of society knows that there are many reasons for this development, and that this is not an isolated phenomenon peculiar to India. Economic realities of modern life force husband and wife to take to jobs; housing is a serious problem in urban localities especially; the job market forces the migration of younger people to far away places where the older people cannot easily be shifted or accommodated. There are old people who are intractable even as there are self-seeking younger people. And there are old people who have no children to take care of them.

There are beggars in front of all places of worship who are probably destitutes.

Statistically, the figures relating to old people are like this:

> The proportion of elderly in the country has risen from 5.6 per cent in 1961 to 6.76 per cent in 1999 and is likely to touch 7.1 per cent in 2001. In absolute terms, the year 1999 saw 55 million elderly persons in the country, 66.7 million in 1999 and the number is expected to touch 75 million by 2001. As such, the country would soon be facing a progressive increase in the proportion of elderly persons-
>
> ('Creating Social Sensibilities for the Aged' by Uma Joshin, *Social Welfare*, October 1999, 46-7, 3-5)

Thus the presence of old people is a reality, and it has to be attended to. And it could also be seen that modern progress in medicine, in living conditions, etc., would contribute to the increase in the number of old people our society has to handle.

Observing the urgent need for some organised effort to help the aged and the ageing, the TTS started the Inba Illam in Pasumalai, Madurai, as far away as 1976. The TTS conducted a first hand survey before launching the home. I am happy to say that the home has learnt that if these old people are properly handled, they can help themselves to quite some extent, help one another, and extend their sympathy and helping hand to others who are even more unfortunate than they are, young or old.

Inistitutionalisation of the care for the aged is thus a controversial issue. While by and large our society still feels critical about people who allow their elders to enter old age homes, the number of institutions is steadily growing. In just one small suburban colony called Tirunagar just 9 km from the city of Madurai, there are three such homes. May be for the present it is an urban phenomenon, but in course of time this trend is going to enter rural areas. Where rural depopulation is not the dominant trend, urban influences are getting stronger progressively, and the problem of care of the old people is going to become serious in those areas also. It is important to note that in this context, some of the research workers especially on rural subjects have come to view the problem with alarm and disapproval:

> The picture of the sixty million aged in India is mostly uncared for, undernourished, unattended, and neglected. . . .
>
> The population in the 60 plus age has risen to a level of 6.65 per cent in 1992 and will rise to 8.3 per cent by 2007.
>
> (— Durairaj, N., and Dr. Kala Rani Rengasamy, 'The Aged: Need Love and Protection', *Social Welfare*, October' 1999, 46-7, 6-7)

In institutionalisation, another important factor inviting our interest is the factor of the target groups. An organisation at the moment at the stage of planning points out that 'no old age home in India currently admits people with ailments . . . .' — (Dignity Homes: Report by Sheilu Sreenivasan, *Dignity: Dialogue*, March 1999, 7-10). Institutions for people with differing needs, backgrounds, etc., have to be planned.

In Western countries, such homes have been in vogue for quite some time, and there is not much of the fear of the stigma that attaches to families with elders in such homes in our country. One reason for this is that many of the Western and affluent countries have been planning for their aged and their unemployed for a much longer period. It is common knowledge that aged Indians in foreign countries like Canada and Australia do not want to get back to their mother land because retirement and old age provisions in those countries are so good. Institutions there are well equipped and are financially sound. They provide their aged inmates with everything except constant family friendship.

But in comparing the conditions in Western/affluent nations, we have to bear in mind the essential differences between them and communities like ours. The concept of individuality has taken root in most of those communities, and the emotional dependence on the younger generation is not quite so rooted there. At least the degree of such dependence is less. The idea of an erning youngster being a paying-guest in his/her own family is not strange there. Such practices have made the separation from the younger generation a more gradual and less painful process. In our circumstances, elders tend to be more protective to their young when they are themselves youngest and middle aged, and tend to be more dependent as they get old. Naturally, they develop a greater sense of the role they have planned in the lives of their young, and naturally have greater demands on the emotions, time and financial resources of their young? Such elders have a characteristic attitude to their Western counterparts, based of course on not-so-well-informed opinion rather than information. It is voiced thus by one person:

> The Westerners are forced to go to old people's homes because when they were young, they had their own pleasures and their own agenda, etc., leaving the children in creche or with baby sitters. Now the children are taking their revenge.

It is not relevant here to speak of the social and other differences between them and us; but it has to be borne in mind that their arrangements are better as of now.

In planning homes for the aged, we must take certain other factors into consideration. The perceptions of the young cannot be ignored in considering the problem. Why do many younger people feel that they are unable to stick to their elders in the normal course of family life? Is it only a problem of finance, accommodation, time etc.? The following views have to be remembered.

Elders tend to be adamant like children in some ways. It is difficult for them to be flexible in their ways. When they are obliged to change their habits — even in simple matters like the timing of their daily schedule, they feel aggrieved and insulted. They feel that they deserve to be more privileged because in their time they have made endless sacrifices for their children. The attitude of self-martyrisation often provokes trouble with the young because the young feel that it is a way of belittling them. This is aggravated when the young are married and bring in somebody from outside the immediate family circle who have their own demands on the consideration of the young. The younger people feel that elders do not have emotional flexibility. Many elders who have independent means want to be on their own as far as possible. Quite often one comes across ageing people who have their children in separate units who do not want to live with their children because they feel that they try to exploit them. They say that children summon their parents to their foreign homes when they want responsible, unpaid baby-sitters and midwives.

On the other hand, there are children who feel that their parents are greedy and grabbing. They want more of everything—privileges, attention, money. They feel that the aged are too demanding and are not easily satisfied. They are possessive and are less tolerant. When the children of their sons and daughters are necessarily members of a new or changing way of life, the elders want to stick to their ways and also want the younger things to confirm to their norms. Inevitably it is a source of tension. Such old people do not easily agree with others; they want others to agree with them.

It could also be seen that elders develop new attitudes. They become more religious, spiritually sensitive, and want to develop new practices and regimens. The young may have no patience or time to adjust themselves to all this. A new formalism or orthodoxy on the part of elders could disturb the family set-up, when the sons and daughters might even feel that their parents did not subject them to such restrictions when they were children. Elders become emotionally more needy and vulnerable as they progress in years.

When elders get sick and immobilised, they develop special psychological problems and needs. They begin to live emotionally in their own worlds, mostly based on their distant past which cannot easily be shared by the children who came into their lives much later. They think of their early days, and begin to live in the past; the physical nearness to others begins to matter more to them. Such needs actually distance them from the younger people while they require greater closeness and attention: as a matter of fact, many elders would be very happy if they are not considered old, as a race apart.

It is not possible to generalise the ways of the old. While some might be arrogant and demanding, and unwilling to take a 'no' from anybody, or incapable of taking any initiative or involving themselves in constructive or remunerative activities even if they have the strength for all that, others might retain their dynamism in every way. There is one resident of the home at Pasumalai who takes a small capital from the management and runs a small shop and manages to repay the loan promptly. In fact, it is even seen that contented residents of the home make a small contribution every month from their pocket-money for causes like looking after mentally retarded children.

What then should be the guidelines for people who interest themselves in the affairs of the aged?

1. They must realise that the old are not a race apart. No human being suddenly loses his contact with the past or the present. They are very much part of the society at large. They have their special needs even as the younger generations have theirs, and they have a right to their ways as the younger ones have to theirs. Institutionalisation should not mean branding the aged as people apart; alienation is bad for any generation. 'The respect and care for the elderly, which has been one of the few constants in human culture everywhere, reflects a basic interplay between self-preserving and society-preserving impulses which has conditioned the survival and progress of the human race' (International Plan of Action of Ageing, para 27). (*Dignity, Diologue* March 1999 vol 4, issue 11). All generations must be able to feel continuity. In other words, the idea of normality should be seen to be a purely relative one. The young and the old should both develop a sense of tolerance for others, for otherness. Society without either category would be incomplete.

2. Those involved with the management of such institutions should realise this link. There are moments in life when the old can give indispensable emotional comfort. The effort

should be to fruitfully tap the resources of the old. There should be no idea of condescension or patronage in the attitude of the young to the old.

Administrators of such homes should be people well-trained in the psychological needs of the elders. They must be capable of seeing themselves not as specially trained benefactors always at the giving end. They must strive to keep their institutions as close to the main community as possible. Such centres should not be areas of isolation; as though the elders are in an inoculation ward, under probation, an institution for the abnormal, etc. In other words, these administrators should undergo special emotional training for their vocation.

What are the limitations of institutionalisation?

Considering the growing number of aged people, we must realise that institutions for many of them is not practicable. The gap between quality and quantity must be realised. It is very necessary that in this branch commercialisation and routinising should be avoided.

That makes the continuous funding a difficult proposition. It is therefore not possible to depend on government. Private resources have to be found. If at all it is possible, old age homes can also develop income generating sections. For instance, those among the inmates who are still able can undertake remunerative work part of which could go to the maintenance of the homes.

It might be worthwhile to make a few suggestions regarding institutions in the context of the limitations. One of the important concepts to be developed would be community-based centres for the old. As many as possible of these could be organised, and be connected for instance with institutions like creches so that the old people could establish relationship with children. That would give them the feeling of being one with the mainstream of society. Other such units that could do with the help of old people could be designed as part of complexes for old people. In other words, old age homes should not be a place where the old unobtrusively move to their inexorable end.

These community centres could be connected with primary health centres where they could get help for their health problems. Local families could be brought into association with these institutions, contributing both financially and otherwise. This could help in developing in the wider society realisation that the old people are still part of their life, and necessary parts, too. The community's participation can also make the process less expensive.

We must take effective measures to see that the community centres do not dilute the quality of the care. It is doubtful whether community centres could afford sophistication of their service: for instance, providing special attention to people who are sick seriously or disabled. Institutions that are run by voluntary agencies will of course be able to do better in these respects. These should co-ordinate their activities with the community projects so that the elders get an integrated service. They may have to organise even counselling programmes for the elders and for the younger generation.

Conclusion

The success of any project depends on the way in which the people respond to it. The general public must be made to understand that the measures taken to help the elders are not measures of a sectional interest. They are measures that concern all society, the present and the future. Project like the year of the old are only efforts in sensitising the world to the problem and challenges in this field, and the relevance of this field to the general population of the world. The Inba Illam of Pasumalai proposes to conduct a Mela on 4 December 1999 to mark this year and its significance.

Media of all kinds should gear to engage in advocacy to achieve awareness, motivation and mobilisations.

Role perception is defective at family system levels. Organised professional counselling services should be made available to deal with individual cases.

Industrial Houses and Companies (for example Coca-Cola) come forward to support programmes for youth but not the 'aged'. This trend must change so that collective action will be possible in changing the environment of the 'aged'.

8

Role of People's Participation in Empowering Families for Care of the Elderly

D. Sivakumar

FAMILY has been the cradle of human civilisations. It is the family which mould and sustains human personality. Family is the abode of human development. Family has been caring all its members including children, women, disabled, destitute, the aged and the chronically ill. Family brings peace and tranquillity, care, rehabilitation and development. Family is the primary group which leads all social processes. With the advent of small family norm in the second half of the twentieth century the membership of the families started to decrease. Families are becoming small and small. The big joint families largely cater to the care of the aged. With introduction of small and single families the traditional family care programmes are facing serious problems. It is the objective of this paper to highlight the role of peoples participation in empowering families for the care of the elderly. With the advent of demographic transition population ageing is a regular phenomena in a large number of countries. This led to intervention by government and non-governmental organisations in the care of the aged. The expansion of care programme for the elderly in proportion to population ageing is a problem facing almost all countries. Certain countries have already developed a continuum of care programmes including health check-up, artificial appliances, medication, food on the wheels, housing, social work counselling, psychosocial and informational preparedness, recreation, personal hygiene, environmental sanitation and beautification, medical nutrition, social work journalism, etc.

It is interesting to analyse the population ageing and care programmes in Kerala (India) and China. Population ageing is widespread and severe in China and Kerala. Developed countries had a severely aged population only after they completed the modernisation process and reached a high level of socio-economic development and had sufficient resources to support and establish adequate social security, social assistance, social insurance and service care delivery system for the elderly.

But in Kerala and China with economic backwardness and under development have to support a severally aged population compared to developed countries.

The following Table 1 shows population aged 65+percentage in China (Census figures and projections)

Table 1 : Distribution of population aged 65+percentage in China[1]

Year	*Aged 65+%*
1953	4.4
1964	3.6
1982	4.9
1990	5.6
2000	6.7
2010	8.1
2020	10.9

Table 2 : Elderly dependency ratio in China (65+population)[1]

Year	*Dependency ratio*
1980	8.3
1990	8.9
2000	11.4
2010	13.6
2020	20.3

Table 3 : Table showing 60 + population Kerala[2] (Census figures and projections)

Year	*Population of age 60+*
1961	5.83
1971	6.22
1981	7.50
1991	8.28
2001	10.73
2011	13.07

Table 4 : Table showing old age dependency in Kerala[2]

Year	*Old age dependency (Aged 60 +)*
1991	13.77
2001	15.79
2011	18.13

When comparing the severity of ageing the figures of China and Kerala do not have much difference. The tempo is more or less same.

Like China, Kerala also provides a large number of social security/welfare fund assistance to the aged. In China in 1981 elderly peasants numbering 4,26,000 collected monthly pension regularly from their Brigade Welfare Fund.

In Kerala 20.4 per cent (1993) of the elderly are getting assistance like destitute pension, aged pension, widow pension, agricultural workers pension and other welfare fund benefits.

While there is very limited institutional services for the elderly in Kerala, China provides a large number of elderly homes.

Table 5 : Institutional services for the elderly in China[3]

Year	*No. of elderly homes*	*No. of elderly*
1982	8800	138000
1987	28014	281056

It is essential that along with institutional care counselling and social work services have to made available to the elderly.

In sociology of health, care of the aged is a growing discipline in providing adequate data for the continuum of services. A multidisciplinary team approach consisting of the geriatrician, the gerontologist, the professional social worker, the clinical psychologist, the social work journalist, geriatric nurse in well organised geriatric centres and their community outreach work through popular peoples participation is a good proposition for the future.

Family empowerment

Services at the sub-centre, geriatric centre, primary health centre should be easily accessible to the family, so that the family is empowered to cater to the needs of the elderly. Similarly poverty alleviation and environmental improvement programmes, social security and social assistance, social work delivery of services, etc., should be available at the door steps of the family.

The family also can play an important role in strengthening daily routine like timely rising from bed, going to toilet, cleaning, personal hygiene, environmental sanitation, physical fitness, taking bath, breakfast, going to/doing work, taking noon meals, evening tea, recreation, supper and sleep. The family can also conduct social diagnosis of the aged patient in the preparation of their psycho-analytical case histories for assisting doctors in the preparation of health plan for every aged. The family can assist the social worker in providing social work treatment, which is very important in balancing of the environment. Social work healing is possible through spouse communication and agreement, inter-generational communication and agreement, social and cultural awareness, cross-cultural counselling, etc. Families can also provide adequate psychosocial and informational preparedness to the elderly against superstition, social deviance, rumours, informational deficiencies and ignorance and make them capable of receiving the services.

Families also can provide individual, group and community experiences and growth opportunities to the elderly. Families can co-operate with public and civic administration, geriatric centres, primary health centres, sub-centres, *anganwadis*, etc., for prevention, treatment and rehabilitation programmes for the elderly. The families have to be empowered, to fight all malice and social and economic maladies, in favour of the elderly.

Provisions of adequate social work literacy programmes are essential to empower families to undertake their specific role in the care of the elderly. The families can play an important role in upgrading the services and quality of life of the elderly. In order to empower families they have to be given sufficient growth opportunities and living, cultural and social work skills.

A study conducted in Kerala shows that peoples participation along with the work of reading rooms, libraries, arts clubs, sports clubs, youth clubs, *mahila mandalas*, *anganwadis*, etc., have a positive role in empowering families to cope more effectively in dealing with the adjustment, health, recreation and economic security programmes in the care of the elderly.

In developed countries like Canada if a family member take care of the aged patient either at home or at the hospital/geriatric centre is provided with salary by the government/local administration or provide special leave with full salary for the period of care. Such facilities have to be made available in all countries to empower the family member to care the aged.

Social intervention

Geriatric committees may be formed for every two thousand populations for rendering geriatric assistance. The committee may consist of health inspector, junior public health nurse, *anganwadi* worker, social worker, sociologist, psychologist, teacher, representative of local body, *mahila mandala*, youth club, reading room, library, sports club, etc., under the co-ordinating influence of the primary health centre doctor.

In each *anganwadi*/family welfare sub-centre one day per week may be designated as aged clinic. Otherwise one geriatric centre may be started for every 5000 population providing facilities like day care, TT immunisation, prophylaxis clinic against anaemia, goitre and blindness. The geriatric centre may be staffed with a junior public health nurse and a social worker considering clinical and counselling needs. The Junior Public Health Nurse (JPHN) may attend to physical ailments while the social worker will deal with individual, group, family and community counselling and social work practice for enhancement of the social functioning of the elderly. Free noon meal services may be provided to the deserving elderly. The geriatric centre may also provide economic self-support facilities, utilising their extra time for income earning vocations or services.

The aged persons suffer from several chronic illness like tuberculosis, leprosy, hypertension, cardiovascular diseases, diabetes, cancer, asthma, allergy, rheumatism, jaundice, meningitis, illness in the joints, urinary disorders, stone, kidney disorders, liver complaints, peptic ulcer, chromes disease, disorders associated with menopause, urinary tract infections, illness in eye, ear, teeth, gums, etc., diabilities, Reproductive Treat Infections (RTSs) sexually transmitted disorders, HIV/AIDS, etc. They also face adjustment problems, alcoholism and drug addiction, idleness, tiredness, fatigue, boredom, family and socio-cultural disintegration, economic handicaps, unemployment, etc. Mental illness like hallucinations, delusions, depression, dementia, fear, anxiety, epilepsy, convulsions, physical illness created by mental disorders, etc., are problems for the aged. Team treatment by doctors of different systems and specialisations of medicine, psychologist, social worker, nurse, sociologist, etc., is essential to upgrade the continuum of services for the care of the aged.

The people of different age group should be given adequate counselling for planning a secure and healthy life in the old age. A curriculum for old age planning should be included in the syllabus of education at different stages. In the treatment and care of the elderly the geriatric committees have to pay an important role.

Special housing programmes like rehabilitation housing, subsidised housing, special housing, aged hostels and care homes, etc., are common in developed countries. Housing for the aged has to be given urgent consideration while preparing plans for the aged.

Let the local geriatric committees and families join hands for upgrading the services of the elderly. Community day care is essential for the elderly in need. Integrated Aged Welfare and Development Projects on the pattern of Integrated Child Development Services has to be organised under government sector for each geographical area for care and protection of the aged. The programme should be based on complete involvement of the families and communities including non-governmental organisations.

Training should be provided to local activists and representatives of socio-cultural complexes, members of geriatric/ gerontological committees, etc., on the continuum of care programmes for the elderly. In order to help intervention by non-governmental organisations (NGOs) the services of governmental pool officers like geriatrician, gerontological social worker, geriatric nurse, clinical psychologist, sociologist, demographer, etc., to help empower families, neighbourhoods to provide enough care and protection to the elderly.

References

Ping, Tu, 1996, 'Population Ageing and Control of Population Growth', *China Population Today*, vol. 13, no. 2, April 1996, China Population Information and Research Centre, Beijing.

Ramakumar, R., *et al.*, 1992, *Demographic Transition in Kerala*, Department of Demography, University of Kerala, Kariavattom, Thiruvananthapuram.

Sivakumar D., 1992, *Progress and Problems of Social Development with special reference to Kerala*, University of Kerala, Kariavattom, Thiruvananthapuram, (Unpublished Ph.D. Thesis in Social Work).

——— 1996, *Social Work Based Health care for the Middle aged and Elderly: Towards a state plan of action*, Population Research Centre, University of Kerala, Kariavattom, Thiruvananthapuram (paper presented in state health educations seminars organised by District Medical Officer of Government of Kerala under Directorate of Health Services.

———, 1999, 'Integration of strategies for care of the elderly' Social Welfare, vol. 46, no. 7, October 1999.

Section II
Problems and Prospects of the Old

9

Integrated Approach to Old Age Care
Problems and Prospects

B. Suguna
Sandhya Rani

Introduction

CONCEPT OF OLD AGE CARE

THIS article is a growing multidisciplinary study in the continuum of care programmes. This merits special significance in the context of the observance of the United Nations International Year of older persons, 1999. The month of October, 1999 'Samaj Kalyan Chetana Parv' is dedicated to the aged and to give them their dignity. The rightful place for the aged is in the family, which is beneficial to all, young and old alike.

Indian thought demarcates four stages of *ashramas* of life namely, *brahmacharya*, *grihastha*, *vanaprastha*, and *samnyasa*. These are student life, life as a householder, early old age that was ideally spent as a forest dweller and late old age spent as an ascetic in prayer and introspection. When the children are married they enter *grihasthashrama* and their parents enter *vanaprastha*. Before the aged left the house as *samnyasis* they were expected to fulfil their parents enter *vanaparastha* by giving their grandchildren the ethics and values of life. Children are a support for old age. The joint family system prevailed in the predominantly agriculture-supported rural areas. Industrialisation has led to urbanisation that has led to consumerism which has profoundly affected our lives. We need state interventions to solve all our problems. Today there is a growing demand for more and more old age homes, but we should not forget for that old age homes did exist in the Indian systems of life. They were called *vriddhashrama* and were present at all places, more so, in pilgrim centres. The old system thus has a new shape and name. The shift in the family structure has created on the other. This shows that changing values are putting at risk two of the most vulnerable groups of society. Our primary focus and need should be to provide space for elders in the family because that is their ideal home and their children are the ideal support system. At the same time we can plan to house old age homes and creches in the same premises so that the young and the old can enjoy each others company.

However, there is a common tendency to foist responsibility on the government for actions that should be tackled on a community and family level. The issue of elder care cannot be addressed to government only nor can it be left solely for families to solve on their own either. So, there is need to develop an integrated approach where the government and the family share the responsiblity to create a space for the elderly that is natural, comfortable and enriching. Of curse, the non-governmental organisations can play a pivotal role in this regard.

Constitutional provisions for the aged

Indian Constitution guarantees the welfare state. Article 41 of the Directive Principles of State Policy lays down that 'the state shall within the limits of economic capacity and development make effective provisions for securing the right to work, to education and to public assistance in cases of unemployment, old age, sickness and disablement and in other cases of underserved want'. Similarly section 20(3) of the Hindu Adoption and Maintenance Act enjoins on persons to maintain his or her aged and infirm parents. In spite of the constitutional guarantee, the positive aspect of the welfare state has not been entirely in favour of the aged. The growing concern with the problem of ageing and constant development of service have brought about demands for a professionalisation of care of older people through manpower development and training.

Social sensibilities for the aged

In a befitting recognition of the year (1999) having been declared by the United Nations as the International Year of older persons, the Government of India approved the National policy for older persons for accelerating welfare measures and empowering the elderly in ways beneficial to them. A national council has been set-up to look into the problems of the senior citizens (above 60 years of age) particularly in matters relating to person and health. It may be recalled that in 1990, the General Assembly of the United Nations designated 1st October as the International Day for the elderly, later renamed the International Day of older persons which was celebrated for the first time the following year. The day has been an annual event in most countries with varied activites organised in conjunction with the official commemoration. The General Assembly adopted the United Nations Principles for older persons in 1991. The eighteen principles provide a broad framework for action on ageing. They are organised into five clusters namely, independence, participation, care, self-fulfilment and dignity of older persons. In 1992, the General Assembly adopted the proclamation which called for the observance of the year 1999 as the International Year of the older persons. The new policy for such persons in India provides for setting up of a pension fund for ensuring security with empowerment of those in the unorganised sector, construction of old age homes or day care centres, establishment of resource centres and re-employment fureaux for the 60 above population and confessional fares for rail and air travel within and between cities. Besides, it aims at enacting legislation for compulsory geriatric care in all public hospitals.

The demographic ageing of the population has serious implications both at macro and the household level, especially when the transition has been accompanied by changes in society and economy. The percentage of elderly persons in the country has risen from 5.6 per cent in 1961 to 6.71 per cent in 1999 and is likely to touch 7.1 per cent in 2001 and will rise to 8.3 per cent by 2007. In absolute terms, the year 1991 saw 55 million elderly persons in the country, 66.7 million in 1999 and the number is expected to touch 76 million by 2001. As a consequence thereof, the country would be facing a progressive increase in the proportion of the elderly persons and it becomes mandatory to provide facilities and support for their well-being.

It is also a fact that industrialisation, education, urbanisation and exposure to lifestyles in the developed countries are bringing changes in values and lifestyles of our younger generation relegating the older person's welfare to the background. In view of these developments, there has been a demand for the last several years that a policy be initiated by the government for its senior citizens so that they do not face any identity crisis. Evidently, any policy for elderly people should lend human touch by viewing the life cycle as a continuum, of which post-60 phase of life is an integral part. By avoiding to assume 60 years as the cut off point for beginning a life of dependency, there has to be major thrust on active and productive involvement of older persons rather than only their care. But how far measures already taken by the government have been implemented is anybody's guess.

It is quite encouraging that the government has recently announced the constitution of National Council for older persons, called 'age well'. It will seek the opinion of oder persons on measures to make life easier for them and also setting up an office to handle the work of the aged including cases in courts. An employment exchange to utilise the experience and talent of older persons is also on the agenda of the council. Attempts will be made to sensitise school children to live and work with them. It will also set-up a round the clock helpline and discourage social ostracism of elders. The organisations formed by a group of eminent persons will reach out directly to families and help the elders by providing companionship, medical support and emergency help.

The government policy recognises older persons as a valuable asset and propagates the cause for their empowerment. The principle area of intervention and action strategies include a significant expansion in the coverage under the old age pension scheme and other retirement benefits to avoid hardship to superannuated persons and also make taxation policies more elderly-sensitive. It also accords high priority to the health care needs of older persons by combining public health services, health insurance, private medical care and health services, offered by non-governmental organisations so that geriatric health is easily available in easy packages. The government has also been contemplating to allot 10 per cent of houses constructed under housing schemes for both urban and rural lower income segments to older persons on easy loan schemes. The policy also provides for meeting the educational, training and information needs of older persons, an area which has remained neglected hitherto. Also special material relevant to the lives of older people will be developed and will be disseminated.

The government also needs to provide a continuous flow of funds to voluntary organisations for construction and maintenance of old age homes. A welfare fund may be created both at the state and central levels and also introduction of special provisions in the Indian Penal Code to protect older persons from lawlessness and crime and machinery provided to attend to all such cases. A review of the tenancy legislation to be undertaken for speedy restoration of rights of occupancy of older persons.

Other areas of action proposed include issue of identity cards by the state government, fare concessions in all modes of travel, priority in sanctioning gas and telephone connections, speedy disposal of their complaints, seat reservation in public transport, cinema halls and entertainment centres with discounted tickets for cultural programmes to senior citizens, states to set-up separate directorates of older persons and review of the national policy at the centre from time to time.

It is absolutely necessary to impress upon the aged the need to adjust to the changing circumstances and live harmoniously with the younger generation. Despite material comfort and psychological security provided to the aged, the twilight years of ageing are far from satisfactory. Life in the greying years becomes all the more despicable when many suffer the agony in silence without letting the world know that their children have neglected them. About 12 per cent of India's ageing population has been officially declared as destitute and forced to live off on meager pension. In this regard mass media could be used to its maximum to sensitise younger generation. Today, the abuse of the elderly is widespread in our society mainly due to break-up of joint family system. In places where large chunk of youths have migrated in search of better life, the aged and the ailing are constrained to lead a miserable life with no one around to take care of them.

To worsen matters, the older women out number the older men. Today 55 per cent women above 60 years of age being widows, and widowhood remains a major problem with the aged population. They are caught in an act of survival having been neglected by the families and shunned by society. Of the 70 million elderly people in India today, about 90 per cent of these are from unorganised sector with 75 per cent living in rural areas. One-third of the elderly are stated to be living below the poverty line. It has been found that old age becomes detrimental to social roles for the aged women and most of them are subjected to social and economic marginalisation to be treated them as 'burden'. Population surveys reveal that 10-15 per cent of the elderly either are childless or do not have children living with them for various reasons.

Despite the fact that most of the countries are having national co-ordinating bodies for social services and non-governmental organisations are doing yeoman service caring the old, family care is still considered to be the main source of social protection for the elderly, because the aged expect not only economic support from younger generation but more of social and emotional support. So, the plausible option could be to strengthen the family system and try to motivate the members of the family to take care of the aged. This may not only help to improve the plight of the aged but also preserve our traditional and cultural values.

The government therefore, would do well to set-up a national commission for elderly people in all that all the problems and issues of the aged are addressed while formulating policies and programmes. The huge population of the aged in the country needs to be given its due place in the society by creating social sensiblities for the aged and only then the country could usher in and implement the concept of welfare state.

Geriatrics and preventive social medicine

Having discussed at length regarding the creation of social sensiblities for the aged, let us consider the crucial problems of geriatric care and preventive social medicine for a comprehensive understanding of the study.

That change is the only permanent truth of life seems to have been the ultimate conclusion of all human experience. Nature changes, from season to season as well as from place to place. Human society changes from one historical epoch to another. It has been the experience of human life that everything in it and surrounding it keeps changing all the time.

Accordingly it, is also seen that 'ageing' is a universal phenomenon. In the words of Seneca, 'old age is an incurable disease'. Sir James Sterling Ross commented 'you do not heal old age; you protect it; you promote it; you extend it'. These are in fact the basic principles of preventive medicine. Old age should be regarded as normal inevitable biological phenomenon. The study of the physical and pyschological changes which are incident to old age is called gerontology. The care of the aged is called clinical gerontology or geriatrics. Another aspect of gerontology is social gerontology which was born on the one hand out of the development of humanitarian social attitudes and on the other out of the problems set by the increasing number of old people (Verzar, F. 1968). Experimental gerontology is concerned with research into the basic biological problems of ageing into its physiology, biochemistry, pathology and psychology. The fields of studies range from studies of populations through individuals, organs, systems, issues and cells, down to the molecular level. Geriatric gynaecology: with the lengthening span of life a new chapter in gynaecology — is fast opening up. More patients are coming for repair of prolapse of varying degrees, non-specific vaginitis, ovarian tumours, psychic aberrations and sexual problems. There is a plenty of scope for research into the generative and other diseases of old age, their treatment in hospital and general practice and finally into preventive geriatrics and the epidemiology of conditions affecting the aged.

Magnitude of the problem

The government aims at enacting legislation for compulsory geriatric care in all public hospitals. Geriatrics, as has been stated earlier is that branch of medicine which deals with the care of the old people. In 1980, the United Nations recommended 60 years as the age of transition to the elderly segment of the population. In many countries the geriatric population is increasing at a faster rate than any population as a whole and thus increasing the dependency ratio of the population. Hence the pro-active approach to geriatric care becomes absolutely necessary.

Discoveries in medical science and improved social conditions during the past few decades have increased the life span of man. Many people in the developed countries are living up to the age of 70 years and more. In England, it was stated, about 12 per cent of the people are over 65 years of age as against 3.2 per cent in India. The age structure of the population in the developed countries has also evolved that the number of old people is continuously on the increase. These trends are appearing in all countries where medical and social services are well developed and the standard of living is high. In India, although the percentage of aged persons to the total population is low in comparison to the developed countries, however, the absolute size of the aged population is substantial.

A rise in the number of elderly has following economic consequences:

(i) It increases the dependency ratio of the population.

(ii) It increases the expenditure on welfare activities of the elderly.

(iii) Due to higher prevalence and long duration of morbidity, the elderly population put a strain on existing health services.

From the social point of view, elderly persons, due to retirement from job and due to reduction in income have a feeling of loneliness, rejection and insecurity. This creates various psychological problems in the elderly.

Health problems of the aged

PROBLEMS DUE TO AGEING PROCESS

No one knows when old age begins. The process is essentially multidimensional. The biological, social, economic and chronological criteria for ageing vary from country to country. The 'biological age' of a person is not identical with his chronological age. It is said that nobody grows old merely by living a certain number of years. Years wrinkle the skin, but worry, doubt, fear, anxiety and self-distrust wrinkle the soil. While ageing merely stands for growing old, senescence is an expression used for the deterioration in the vitality or the lowering of the biological efficiency that accompanies ageing (Viswanathan, R. 1969). With the passage of time certain changes take place in an organism. Our knowledge about the ageing process is incomplete. We do not know much about the disabilities incident to the ageing process.

However, the following are some of the disabilities considered as incident to it:

(a) Senile cataract,
(b) Glaucoma,
(c) Nerve deafness,
(d) Bony changes affecting mobility,
(e) Emphysema,
(f) Failure of special senses and
(g) Changes in mental outlook.

This list is not exhaustive we need to know a lot more about the disabilities incident to the ageing process.

PROBLEMS ASSOCIATED WITH LONG-TERM ILLNESS

The longevity of aged persons gives rise to certain chronic diseases which are more frequent in the elder section of the population than in the young one. These are:

Degenerative Diseases Of Heart And Blood Vessels

Of particular importance after the age of 40 years are the degenerative diseases of the heart and blood vessels. The inner walls of the arteries break down and a lipoid material is deposited. This incourse of time is replaced by calcium which leads to narrowing of blood vessels or atherosclerosis. This leads to diminished blood supply, thrombus formation, rupture of blood vessels and high blood pressure. No single factor has been identified as the cause of atherosclerosis. Diet, heredity, over weight, nervous and emotional strain have all been implicated. Cardiovascular diseases are the major causes of death in the developed countries. A reduction of body weight and modification of the habits of life are needed to decrease the strain on heart and blood vessles. By these, it is possible to lead a longer and useful life.

Cancer

The danger of cancer looms large past middle life. In the developed countries, cancer is a leading cause of death (Raman' M.V. 1968). The incidence of cancer rises rapidly after the age of 40 and cancer of the prostage is common after the age of 65 years.

Accidents

Accidents are a health problem in the elderly. The bones become fragile due to a certain amount of decalcification as a result of which they break easily. Accidents are more common in the home than outside. Fracture neck of femur is a very common geriatric problem.

Diabetes

Diabetes is a long-term illness due to faulty carbohydrate metabolism. It is a leading cause of death as the population grows older. About 75 per cent of diabetics are over 50 years of age.

Diseases of the locomotor system

A wide range of articular and non-articular disorders affect the aged-fibrositis, myositis, neuritis, gout, rheumatoid arthritis, osteoarthritis, spondylitis of spine, etc. These conditions cause more discomfort and disability than any other chronic disease in the elderly.

Respiratory illnesses

In the upper decades of life, respiratory diseases such as chronic bronchitis, asthma, emphysema are of major importance.

Genitourinary system

Enlargement of the prostate, dysuria, nocturia, frequency and urgency of micturition are common complaints.

PSYCHOLOGICAL PROBLEMS

Mental changes

Impaired memory, rigidity of outlook, and dislike of change are some of the mental changes in the aged. Reduced income leads to a fall in the living standards of the elderly. It does have mental and social consquences.

Sexual adjustment

Between 40 and 50, there is normally stoppage of reproduction by women and reduction in sexual activity on the part of men. During this period, physical and emotional disturbances may occur. Irritability, jealousy and dependency are very common and frequent.

Emotional disorders

Emotional disorders result from social maladjustment. The degree of adaptation to the fact of ageing is crucial to man's happiness in this phase of life. Failure to adapt can lead to bitterness, inner with drawal, depression weariness of life and even suicide.

Implication of the ageing population in terms of preventive and social medicine

The ageing population is both a medical and sociological problem. First, it makes a greater demand on the health services of a community. It is a huge economic burden on the community to meet the cost of retirement pensions and support vast medical social services. Besides, a great strain is placed on the younger generation to look after them. The modern philosophy is that the old must continue to take their share in the responsibilities and in the enjoyment of the privileges which are an essential feature of remaining an active member of the community. The community must assist the aged to fight the triple evils of poverty, loneliness and ill health.

The health promotional measures required by the old people are:

- Good housing, health and freedom from disability
- A balanced diet.
- Reduction in physical and mental strain.
- Some intellectural activity — a variety of interests, activities and hobbies .
- Intra-familial cordial relationship, understanding and co-operation.
- Efficient geriatric service and welfare services such as access to clubs, hostels and homes.
- Cordial Social relationship, number of social contacts with friends and others.

The specific preventive mesures are:

- Avoidance of injuries and falls.
- Careful dieting and reduction of obesity.
- Periodic health check-up for early diagnosis and its treatment.
- National assistance and supplementary pension.
- Home services, home care services, meals on wheels services, old folk homes, sitters up service and provision of services of health visitors.

Integration of strategies for the care of the aged

Health-care and development of older person is a growing discipline in the continuum of care programmes which merits significance in the context of the observance of United Nations International Year of older persons, 1999. Since the publication of Social Diagnosis in 1917 by Mary Richmond, the role of the psychologist and professional social workers in psychosocial work treatment has attained supreme importance.

With the advent of demographic transition population ageing is becoming a serious problem in almost all developing countries. Integration of strategies is essential for the comprehensive and sustained social development of older persons. Improvement of quality of life and levels of living and enhancement of social functioning of individuals, groups, families and communities are the sum total of social development. Ageing of population as a branch of socio-psychological and social work study is getting worldwide attention.

Social work treatment

Medical and psychiatric social workers working in geriatric settings play a key role in social work treatment. The important methods include the following:

- Preparation of psychoanalytical case histories of the aged is essential in social diagnosis.
- Diagnosis of physical and cultural environment of the aged and understanding their felt needs for adjustment and enhancement of their social functioning.
- Finding out ultimate courses of illness and immediate, intermediate, and ultimate treatment models based on living and working conditions.
- Counselling and social work treatment are important in balancing of environment.
- Healing is possible through spouse communication and agreement subling communication, intergenerational communication and agreement, social and cultural awareness, cross-cultural counselling 'etc.

- Social work clinics and psychosocial and informational preparedness are essential social work healing is possible in social work clinical settings.
- Integration of social work and journalism strategies in technology transfer and technology utilisation are essential in the care of the aged.
- Provision of individual, group and community experiences and growth opportunities as a challenge in social work treatment of the elderly.
- Collaboration, co-ordination and linkage with other professions like nutrition, psychology, psychiatry, nursing, pharmocology and community participation are required.
- Policy analysis and co-operation with public and civic administration for care of the aged and for full development of their personality.
- Promotion of health and welfare, literacy campaigns for the enhanced social functioning of the elderly.
- Fighting social maladies like superstitions, human and substance abuse, cheating, crime, delinquency and squalor and preventing of social deviance, information deficiencies, suicides, conflicts, violence, etc.

Policy recommendations

1. The medical teams consisting of the demographer, the gerontologist, geriatric doctor, the clinical psychologist, the medical/psychiatric/geriatric social worker and geriatric nurses should have to be promoted in the healthcare of the older persons.
2. Non-governmental organisations (NGOs) and para professionals may have to be actively involved in healthcare efforts of older persons (both men and women) providing support services for their care, health check-up, nutrition, follow up of medical treatment, etc. Local NGOs could also run day care centres at the gram panchayat, *mandala* and

district levels.

3. Training and research programmes on community based health care for the elderly in clinical psychology, geriatric, medical and psychiatric social work, geriatric nursing has to be promoted so as to upgrade the programme.
4. Professional and scientific social work intervention has to be promoted in the prevention, treatment and rehabilitation of psychical, mental and social ill health.
5. Geriatric health awareness programmes have to be mandatory and inevitable part of social work literacy.
6. Excessive dependence on drugs in geriatric mental health care has to be changed with inter-personal, group and community counselling, community health programmes, social psychiatry and psycho-social work treatment.
7. Geriatric experts may be mde readily available at all levels of service.
8. Inter-personal communication, spouse communication, intergenerational communication, etc., should be strengthened so as to promote sustainable standards of geriatric health.
9. The family and the community have to take the responsibility for the care of the elderly as a challenge and more growth opportunities may be made available for improving the quality of their life.
10. Workshops, seminars and conferences on the care of the aged may be organised frequently at various levels as a multi-diciplinary and multi-professional programme.
11. The care programme should include family social work, family therapy, counselling, etc., to prevent family disintegration and to uphold human resource development.
12. Geriatric committees and families to join hands for upgrading the services of the elderly, community day care centres should be scientifically run and professionally

equipped. Integrated aged welfare and development projects on the pattern of ICDS has to be organised under government sector for each geographical area for care and protection of the aged. The programme should be based on complete involvement of the families and communities including NGOs.

13. Frequent demographic surveys to be conducted to determine the nature and extent of population ageing in various regions and various socio-cultural groups. These surveys are essential to assess the nature and extent of destitution, disability and chronic illness among older persons. Sample surveys are also required to assess morbidity patterns and healthy/disease-free life expectancy.

14. Physical beautification, environmental sanitation, personal hygiene, horticultural therapy, music therapy and occupational therapy have to be promoted and strengthened.

15. Strengthening of family betterment committees.

16. Including detailed care programmes of the elderly in family social work courses.

17. Psychosocial and economic betterment and empowerment of women and families are essential to cater to care of the older persons.

18. Journalist and mass media should cover care programmes of older persons in totality.

Conclusion

Thus, a continuum of care programmes for the aged including special housing schemes, food on wheels, both family faced care and institutional care have to be upgraded. In the twenty-first century, the proportion of the aged will be much higher in most populous, countries like India and China and social work strategy on the care of the aged is absolutely essential. Population profiles as older persons belonging to each socio-cultural stratum have to be prepared and analysed to systematise care programmes for the elderly.

When all is said and done, our attitude towards the old determines our actions for them. The old, are to be cared for cherished and comforted because they are 'valuable human resource' that have done with voyaging and are laden with the wealth of experience. Give them respect for they richly deserve it. By providing the onerous services to the aged, the individual, the family, the society and the state ensures that the years of retirement as those who have worked and toiled hard in its service shall be free from anxiety, want and boredom.

References

Baldev, Raj and Prasad, B.G., 1970, Geriatrics, 25, 142-58.

Park, J.E., 1983, *Textbook of Preventive and Social Medicine*, Banarsidas Bhanot, Jabalpore (India)

Raman, M.V., 1968, *Ind. Jourl.* Public Health, 12.1 give them their Dignity: the *Hindu* dated Sunday, March 28, 1999.

Social Welfare, *Samaj Kalyan Chetana Parv — 1999*, vol. 46, no. 7, October 1999 — Social Spaces for the Aged.

Siva Kumar, D., *Ageing of women in Kerala and Canada: Integration of Strategies for Their Social Development*, 26th All Kerala Sociological Conference, Tiruvananthapuram, February 5, 6 and 7, 1999.

———, *Aging of population in China and Kerala : Care of the Aged — The challenge of twenty-first century*, International Workshop on Population Issues of India by the down of twenty-first century, Tiruvananthapuram, 1998.

———, *Social work based Health care for the middle age and elderly — a state plan of Action*, presented in Health Education Seminar under the Auspices of Government of Kerala, 1996.

———, *Role of peoples participation in Empowering Families for the care of the Elderly*, International Congress on Ageing, Centre for Gerontological Studies, Tiruvananthapuram' 1996.

Viswanathan, R., 1969, *Medical problems of old age*, Current Technical Literature Co, Bombay.

Verzar, F., 1968, *Triangle*, the Sunday, *Jr. of Med. Sc.*, 8, 293.

10

Problems and Prospects of Old Age

R. Moorthy

OCTOBER Second is being celebrated as World's Elders Day, yet many senior citizens live a life of loneliness and despair.

Ageing is not a new phenomenon. But the problems that occur with ageing appear to be a product of the modern age. In the context of the dynamic changes taking place in Indian society, the problems of the aged have assumed grave importance (Joseph Subian, *et al.* 1989). Our ancient, culture demands that the aged should be respected. In fact, the order of prevalence in India has been mother, father, teacher and god. Since time immemorial most traditional families in India cling fast to the belief that, while it is the duty of the parents to look after their children, it is equally incumbent upon the children to look after their dependent parents. However, the changes taking place in Indian society due to urbanisation, industrialisation and modernisation have created problems for the aged in rural India (Pati, R.N. *et al.* 1989).

Better medical facilities, better nourishment improved standards of public health have all contributed to prolonged life. The population of elderly has risen rapidly both in developed and developing countries. While the developed nations have made serious efforts to provide for the ageing population, countries like India have hardly been taking effective measures to cope with the increasing number of senior citizens. Many thousand of them are still neglected by society. Their final years are grim, and lonely (Hindu 1999).

It is common knowledge that in the past joint family was the common pattern of family life in India, with head of the family enjoying rights, responsibilities, commanding obedience and respect from other members of the family. Today, nuclear family prevails with deteriorating the position of the elders in the family. They no longer enjoy the rights and responsibilities they once had. Apart from facing specific difficulties like scarce accommodation, high cost of living and expensive medical care, many elderly people also await the grim prospect of being unloved and unwanted.

The problems are different for different categories of elderly. The problems of elderly differ with respects to income, residential pattern, age, sex, education, occupation, health, marital status, family pattern, family support and whether living in urban, rural and tribal areas.

Today old age contributes one of the major social problems in developing countries. This is because while the number of the old age is increasing, social welfare measures for the support care and treatment are inadequate. The worst affected are the weaker sections of the society, i.e.' scheduled castes, scheduled tribes, and most backward communities. The aged among them are malnourished in their infancy, begin to work in their childhood, are underpaid and lack of job security in their adulthood. They cannot think of retirement in their old age and are victims of what is known as cumulative inequality. The general problems, the elderly face are loneliness and despair. It is not only that their bodies are weak but also the psychological effect, this has over will-power to live. They generally become dependent on others while all along they were independent. Due to various problems they are left alone and this leads to frustration, uselessness and helplessness.

Apart from the general problems faced by the elderly, there are problems related to specific sections.

Women

For women widowhood has greater impact than for men. It makes them dependent on sons, and simultaneously loss of status in family.

Childless couples

For them, old age is rather lonely and frightening. Their problems are not very different from couples who have children abroad. These prople are at the mercy of strangers, neighbours, watchmen, milkmen and domestic servants. They have all the material comforts but lack of family support.

Today society has to help the elderly and confront the reality of lonely living. A multi-prolonged effort from varied quarters is needed to help the elderly cope with the growing demands of situation. In 1991, India's population of the aged 60 years and above comprising 6.2 per cent of the total population, is estimated to increase according to the expert committee, to 7.7 per cent in 2001. In absolute members, persons 60 or more years of age were 56 millions in 1991. It is expected that this number will increase to about 76 million, in AD 2000, one of the every twelve Indians will be aged 60 years or more (Singh, R.R. 1998). According to recent UN reports, India would become an ageing society by the turn of century. The aged would be more than 7 per cent of total population. There are 70 million old people in India alone 60 years of age. Of this 40 per cent live below the poverty line, 55 per cent of women are widows and over 60 per cent of them are without any support, 75 per cent of them are illiterate and have to depend on physical labour even during their last days (Saraswathi, S. 1998).

There are certain measures required to cope with this problem of elderly.

Need for family support

There is definit need for family support. The members of the family have to be satisfied and made aware that they would also one day be in a similar situation.

Counselling

Counselling to the elderly would solve certain of their problems. While the members of the family could also be counselled to take optimum care of their ageing parents and still maintain a personal life.

Community oriented projects

The society could help the old to help themselves; society has to sensitise itself to the problems of the old and elderly and help them to lead a life of dignity and independence. Alternative living arrangements for the elders could be provided by NGO, NRIs and social service organisations. Much could be achieved if such people and their ideas are taken as resources to tackle this problem.

The Probus Club of Chennai has brought out a publication which gives useful information to senior citizens. A list of elder care homes and information on medical facilities, nursing care, and about caterers who will provide daily meals is available in the publication.

NRIs with ageing parents have thought of projects to provide information for the elders on similar lines. A network which provides interactive support on medical, nutritional, rites, and religious information is being worked out. Another idea planned is the formation of an experience bank which can collect and codify oral social history from the eventful lives of many seniors. Other areas where counselling is provided include civil affairs, legal matters, financial and banking advice, health and medicare and personal administration.

Psychological support

The Geriatric Counselling Centre in General Hospital, Chennai, was found by Dr. V.S. Natarajan to help the elderly face old age with dignity and courage. Apart from gerontology, the centre provides information on geriatric care and elder care management. Organisations like Helpage India have tried to include care of the elders in their agenda. Apart from providing homes to the aged and caring for their medical needs. Helpage India also has schemes for productive employment of the elderly. This helps them lead a life of dignity and courage and to die with grace.

Medical support

Medical care is also expensive. The government has been trying to solve this problem in hospitals and nursing homes but much needs to be done. Health costs are again high with the government unable to provide assistance to the aged, leave alone the suffering poor and sick. The Tamil Nadu Hospital has a service exclusively for elders who need medical help. The vision for the elderly depends on empowering them.

References

Joseph, Julian, William Korbulun, 1989, *Aged in India : Social Problems*, Englewoods: Prentice Hall.

Pati, R.N., Jena, B. (ed.), 1989, *Aged in India Socio-Demographic Dimensions*, New Delhi: Ashish Publishing House.

Saraswathi, S., 1998, 'Now, a policy for the aged', *The Hindu*, 24 March.

Singh, R.R., 1998, 'Approach to National Policy formulation ageing', *Research and Development Journal*, vol. 4, nos 2 and 3.

The Hindu, Sunday, 10 October, 1999.

11

Elderly Life Span: Enigma and Viewpoint

R. Shankar

Introduction

ELDERLY life span is an universal phenomenon. With varying degrees of probability, individuals endure childhood, grow to ripenness, and become old in all societies. But the enigma of elderly age are different in different societies. In most Western countries old age is associated with illness. The person who is old is thought to be sick. But 'elderly life span' and illness are not synonymous. Some people accept old age flowingly and they are happy with their children. But the condition of the preponderance of the elderly people invoke pity. In courtaneous age the rate of the old people is augmenting and the process of decline during the part of life becomes an enigma not only for the person concerned but also for the close relatives and the society as a whole. With the rise in population of the elderly people throughout the world, concern and care of the aged have attracted global attention of the social scientists and the administrators. When the elderly province quotient of a country is very high, it will create unusual and different types of puzzle.

What is elderly life span?

Bipedal life cycle is assuredly based on the biological method of ageing. But at what age people become elderly in the life cycle is not clear. There is no single point at which people automatically cross a magic line and become 'elderly'. To the people who turn 40, 50 seems old; at 50, 60 looks old. Thus the 'elderly' life span depends in part on the life span of the viewer.

However, more objectively, the 'elderly' life span depends on the average life anticipation in a particular society. This, in turn, is related to the society's overall standard of living and its technological ability to control diseases and other threats to human life. Throughout most of bipedal history, people's lives were quite short by the current standards of the developed countries. People married and had children at teen-age. They became middle-aged in their twenties and old by about thirty. Reaching the age of forty was rare until the late middle ages when a rising standard of living and technological advances began to bring about mortality decline and augmentation in the life anticipation.

Momentarily, gratitude to the rise in the standard of living and control of killer-diseases, in many countries, the average life expectancy has increased to 60 and this age is viewed as the old age and those who reach this age are labelled 'old'. Even this age will not remain fixed a will likely to change. With the further increase in the average life expectancy, the standard of old age will go up. In Japan, for example, a few decades back, the age 60 was so firmly marked as the beginning of old age. They called it *Kanreki* which literally means 'return to calendar', a time at which people were expected to become dependent. Momentarily they have advanced their idea of the onset of elderly life span to 70.

Thus, whether one is elderly or not depends on the prevailing standard of old age. Those who are once 'elderly' at 50 are not so at the same age today. Those who are 'elderly' at 60 today will not be so at the same age tomorrow. At the same point of time, there is a variation in the standard of elderly life span among the societies of the world. In much of the industrialised northern hemisphere, the average life span is 70 years and it is viewed as the elderly life span. But on the other hand, in many societies — primarily in the less industrialised and poor nations of southern hemisphere — life expectancy is less — around 50 to 60. The people in this age group are viewed as the 'elderly life span'.

Elderly life span — a general view

Throughout bipedal chronicle it has been evident that as some people get older, their activities wince in number and range. Old people are more likely to be infirm and, therefore, unable to travel about easily. They are more likely to be poor and to lack resources, which make taking part possible. Some theorists have gone further in explaining the limitation of activity in old age. Rene Knoing and others have used the concept of 'desocialisation' in contrast to the concept of 'socialisation', in childhood and adolescence, for the social and psychological change in old age.

Cumming and Henry have developed the concept of 'disengagement'. Independent of ill-health and poverty, normal ageing is a mutual withdrawal or disengagement between the ageing person and others in the social system.

Bipedal evolvement refers to the series of changes that individual characteristically show as they progress in time toward ripenness (growth and maturation) and through adult phase toward elderly life span. Ageing may be regarded beginning when the forces of growth bring the organism to a relative equilibrium. The term like 'maturation' and 'ageing' imply direction to events, direction that is controlled by psychological, social and physical and environmental forces common to the species and unique to a particular individual.

As a mankind grows elder, he is said to become 'more like himself'. This is meant to imply that the individual increasingly shows a pattern of appearance and behaviour that is characteristic of him. He is, of course, always moving forward in time and is in a dynamic transformation from his past to his future. The individual is a biological, psychological and social constellation moving forward in time. The dynamics of the transformation of the individual from childhood through adulthood are such that mixtures of stability and change, persistence and adaptation, and emergence of new features are seen in the wide range of bipedal characteristics.

Metaphorically, man's evolvement over the life span might be linked to the growth and branching of a tree. Once breathing has occurred, the pattern is somewhat determined, and the growth proceeds on previous growth. Behaviour also develops by branching and selection at choice point. Unlike the tree, however, man is both the result of and a determiner of his environment. His choices of behaviour lead to further differentiation and to a more ensemble of behaviours.

The term 'ageing' refers to something closely related to chronological age, but not identical with it. By itself, chronological age is one of the most useful singly items of information to know about an individual. Knowing an individual's chronological age, one can make a number of predictions about his most likely anatomical, physiological, psychological and social characteristics. Ageing is useful and power index in classifying large amount of information; but ageing is used in a broader sense.

Ageing is a natural phenomenon with not only broad scientific implications for all living forms, but also with profound personal implications for each individual. Man has been reflective about changes occurring in behaviour and temperament with advancing age, and the record of his subjective reactions to ageing are well in sculpture, painting, prose and poetry.

Primary scientific interest in ageing has focussed on the time-related changes in the individual organisms and personality. As the field developed, four principal factors have emerged:

- Biological changes.
- Changes in the psychological performance.
- Alternation in the situation and position of the individual in society.
- The manner in which ageing individual organises his feelings, self-concepts, and behaviour in response to internal changes and to the pressure and definitions of society.

Sociological life span

The sociological aspect of individual ageing is concerned with changes in the circumstances or situations of the individual as a member of the family, community and society. The changes and events associated with include age-grading and social attitudes and behaviour of society toward the ageing individual, completion of parental and work roles, reduced income, restricted activity and mobility, loss of spouse and associates, large increments of free time and relative absence of clearly defined societal expectations.

The enigma of ageing is, therefore, one that well merits study, both from the point of view of the individual and from that of the nation. Those who say that is the lot of mankind which must come, or elderly life span comprehends later part of the cycle of individual life, a period during which the symptoms of physical deterioration are apparently visible, and that nothing can be done are greatly mistake. Each phase of life is a preparation for the one, which follows it. The foundation laid on in our childhood determines to a great extent the success or failure of our mature life, so also does a behaviour in 'mid-life', which decides the natures of our elderly life span. So if entire life is itself planned, old age is automatically planned.

Continued participation of elderly people in their workforce and withdrawal from it has become a major interest of social gerontologists. A principal challenge and problem to elderly people in how to make use of the increments of free times resulting from shorter hours of work, earlier completion of parental responsibilities and retirement. Social gerontologists have become interested in persistence of earlier roles and role changes, activities and lifestyles in retirement, and in the conceptualisation and meaning of leisure to elderly people.

Retirement from work is rapidly becoming an institutionalised pattern in highly developed societies. The shifts from the work to the retirement role is recognised as one of the most drastic changes in the later years, with the consequence that a fair amount of research is being done one of the processes of retirement, anticipating attitudes and behaviour, and adjustment of retirees and family members.

Elderly life span has also been termed as social gerontology, which is concerned with changes in the social characteristics, status and roles of individuals. Over the second half of the life span, with the nature and process of adjustment, personality development, and mental health in the ageing individual, and with the biological and psychological processes of ageing in so far as they influence social capacity in later life.

Social gerontology seeks to discover the role of milieu, culture and social change as determinants of ageing and of the behaviour and position of elderly people as groups and in the aggregate; and their impact on social values and institutions and on economic, political, and social organisation, structure and function.

Social gerontology represents a confluence of several interests, which had their origins at different stages of social evolution. Simmon's (1945) survey of ethnological literature revealed that men in pre-literate societies were much concerned with extending of life, with getting a living with less energy, expenditure, and retaining opportunity for social participation and continued exercise of prerogative into elderly life span. Rather elaborate systems of intergenerational accommodation were developed in order that all age groups might like to take advantage of the experience and quality of judgement among the old while, at the same time, safeguarding the expectations of the younger men and protecting the postition of the old.

Elderly life span: present enigma of the elders

The enigmas of the senior citizen in India and for that matter in most of the Third World countries are different from the problems of the elderly persons in the developed and Western countries. The social institutions, cultural milieu, customs, traditions, religion, community controls and individual as well as group psychology of the two world are quite different.

Whenever the problems of the aged are discussed from academic and [1]or policy orientation point of view, in India it is, by and large, middle class and the other peripheral elite whose problems get highlighted. For example, there has, hardly, been any effort to measure the problems of the aged in poorer sections of the society.

It is imperative to mention here that in a society where more than 70 per cent population lives in the villages and an aggregate of more than 50 per cent of the rural and urban population merely exist below poverty line, it is not the problem of the aged that becomes important but it is the problem of poverty that also needs urgent attention.

I. Biological and physiological problems

- Problem in mobility.
- Problem in following routine work.
- Dependency.
- Senescene.
- Senility.

II. Health care and medical services

- Minor health problems due to negligence and lack of care, such as: defective eye-sight, general weakness, pain in joints, cough and cold, defective hearing, blood pressure, digestive complaints, breathing trouble, trembling of limbs, etc.
- Chronic diseases.
- Accidents.
- Non-adoption of preventive measure.
- Lack of health insurance scheme for the aged.

III. Nutritional problems

- Lack of awareness, education, non-availability of nutrients.

IV. Psychological problems.

- Maladjustment, lack of regard, affection, love, feeling of isolation loneliness, neglect, insecurity, humiliation and frustration.
- Intergenerational relations and generation gap.
- Rigidity.
- Dissatisfaction with life.

V. Socio-cultural problems

- Socio-cultural problems role diffusion, change in status, disintegration of joint family system, non-participation in decision-making, increasing materialism, individual orientation in place of family, urbanisation, industrialisation, displacement from rural to urban areas, changes in values, norms, culture and acculturation.

VI. Occupational and financial problems

- Problems in arranging suitable part-time job to supplement their income.
- To involve them in some productive and creative work which is useful for them and society as well.
- Creating economic independency.

VII. Environmental hazards susceptible to environmental change (heat and cold), (noise and air, etc.), ecological imbalances.

VIII. Housing problems.

IX. Social security measures for aged.

X. Communication and transportation.

XI. Recreation psychological problems.

Psychological enigma of personal alienation of the elderly may be due to a number of factors. Firstly, there is a sudden change from the occupational retirement and, apart from economic consequences; there are social and personal consequences of withdrawal from active life, e.g., depression, loneliness, frustration, rolelessness, powerlessness and unhappiness. As says John B. Martin former U.S. Commissioner of Ageing 'Forced retirement of Ageing can be no less devastating a blow than cancer'. Secondly, the death or migration of close friends and relations also involves loneliness. Specially in case of widows in India who are used to relying on the support of their husbands and other close relations. Thirdly, longevity involves living in different social, economic and value systems from those prevalent during the individuals' prime time together with reduced ability to change and reform attitudes. The intelligence, memory, learning, reasoning, judgement and creativity tend to decrease with age; some other unfavourable aspects of personality, *vis-a-vis*, tough-mindedness, narrow-mindedness, religious rigidity in behaviour and selfishness augmentation.

Elderly life span in developed and developing countries

The method of ripening is a communal phenomenon. Its frequency may vary from country to country and society to society. Its relative amount and conjuncture are extremely different. Being ahead in the process the matured regions have experienced this position and the maturing countries is well on its way to face a similar scene.

In matured nations, where family set-ups are no more considered, and the plight of the aged are wretched. The younger members of the family spend no time with their aged parents or relatives. They are more business-minded and they are busy always. So that nowadays in all developed countries institutional care for elderly has become common. But in developing countries this problem has not become so strong. Even momentarily majority parents live with their children and younger generation shows somewhat respect, love and protection for them.

Elderly life span — metropolitan and bucolic areas

In India greater number of the people live in villages. They are traditionally trained to respect love and alimentation the elderly people. The position and condition of bucolic the elderly is better than the metropolitan because they enjoy property and dominating power. One recent document reveal that four out of five of the total elderly are found in bucolic areas and the remaining live in metropolitan areas (irudayarajan, S. 1993). In metropolitan areas, they feel loneliness because their children are mostly employed, and grandchildren are admitted to school at an early age. Hence, they do not get a change to interact with family members and they have no work in the metropolitan house. This situation alienates them from family, society and more, from himself because of the aspiration and the attitude of independence of the younger generation. The rural elderly is a little more comfortable than their metropolitan counterparts. Yet lower economic position creates problems for the rural aged (Sabita Guha 1992).

Elderly life span — a multi-dimensional enigma

Elderly life span is an inevitable and universal process. There has been a rapid augmentation in the number of elderly people due to low mortality rate and medical advancement. Psychologists, sociologists and anthropologists are trying to solve the enigma of ageing from their own angles. A few studies (Birren 1959), (Tibbitts & Donshuse 1962), (Twoensend 1971), (Desai 1982), (Rao 1975) have highlighted the family social roles and physical and psychological aspects of ageing. In the past, they were taken care of by the individual concerned took them care of and his immediate circle of relatives took them care of and as such, elderly life span did not constitute a social enigma. In recent times, as a result of the changing circumstances the elderly people have become increasingly vulnerable to their natural circumstances the elderly people have become increasingly vulnerable to their natural disabilities and have been compelled to have recourse to societal organisations to solve their difficulties. The problems of bipedal beings are intimately connected to the milieu in which they live. Bipedal milieu is not only physical but also social and psychological. The enigma of ageing also have its own dimensions. Really no one compartmentalises the problem of the elderly, the physical and other problems will augmentation the rate of psychological problems. Therefore, all problems are interrelated. For the study purpose, social scientists, watched the different dimensions of the ageing problem. If we try to analyse the problem of ageing, we must analyse it, through different dimensions such as, biological or health, psychological, economical, cultural, political, demographical and social. This is well explained in the subsequent passages.

Biological or health enigma

In elderly life span physical and biological changes take place like hardening of the arteries and changes in the bone structure of mobility, problems in thinking strokes, prostate and heart problems, eye diseases and many more. The health status of the aged is generally poor becasue of natural wear and tear. Their weak financial position does not permit them either to take nutritious food or to get proper treatment with the result that there is a sharp deterioration in their health.

Pathak (1975) estimated that 25 per cent of the aged from middle and upper classes of the society suffer from multiple disorders. Sen Gupta and Chakraborty (1982) found that 92 per cent of the aged covered in their study were chronically ill. Gupta and Vohra reported that out of ever 10 aged mental patients, one suffered from organic disorder and the rest from functional disorders. Ahmad (1992) found that the problem of vision of foremost (82 per cent) followed by psychomotor problems (78.8 per cent), bone joint problem (78 per cent), memory problem (58.8 per cent) and sleep problem (58 per cent).

Psychological enigma

Psychological enigma of personal alienation of the aged may be due to a number of factors. Lehner and Kube (1955) have highlighted three fears that come with the old age. These are:

- *Fear of dependence and usefulness*: As a person ages he begins to fear retirement, unemployment, financial insecurity, loss of mental keenness and manual skill, and the possibility of having to rely on children to support.
- *Fear of illness*: As one gets older, fall in health often becomes a problem. An old person is no longer able to see or hear as he used to, his reflexes slow down, strength begins to ebb and such things as digestion and circulation grow sluggish.
- *Fear of isolation*: The elderly develop the fear that in case they are afflicted by any infectious disease, they may be isolated. The unpleasant specter of invalidism also moves step by step, threatening them to shut themselves off completely from their already shrinking social contacts. The loss suffered due to death of friends, of spouses and of colleagues aggravates the older persons' feeling of isolation.

Lemkar (1955) has clarified that elderly life span brings a reduction in memory and subjects the aged to varied kinds of mental illness. Cavan (1946) has made it clear that old age comes with worry over finance, anxiety over health, feeling of being unwanted, isolated and lonely, feeling of guilt, irritation, untidiness, uncleanness, inability to adjust to change conditions and decreased social contact and participation. Beard and Wagner have observed that forgetfulness hallucinations, feebleness, dizziness and pain may be unconscious mechanisms used by old people to attract attention, avoid boredom and upleasant reality and escape from the perplexities and disappointments of life.

Chowdhry (1992: 101) has pointed out that

> an old person begins to feel that even his children do not look upon him with that degree of respect which he used to get some years earlier. The old person feels neglected and humiliated. This may lead to the development of psychology of shunning the company of others. Loneliness in turn may give rise to depression and may eventually lead to worsening of sickness.

Thus, the elderly life span are facing a number psychological problems. Noteworthy among them are:

- Loss of memory.
- Difficulty in learning, particularly complex matter.
- Lack of confidence in one's own ability and judgement.
- Tendency to blame others.
- Feeling of being unnecessary.
- Unwanted and useless.
- Reduced interest.
- Mental rigidity.
- Feeling of isolation and loneliness.
- Tendency of hoard.
- Feeling of monotony and boredom.
- Feeling of inadequacy.
- Conservatism.
- Irritation.
- Sudden emotional outbursts.

- Feeling of uncertainty and insecurity about future.
- Tendency to brood over trivial matters.
- Fear of disease and death.
- Constant feeling of tension, worry and anxiety.

These psychological problems are further aggravated by constant pressure exerted by family members and close relatives to provide them financial help for realisation of their different types of plans out of their meager savings made with great difficulty and sacrifice and to transfer their property, particularly immovable, in their name, may be writing a will in their favour.

Economical enigma

Economy is another enigma in the lives of the aged. Diminished economic productivity of the aged, inflationary trends and changes is socio-economic values may give rise to varied economic problems. There is a reported nexus between economic stringency and nutrition and medicare.

Elderly life span become more disturbing in a society whose culture provokes irreverence towards the elderly and where the economic competition works to their disadvantages (Barron, Streib and Suchman 1952). Owing to the rapid advance in industrial technology for the expansion of productivity through high energy system, in the twentieth century the American society restricted the participation of older employees in the labour market (Burns 1954; Orback 1962; Hauser 1954). And it is only for the last few decades that the retired people are being regarded as a new category of persons in society being regarded as a new category of persons in society (Danshue, *et al.* 1960). The environment of the present industrial society is not conducive to the old people to get satisfaction of their physical and social psychological needs.

In the pre-industrial Indian society, most of the elderly people used to remain economically independent till they lived. They retained ownership of land holdings and other occupational establishments, and participated in productive activities according to their physical fitness.

Political

Conventional style of house dominance in joint families are helpful to older people. In the case of female elders, when they enjoyed the power and dominance under matriarchal system, their condition was very good. When this matriarchal joint families disappeared, their condition started deteriorating.

Demographical

The demographic component of elderly people in a population is a very important matter for all concerned. It becomes a problem when we ask the question; what is the use of these groups? Actually, these groups are uproductive in a particular country's population and hence cannot expect more developmental action from them. Because preponderance people come under the dependents. The working people's rate is very low. These group relays take more risk in their life to feed the dependents. That is, if the dependent ratio is higher, it is a enigma for any country. Especially, the female dependency ratio is higher because of their life anticipation rate rather than males and these widows remain unmarried ever after.

Social

When we consider the social enigma, we mean anything that shakes the social order and structure of the society. It will make changes as well as problems. The changes in the position and status lead to changes in the social structure. When people become old, they have to change their positions, which would ultimately change their social status. Consequently disroder creeps into the society that would impair the developmental activities. Thus, it is considered to be a great social problem by the administrators and sociologists. Since the individuals could not solve the problem, they hand it over to society. So solving the enigma of the aged is the duty of society.

Elderly life span — worldwide and federal viewpoint

The worldwide action was initiated in 1982 for the care of the aged by organising World Assembly on Ageing in Vienna under UNO. This World Assembly proposed a Plan of Action for Elderly to create awareness in the countries about the problem of ageing. Since then, there have been a number research studies, conferences, seminar in India with the financial assistance from the Government of India. The Government of India has also set-up an inter-ministerial committee on the welfare of the aged to consider a federal policy for the aged, their problems and programmes in the context of the changes taking place as a result of overall evolvement.

India's Constitution accepts the concept of a welfare state and Article 41 lays down the duty of the state towards all citizens including the aged, to 'make effective provision for securing the right to work, to education, and to public assistance in cases of unemployment, old age, sickness and disablement and in other cases of undeserved want'. The implementation of this Directive Principle of State Policy is subject of the limits of the country's economic capacity and evolvement. With the overall developmental process more and more services are likely to be available to the elderly.

It is now well recognised that the conventional approach of caring for a providing only for the destitute and poor aged needs to be reviewed. The new approach has to be in consonance with the recommendation of the World Wide Conference on Population (1984) that the

> Governments should view the ageing sector of the population not merely as a dependent group, but in terms of active contribution that older persons have already made and can still make to the economic, social and cultural life of their families and communities.

There are now a large number of aged who are active and healthy. They may be well-off also. The new approach, therefore, is to keep them usefully engaged through part-time, casual or consultancy services in spheres, which help the country in its march towards socio-economic evolvement. The elderly who have lot of experiences in coping with problems of life could help in providing social services. They could be effectively utilised in stemming the increasing tide of delinquencies and crime amongst younger groups.

The existing programmes in most cases do not meet the socio-psychological needs of the aged. The emphasis is, therefore, not only on physical and economic services but also on the integration of the aged by providing them leisure time and entertainment activities. The future homes for the aged should be centres of activity for the community as a whole. There should be constant interaction between the inmates of the homes for the aged with the inmates of children of women's homes. The residual work capacities of the aged have to be utilised in making the homes self-reliant and as centres of services to the aged living in neighbourhood. Day Care Centres for the aged where the aged meets to discuss and solve their own problems have to be encouraged. The Government of India since 1983-4 implements as central sector schemes whereby the voluntary organisations are helped establishing and running also of Day Care Centres for the aged.

Another requirement is to make the programme community based. Not only the voluntary organisation but even the municipal and village level local bodies have to be involved in providing welfare services to the aged.

Role of voluntary organisation

Voluntary organisations have to play a very consequential role particularly in effective implementation of a strategy which places a great premium on the care of elderly through the family and the community and non-institutional services. This role should encompass advocacy, promotion, evolvement and cater different types of needs in bucolic as well as metropolitan areas. Some of the services which they can offer are arranging health care through mobilising private medical practitioners/facilities; transportation services to hospitals/dispensaries; mobile medical services; supply of aids and appliances, Day Care Centres serving multiple needs, creating community awareness of the needs of the aged educating the family members and the elderly themselves on relevant matters to facilities understanding the harmony; arranging pilgrimage and domiciliary services; developing referral information systems; extending health and nutrition education; hold discussions to sensitise public opinion and bridge inter-generation gaps. VOs can also help in raising funds, mobilising manpower resources and supporting the participation of institutions (banks, trade unions, etc.) for extending services to the elderly. Organising the training and refresher courses for the people engaged in the care of the elderly is an emerging needs; the existing training institutions in different fields needs review to train these workers. Further there is urgent demand of the situation that some concrete short-term and long-term measures must be taken, otherwise the time is not very far when situation will be out of control. Following strategies may be useful in this connection.

Short-term strategies

- Creating more and more cognisance and education among the aged and the community regarding realities of this age-group and the role community as well as aged to reduce the problems.
- Providing health and nutrition, education and early detection of diseases and prevention from secondary complications.
- All community centres established by government, corporations, municipalities, NGOs and social and religious institutions should earmark reasonable space for day care and recreational facilities for senior citizens.
- Mobile medical care unit should be opened.
- Preventive measures should be adopted and physical exercise like *yoga* classes, etc., should be organised.
- Voluntary organisation's services should be encouraged.
- Utilisation of senior citizens as a resource of community work.

Long-term strategies

- Preparation of psycho-social and health profile of the aged of rural as well as urban areas.
- Development of programmes to improve the status of elderly such as creating adequate opportunities for gainful employment for the capable elders.
- National policy for the health of the aged should be formulated.
- Development and organising training for health, para-social work professionals, committed to work with this group.
- Inter-sectoral, multidimensional, mutual functional approach is needed.
- There should be creation of separate geriatric wards as well as department for the elderly with specialists' provision.
- Research activities should be carried out to have more knowledge regarding problems and solutions of elderly involving different disciplines.
- Housing should be provided by the evolvement authorities of different districts, which are constructing thousands of flats for middle and low-income group. There should be reservation of flats up-to some fixed percentage for the aged.
- Discourage the displacement of people for employment or other reasons, which is affecting joint family system.
- Tax exemption should be given to those individual as well as organisations who are providing funds to run the programme for aged.
- More travelling concession for aged. With these suggestions and comments it is concluded that we must go with full commitment not only to think or discuss this issue but also to contribute somethings constructive in this regard to minimise these state of affairs.

Elderly life span in future

The percentage of the elderly person in the age group of 60 which was 4.57 in 1961, went up to 3.14 per cent in 1981. It is likely to be 7.11 per cent in 2001.

The age group of 55 per cent is estimated to be around 85 million, which is considerably more than the population of several countries. Thus population explosion coupled with longevity due to better health and medical facilities on the one hand, nutrition, education and literacy on the other, will result in the aged being a very big group in India, which the nation cannot afford to neglect despite the gradual disintegration of the joint family system. On the other hand, urbanisation, industrialisation, economic factors and diminishing value system are likely to make welfare of the aged as the most critical area of social welfare, social schemes and geriatrics. Hence, there is a need for not only undertaking inter-disciplinary research in social sciences like the social, economic and psychological problems of the aged but also in combination with other natural and biological sciences before the close of the twentieth century, but also a twenty-year perspective plan for the welfare of the aged has to be prepared. A co-ordinated organisation structure also needs to be created to help in its implementation.

Conclusion

Ederly life span brings in its wake a host of changes in body and mind of individuals with consequent impact on the lifestyle and social relations. Enigma of elderly life span are different from country to country. However, a person's usefulness in the society diminishes because of ageing. Thus, the aged are one of the most vulnerable and high risk groups in terms of health, development and economic status in society today.

Better elderly life span: few suggestions

Havinghurst (1963) in his book, *Human Development and Education* (New York: Longman) gave the concept of 'Developmental Taste' which he defined as the taste at a certain period of an individual's life, successful achievement which leads to his happiness and success in the later tasks, while failure leads to unhappiness in the individual, disapproval by the society and difficulty with later tasks. The Western thinkers have not utilised the concept of 'developmental task' in psychologically tackling the problem of old age. But this concept may give us some insight into the forgotten usefulness of division of lifespan into four *ashramas*, viz.:

- *Brahmacharya ashrama* - Where the aim of a man should be to get education and observe celibacy.
- *Grihastha ashrama* - Where the aims of a man should be to earn wealth and fully satisfy his sexual needs.
- *Vanaprastha ashrama* - Where the aims should be to develop detachment and train his son, grown up by now, to look after his house or kingdom.
- *Samnyasa ashrama* - Where the aim should be to renounce the world and prepare for peaceful death.

If one does not maintain celibacy and seeks education during the *brahmacharya ashrama*, he may not be able to earn enough wealth and satisfy his sexual needs during the *grihastha ashrama* and this would leave him unprepared for the *vanaprastha ashrama* ultimately for the *samnyasa ashrama.* Thus, to avoid old age problems one must start preparing for the ultimate aim of life which is peaceful death and this could be successfully achieved only if one has adhered to aims of these four *ashramas*, one must also learn the reality that birth and death are the two doors of life the first for the entrance and latter of his exit. One must also learn how to die peacefully and successfully, this learning would considerably depend on well one has adhered to and observed the prescribed roles of these four different stages of life.

References

Bhattacharyya, S.K., 1989, 'The Problem of Aged', *Employment News*, Sept. 22-9.

Cary S., Kart, 1981, *The Realities of Ageing, An Introduction to Gerontology,* Allyn and Bacon Inc., London.

Desai, K.G. (ed.), 1982, *Ageing in India*, Tata Institute of Social Science, Bombay.

Dooghe, G. and Helander J. (ed.), 1979, *The family Life of Old Age*, Martinus Nijhoff Publishers, London.

Herman, J. Loether, 1967, *Problem of Ageing*, Dickenson Publishing Company, California.

Pathi, R.N. and Jena, B. (ed.), 1989, *Aged in India*, Ashish Pulishing House, New Delhi.

Sharma, M.L. and Dak, T.M. (eds.), 1987, *Ageing in India: Challenge for the Society*, Delhi: Ajanta Publications.

Soodam, Kirpal Singh, 1973, 'Economic Status of Aged', *Social Welfare*, vol. 20(6) Sept.

Suresh Chandra, 1970, 'The social challenges of Old Age', *Social Welfare*, no.17(6) Sept.

Townsend, Peter, 1957, *The Family Life of Old People*, Routledge and Kegan Paul, London.

12

Problems of the Aged
A Sociological Analaysis

Padma Mohanan

Introduction

THE human body is the most wonderful machine which nature has ever produced, but it also wears down with use and time. Ageing is a complex process involving biological, psychological, social and environmental components. Biological changes which are insidious and degenerative in nature constitute the basis of ageing and in turn modify the psychological and social function. There is a concomitant reduction in the resistance to illness and limitation in adaptability to environmental changes (physical and social) as well as to stresses and strains of daily life. Thus, it is necessary to adopt a holistic perspective to human ageing (Clymant' *et al.* 1986).

The scientific study of all apsects of ageing — health, economic, psychosocial and environmental has been termed 'gerontology'. It is a multidisciplinary field. That branch of gerontology and medicine which is concerned with the health of the elderly in all its aspects (preventive, curative, rehabilitative and continuous surveillance) is termed 'geriatrics' (WHO TRS 1974).

The ageing of the population means an increase not in the number but an increase in the proportion of the aged in the total population. However, due to improvements in the mortality figures and a decline in fertility levels, in the twentieth century the population of all the major regions of the world except Africa have been growing older at a much faster rate than ever in the past. In 1990 almost half a billion people slightly more than 9 per cent of the world's population were over 60 years. By 2030, the number will triple to one to four billion (World Bank Report 1994).

India, a subcontinent which carries 15 per cet of the world's population is gradually undergoing a demographic change as a result of many factors including specific development programmes. In 1951, the population over 60 years was around 21 million (Census of India 1954). Three decades later in 1981, it was a little over 43 million (Census of India 1983), a further decade later in 1991 this has increased to 54.7 million and for 2001 it is projected to be 76 million (Census of India 1984). Calculations also based on census reports (Bose 1988) show the decadal rate of growth of the population in the age category 'sixty plus' to be higher than that of the general population.

When the elderly were relatively few, there was a conspicuous place for them in the social structure of the community. Past values and traditions supported older person at the level of the family and community. It was the traditional practice of elderly being cared by the family members with love and respect, but over the years it has changed and a need was felt to study the family life of the aged with a view to identify areas of neglect and abuse. Interaction of the family members with the aged regarding their care were seen in the light of the expected social norms in order to determine the degree of neglect or abuse. Simultaneously, the aged respondents view of their life-style interaction pattern and feeling of neglected or abused was of central importance to the investigator.

Universe and the sample

The population under study were individuals aged 60 years and above living in the semi-urban of Mangalore municipal corporation area. A total of 200 subjects out of 176 houses, 86 males and 114 females were selected from the community using simple random sampling method and studied in detail.

It was a descriptive cross-sectional study done by the investigator during the period January to September 1998. A pre-tested, predetermined questionnaire was used for data collection. The schedule comprised of family information and individual information for geriatric subjects. It was designed to obtain demographic and socio-economic characteristics of all family members such as age, sex, education, occupation, present health status, particulars regarding environment, housing, family income and expenditure, type of family and intra familial relationship. Other than this, a detailed inforamation on the physical and psychological conditions of the geriatrics subjects were collected through the individual information schedule. A house to house survey was conducted to collect the data. Health examination of the subjects were done on the spot and assessment was done from the data gathered from the physician's record. Finally the data was analysed and appropriate statistical tests were applied.

Results and discussion

The health problems of the aged in this semi-urban area was found to be an integral part of the social and economic milieu of the general urban community-poverty being the basic factor. As the aged population are the non-productive or underproductive, economically weak with little or no income, they are considered a burden by their families and subjected to neglect or indifferent attitude. This made the age population adopt a pessimistic attitude with regard to their life in general and their health status in particular.

The details of the findings in the survey are presented below. The demographic profile of the population studied in the age group of 60 to 75 years, 48 per cent were females and 35 per cent were males (Table 1). A detailed information on the marital status of the elderly were collected and was found that majority (65 per cent) of the population were widowed, separated or unmarried (Table 2). Among these most of them were living with their sons, sons/ daughter-in-law or other close relatives and a minority lived alone. The educational background of the aged irrespective of the sex showed that only 26 per cent were illiterates. It was surprising to note that four women possessed professional qualification (Table

3). The occupation of the aged prior to their retirement has significant bearing on their social life as well as on health and psychological needs. The occupation of the aged were analysed to find that 65 per cent of the males were employed full-time in petty jobs and 16 per cent were employed part-time whereas 18 per cent of them were retired government servants. Among the females only 26 per cent were employed. Most of the women (74 per cent were unemployed and dependents (Table 4).

Table 1 : Distribution of subjects

Age	*Male*	*Female*	*Total*	*Percentage*
60-65	40	53	93	56.5
66-70	18	29	47	23.5
71-75	12	13	26	12.5
76-80	10	11	21	10.5
80+	6	8	14	7
Total	**86**	**114**	**200**	**100**

Table 2 : Marital status

Status	*Number*	*Percentage*
Married	70	35
Unmarried	2.5	12.5
Widow	62	31
Widower	29	14.5
Separated	14	7
Total	**200**	**100**

Table 3 : Educational status/sex

Educational status	*Male*	*Female*	*Total*	*Percentage*
Illiterate	14	38	52	26
Primary	26	58	84	42
Secondary	21	8	29	14.5
High school	6	6	12	6
College	19	4	23	11.5
Total	**86**	**114**	**200**	**100**

Table 4 : Occupational status/sex

Occupation	*Male*	*Female*	*Total*	*Percentage*
Unemployed (dependent)	20	84	104	52
Skilled workers	12	10	22	11
Unskilled Workers	21	9	30	15
Traders	10	2	12	6
Retired Govt. Servants	12	6	18	9
Part-time workers	11	3	14	7
Total	**86**	**114**	**200**	**100**

The status of the aged in the family depends on their contribution to family and also how they engage themselves after retirement. The economic crisis has forced many of the aged to reduce/adjust their needs eventually leading to psychological depression. As members of society they too have to fulfil certain social obligations like attending marriages, deaths of kins or friends, giving gifts to their daughters and grandchildren at the time of their visits. To meet such obligations their economic dependency certainly and gradually gives rise to conflicts in the family and to avoid this they ought to go for small employment. Thus, 65 per cent of the men were employed. On the contrary majority of the women respondents have a feeling that old age marks a period of rest for them. Hence, they are not productively engaged.

Ageing is associated with health unless there is disease or disability. It is important not to assume all ageing to be the equivalent of disease and disability. Majority (56 per cent) of the respondents view their health as being good or fairly good since they are not suffering from any major illness as known to them. Those suffreing from diabetes, arthritis, asthma, paralytic stroke and fracture were 44 per cent and they considered their health as bad or not so good. The association between ageing and health status was found to be statistically significant $P < 0.01$ (Table 5).

Table 5 : Agewise health status

Health status	*60-65*	*66-75*	*76-85*	*85+*	*Total*	*%*
Good (no major illness)	22	19	9	3	53	56
Fairly good (illness backache, cold, fever,etc.)	23	28	6	2	59	
Not so good (arthritis, backache, cataract, breathlessness, asthma, anemia, diabetes, hypertension, filariasis)	46	16	4	8	74	44
Bad (paralytic stroke, ischaemic heart disease, tuberculosis)	2	9	2	1	14	
Total	**93**	**72**	**21**	**14**	**200**	**100**

A large proportion of the households was headed by the sons where the aged do not receive the same defence and care as in the olden days and very often they are not consulted for major decision-making in the family. This is true in the present study where only 59 per cent of the respondents accepted that due importance was not given on their decision at the family level (Table 6). This is in confirmity with the findings of Vasvani and Dave (1996) and Rathi Devi (1996).

When asked about the type of care received from the family, 37 per cent of the respondents were of the opinion that family helps in time of need and advise rest and bring the necessities for them (Table 7). When interviewed about the medical care attended to by the family majority (74 per cent) of them felt that adequate diet and medicine were denied to them during illness. The caretakers showed lack of interest to prepare separate food for them even during illness. These repondents were longing to have their traditional food pattern not only during illness but at other times (Table 8). A few (29 per cent) who were living with their spouse and a few who were with the family like sons or daughters never felt worthlessness since they were taken care of properly (Table 9).

Table 6 : Family's consideration/non-consideration regarding decisions

Family considers opinions and advice	*Number*	**Percentage**
Family considers opinions and advice	82	41
Family sometimes consider opinions and advice	31	15.5
Spouse give opinions to each other (family has abandoned)	28	14
Respondents do not give advice (considering it as an interference)	32	16
Family never considers (shows neglect)	22	11
Lives alone (family has abandoned)	5	2.5
Total	**200**	**100**

Table 7 : Family helps/does not help in need

Family helps/does not help	*Number*	*Percentage*
Family helps (advice rest and bring the necessities)	75	37.5
Spouse helps (family has abandoned)	21	10.5
Family sometimes helps (shows neglect)	33	16.5
Family does not help (shows neglect)	66	33
Lives alone (Family has abandoned)	5	2.5
Total	**200**	**100**

Table 8 : Family takes/does not take for medical check-up

Family takes/does take	*Number*	*Percentage*
Family takes (thinks it to be a necessity)	52	26
Family sometimes takes (depends on the financial situation)	38	19
Family does not take (family finds it to be expensive and not necessary)	61	30.5
Does not go (finds it to be a waste of time, does not like to ge to hospital)	44	22
Does not go (has no family)	5	2.5
Total	**200**	**100**

Table 9 : Perception of experiencing worthlessness

Experiencing worthlessness	*Number*	*Percentage*
Money constraints (not caring and don't ask from family)	44	22
Family's disregard (in health, illness and old age)	52	26
Experiencing worthlessness sometimes (due to old age)	18	9
Experiencing worthlessness as still working (in spite of old age)	14	7
Leaving alone brings feeling of worthlessness (family has abandoned)	13	6.5
Not feeling worthless as family takes good care advising rest and getting required necessities	22	11
Not feeling worthless happy with spouse	37	18.5
Total	**200**	**100**

Co-residence was closely linked to care giving especially in the elderly's more advanced years when their health deteriorates. Living arrangements at this stage reflect the pattern of care giving within the family. Increasing longevity of individuals and the effect of younger age at marriage of women has resulted in wives ending up as care givers for their older husbands (Garret 1992). Table 10 shows that spouse was the main care providers when the elderly were in need of care. 35 per cent of the males reported their spouse as the care providers compared to 10.5 per cent among the females.

The attitude of the subjects to their life in general and their health status in particular was reported to be pessimistic by the majority (49 per cent) of the surveyed population (Table 11). The major recreational activities of these population were (1) conversation and gossip with elderly neighbours and friends (93.5 per cent), (2) participation in local fairs and festivals (82 per cent). Other recreational activities in which the aged had reported to be part taking were listening to transistors, participation in religious discourses and viewing cinema.

Table 10 : Care providers for the elderly when ill/needing care by sex

Care provider	*Male*	*Female*	*Total*
Self	21	25	46
Spouse	30	12	42
Son/daughter-in-law	15	43	58
Daughter/Son-in-law	7	12	19
Grandchildren	6	5	11
Others	7	17	24
Total	**86**	**114**	**200**

$x^2 = 23.697$: $p < 0.01$

Table 11 : Social history

Attitude to life and health	*Number*	*Percentage*
Optimistic	60	30
Pessimistic	98	49
Indifferent	42	21
Total	**114**	**200**

Table 12 : Social interaction

Attitude to life and health	**Number**	**Percentage**
Participation in fairs and festivals	164	82
Conversation with right friends	187	93.5
Listening to transistor	57	28.5
Viewing cinema	88	44
Partaking in religious discourse/programmes	192	96

Conclusion

The position of the elderly in a family was determined by a complex mix of the socio-economic and cultural development, material and economic interrelations and traditions. It may be concluded from this study that almost all the aged in the study experienced one or the other form of neglect, lack of attention, denial of freedom, food and health care. Though the traditional family bonds and solidarity were changing any improvement in the general well-being of the aged must begin within the context of the family. There was a great need to consolidate the family bonds in the society where these have been snapped and where the process of loosening of their bonds has already started. There was a need of proper social intervention so that these bonds get consolidated and strengthened.

The national policy has to be framed in such a manner that it includes all social security measures of the aged so that they need not depend on their children to look after them in old age. A large family was always considered as insurance against neglect of the old parents. Limiting family size in India could be effectively only when there is a comprehensive social security scheme applicable to the senior citizens in our country. The future of the aged in India as in any other country depends to a great extent on how the aged look at their own predicament and prepare for the sunset years.

References

Bose, A.B., 1988, *Ageing in India, Demographic Dimensions, Problems and Potentialities,* Abhinav Publications, New Delhi.

Census of India, 1954, Age Papers - 1951 Census Paper No. 3, Registrar General India, New Delhi.

Census of India, 1981, series 1, India paper 2 of 1983, Registrar General and Census Commission of India, New Delhi.

Census of India, 1981, series 1, India paper 1 of 1984, population projections for India 1981-2001, Registrar General and Census Commission of India, New Delhi.

Clymant, M.C. *et al.,* 1986 '*Health Visiting and the Elderly*', 1st edn., p. 30.

Garrett Mario, D. 'International Conference on Population Development', Paper submitted to the Expert Group Meeting on Population Growth and Demographic Structure, Paris.

Rethi Devi,K. 'Abuse in the family paper', Paper presented in the International Congress on Ageing, Trivandrum.

Vaswani, T.G. & Viraj Dave, 'Neglect and Abuse of Elderly in the Family', Paper Presented in the International Congress on Ageing, Trivandrum.

World Bank, 1994, 'Averting the Income Crisis for the Old' 'World Bank Policy Research Bulletin' 5 {4}.

WHO-TRS, 1974, 'Planning And Organisation of Geriatric Serivices' no. 548, pp. 11-12.

13

Aged — Problems and Prospects

Usha John

AGEING is an inevitable phenomenon in all living organisms. It is an inexorable process in life, leading to its extinction.

Definition of concepts

The term gerontology comes from the Greek word *geras* meaning 'old age' and *logos* referring to the study of a subject. The term, gerontology is very broad and encopasses the psychological, socio-economic and physiological aspects of old age. Social gerontology is concerned with reciprocal relationship between the individual and society. The term geriatrics deals with causes and amelioration of physical pathology in old age. Senescence, a biological term refers to the physiological aspect of growing old. Gerontocracy refers to government that is ruled by elders. Ageism is discrimination against individual on basis of old age. The term gerontophobia is used to designate the fear of growing old or the fear of hatred of the aged. The term ageing refers to the process of growing old.[1]

---

1. James, E., Birren, K., Warner Schaie, *Handbook of Psychology of Ageing* (4th edn.), Margret Gatz and Timothy (eds.), New York: Academic Press, Pandiego, 1996: 6-10.

   James, E., Birren, K., Warner Schaie, *Handbook of Psychology of Ageing* (1st edn.), Van Nostrand, Reinhold: Lilton Educational Publishing Inc, 1977: 95.

→

History

ORIGIN OF GERONTOLOGY AND GERIATRICS

The father of modern geriatric medical research and practice. Ignatz Z. Nascher, coined the word 'geriatrics' in 1909 and gave a new name in the medical field.

The field was still called ageing and apparently unnoticed until N.A. Rynikov the originator of the term outlined the nature of this new discipline. Gerontology aims at the investigation of the conditioning causes of old age as well as the study and careful description of the regular progress of the changes in behaviour peculiar to age. Although research and publication of studies on various aspects of ageing grew rapidly in the late 1920s and 1930s, the discipline of gerontology was not formally recognised nor was the name used in any form until 1940. In 1945, the gerontological society was organised and in 1946 the Journal of gerontology made its first appearance. [2]

Edward J. Stieglitz in the initial chapter of his book *Geriatric Medicine* published in 1954 used the expression of social gerontology. He divided gerontology into three major areas, (1) geriatric medicine, (2) biology of senescence, and (3) social gerontology. All economic and cultural factors of ageing such as employment, retirement, chronic illness, housing, education for senescence, marriage, family attitudes towards aged, social attitudes, cultural maturation and international aspects of maturing population comprise social gerontology.[3]

The growing interest and attention of social scientists in 1940s

---

Reymond' J., Corsini, Bonnie D. Ozaki, *Encyclopaedia of Psychology*, vol.1, John Wiley and Sons Inc. 1984: 39-40.

Frank. N., Magill, Jaclyn Rodriguez (eds.), *International Encyclopaedia of Psychology*, vol.1, London: Filz Roy Dear born Publishers, 1996, 105-39.

2. P.N. Sati, *Retired and Ageing People*, Delhi, Mittal Publications, 1988, p. 6.
3. *Ibid.*, p. 8.

and 1950s to gerontology led to the creation of an Inter-University Training Institute in Social gerontology in 1957.[4]

The publication in 1948 of Social Science Research Council's planning report Social Adjustment in Old Age edited by Otto Pollak marked another important transition from concern about the aged to the study of ageing as a process. The report reflected almost a decade of work by an interdisciplinary committee which began in 1941. By 1943, the committee had focussed its attention on social adjustment in old age as the most significant issue for social scientific research.

At the end of 1950s, a multi-university consortium projected three volumes which would document the scope, methods and conceptualisation of studies on ageing. The first of these volumes to appear was the *Handbook of Ageing and the Individual, Psychological and Biological Aspects of Ageing* edited by Clark Tibbitts and *Ageing in Western Societies* edited by E.W. Burgess (1960). These volumes constitute excellent bibliogrphic coverage of studies on ageing in the two decades prior to their publication and document the principal characteristics of studies of ageing.[5]

Sociologists in Duke and Chicago concentrated a substantial degree on adaptation in late life, comceptualised variously on morale, mental health or life satisfaction. The dominant perspective which emerged in these studies was that social integration in late life is not only possible but also probable and that social integration predicts morale. The exception to this dominant perspective was of course Cumming and Henry's (1961) concept of disengagement. Irving Rosow's *Social Integration of Aged* states that the probability of social interaction of older persons is significantly affected by the availablility of age peers of similar social status.[6]

---

4. L.L. Frank, 'Gerontology', *Journal of Grerontology*, Michigan: Ann Arber, 1946: 1 (1) (1-12).
5. P.N. Sati, 1988, *op.cit.*, p. 9.
6. *Ibid*, p.11.

Problems of aged

An aged person may be confronted with a legion of problems: economic, psychosocial, familial and health. A miserable state of deprivation, dependence, desertion, depression and disengagement inexorably pervading the aged persons mind takes him through an uncanny experience of orphanhood even in the presence of offsprings. The conternation and agony are never ending. It is important that the aged person makes an attempt to cope and reconcile with the various stresses and strains of ageing. It calls for necessary adaptation by the aged person to the changed scenario, readiness for sacrifices and adjustments in order to live in perfect harmony as per the Zeitgeist and with the interests of the future generation.

Global situation of aged

Ageing of population is a by-product of demographic revolution which is a consequence of industrial revolution, change in public health and education.

The world demographic situation shows that the percentage of age 65 + is increasing from 5.5 per cent in 1970 to 5.77 per cent in 1985 and it will be 6.39 per cent in AD 2000. The rate of incidence of ageing has been higher in developed regions and less in developing countries. As against 38 per cent increase in the total world Population for the period 1981 to 2000, the increase of population of 60 + age is 5.71 per cent.[7]

The ageing of populations is now a global phenomenon. It is manifest in several parts of the world and incipient in all the rest. In 1950 there were 200 million persons aged 60 and over in the world constituting 8 per cent of the total global population. By 2025, there will be sixfold increase in this number, the world elderly population is projected to be 1.2 million people about 14 per cent of the total figure. The median age of the world population will jump from 23.4

7. D.P. Chowdhury, *Ageing and the Aged: A Source Book*, New Delhi: International Publications, 1992, pp. 26-7.

years in 1950 to 31.1 years in 2025[8] (world population prospects). By 2025, 72 per cent of the elderly, about 858 million people will be living in developing region.[9] By 2025 the very old will number about 137 million, 11 per cent of the total elderly.[10] Between 1985 and 2025, projected increase for persons aged 70 and above are 32 million for males and 317 million for females in the developing regions. Sex differences in absolute increments are more apparent at older ages. Thus, over the same period, projected increase in the number of persons aged 80 and above are 8 million for males and 14 million for females in the developed regions and 24 million for males and 35 million for females in the developing countries.[11]

The ageing of population and social development

The developmental impact of the ageing of populations must extend beyond economic issues. The social component of development encompasses the equitable distribution of economic growth to all sectors of the population and even more broadly is concerned with improvements in the intangible social, cultural, psychological and political factors that shape the quality of life. Elements of social development include promotion of human dignity, the provision of social process of development. Factors that have been suggested as measures of progress in achieving social development include (1) the responsiveness of development to human needs, (2) the extent to which the entire population participates as agents and beneficiaries of the development process, and (3) spatial distribution of the benefits of development.[12] The extent to which population ageing will cause serious economic problems is not as clear as is commonly believed. There is need to understand ageing phenomenon and assess policy options related to demographic change. While pondering over the

8. United Nations Publication, *The World Ageing Situation* — 1991, Vienna: The Centre for Social Development and Human Affairs, 11.
9. *Ibid.*, p. 11.
10. *Ibid.*, p. 10.
11. *Ibid.*, p. 19.
12. *Ibid.*, p. 48.

issue of the ageing of populations and social development the key points to be considered are the effect on the capacity of family to support older persons, promotion of education and training, promotion of work roles, strengthening the indirect economic contributions of the ageing, the promotion of participation in community life. A reduction in family resources will be accompanied by an increased need for public services.

Situation of ageing in India

According to census figures, the population of people of 60+ age in India was 425 million in 1981. This constituted a 34.87 per cent increase in the population of this group from that of 1971 census figurs. This constitutes over 5 per cent of the population of country. In India, persons in the age group 60+ is more than 6 per cent of the population in 1991 and is likely to be 7.11 per cent in 2001. The average life expectancy of an Indian in 1991 was around 60. The level is expected to rise to 65 years in 2001.[13]

Relevance of old age support in Kerala

The old age population in Kerala is growing more rapidly than all other states of India with more than 9 per cent of the population already 60 years old as per 1991 census (all India 7 per cent).[14] The elderly will constitute about 20 per cent of the states population by 2021 (All India — 14 per cent). Like most of the industrialised nations Kerala will be poised to become an aged society in another 10-15 years.[15]

In Kerala, families still continue to be the major source of bulk of support given to the elderly population. But society has a major

---

13. International Federation of Ageing, 1992, *The Report of the First Conference on Ageing*, Pune.
14. P.K.B. Nair, 'Demographic and Social implications of Population Ageing in Kerala', Paper Presented at a Symposium. (Population Research Centre, University of Kerala, Trivandrum: 16th June 1994.
15. *Ibid.*

stake in the ability of families to care for their elders, in the context of emergence of nuclear families, migration for job purposes and increasing number of women finding career outside the household which may lead to institutionalisation which has its own short-comings.

Unfortunately an adequate social support system for a society ageing rapidly is not-existent in Kerala.

The wrenching trauma and dilemma convulsing the rapidly ageing in Kerala, their frustrating emotional and social vaccum, their orphanhood despite offsprings and their increasing medical needs call for comprehensive action plan which must go beyond minimum financial support in the form of old age pension or family pension and provisions for institutionalisation.

Empirical study

It is against this background an empirical study has been made to identify the problems of the aged, i.e., health, psychological, social, familial and economic problems and the subsequent coping style, *geographical universe of the study* is Karavalloor Panchayat, a rural area in Kollam district, Kerala, India. Aged persons in the family setting is the unit of study. The universe comprise 80 aged persons 40 males and 40 females, 40 in the age group 60-9 and 40 in the age group 70-9, 40 below the income Rs. 1000 and 40 aged persons above the income Rs. 1000 chosen by adopting purposive sampling. The design is descriptive.

Major findings

I. Health problems have significant association with income and educational status and not with gender and age.

II. Psychological problems are not associated with age, income, marital status and educational status.

III. Social and familial problems are not associated with gender, age, income, marital status, educational status.

IV. Financial problems are associated with age, educational

status and income but not with gender or marital status. 68.75 per cent of the respondents were coping with physical discomforts by taking medicine, 21.25 per cent were not taking medicine, 8.75 per cent of the respondents by controlling diet and 12.5 per cent by changing lifestyle.

3.75 per cent of the respondents were coping with the psychological problems by visiting temples, 12.5 per cent of the respondents by attending prayers, 47.5 per cent of the respondents by praying, 18.75 per cent by tolerating and 1.25 per cent by doing some work. 16.25 per cent didn't respond.

20 per cent of the respondents were coping with the social and familial problems by spending time with someone, 33.75 per cent by praying. 11.25 per cent by doing some work and 10 per cent by tolerating, 25 per cent of the respondents didn't respond.

47.5 per cent of the respondents were coping with the financial problems by asking money from children, 8.75 per cent by doing some work, 10 per cent by asking money neighbours, 10 per cent by praying and 47.5 per cent by tolerating. 16.25 per cent of the respondents didn't respond.

Issues

Discussion: To strengthen the economic capacity of family to perform its caretaker role and whenever necessary to substitute for traditional family support. The effect of the demographic transition on ratios of surviving children to serving parents implies an increased need for public support to families caring for older age groups. An important issue concerns how best to strengthen the resources of the most under privileged and often less visible and least articulate subgroups among the ageing, including racial, ethnic minorities, migrants and refugees.

Table 1 : Personal background of respondents

Gender			
	Male	40	50%
	Female	40	50%
Age			
	60-9 yr.	40	50%
	70-9 yr.	40	50%
Marital status			
	Married	47	58.75%
	Unmarried	2	2.50%
	Separated	3	3.75%
	Widowed	28	35%
Edcuational status			
	Illiterate	47	58.75%
	Primary	25	31.25%
	Matriculation	2	2.5%
	Graduate	6	7.5%
Family income			
	Below Rs.1,000	40	50
	Above Rs. 1,000	40	50

Table 2 : Health problems

1. Health problems and gender	1.84	Not significant
2. Health problems and age	4.54	Not significant
3. Health problems and income	6.205	Association
4. Health problems and educational stutus	13.52	Significant associated

Table 3 : Psychological problems

Variables	x^2	*Significance*
Psychological problem and gender	0.0779	Not significant
Psychological problem and age	2.646	No association
Psychological problem and income	1.764	Not significant

Table 4 : Social and familial problems

Variables	x^2	*Significance*
Social and familial problems and gender	5.495	Not significant
Social and familial problems and age	1.9782	Not significant
Social and familial problems and income	5.495	Not significant
Social and familial problems and marital status	10.31	Not significant
Social and familial problems and educational status	7.064	Not significant

Table 5 : Financial problems

Financial problems and gender	1.5834	Not significant
Financial problems and age	5.991	Significant
Financial problems and income	12.48	Significant
Financial problems and marital status	4.35	Not significant
Financial problems and educational status	45.36	Significant

Promotion of education and training

Education is a pre-requisite for the integration of the aged into modern society. In the occupational sphere, adult education including functional literacy and training in new technologies is needed to help older persons especially the most disadvantaged. They play an active economic role either continuing older ones or acquiring the skills needed to generate other forms of income. Older people need to be taught ways of preventing unnecessary illness and how to avoid accidents so that they can remain healthy enough to continue working.

The population as a whole should be given a better understanding of ageing processes and made aware of the skill and abilities of older persons. Overall education acts on stereotypical notions existing between the older and younger generations and gives older people the resources to reduce their dependence. As a means for tapping the knolwedge and skills of the ageing education becomes a catalyst for their productive contributions to development.

Continuing to work within their capacities permits older people to remain socially integrated. It also permits them to retain a sense of independence and contribute to their own support. Old persons contribute to economic development by assuming domestic responsibilities, freeing younger persons for other work.

The promotion of participation in community life ensures the enhancement of social communication between administrators and beneficiaries. The intended beneficiaries perceive the need for change, the utilisation of local knowledge and experience to anticipate problem that may arise during the implementation of development projects and the mobilisation of talent potential such as under used human and physical resources. The active involvement of intended beneficiaries in planning for new technologies helps to encourage the necessary changes in perceptions and behaviour the reversal of dependency by actively involving people in their own development and finally the promotion of the equitable distribution of benefits accuring from development measures. From an economic viewpoint, the continued participation of able older persons has been identified as one means of reversing the burden of dependency and providing additional human resources for productive alternatives.

World assembly on ageing and Vienna plan of action

In view of the global dimension of the problem of the aged, the United Nations organised the World Assembly on Ageing in Vienna in 1982 as a forum to launch an international action programme aimed at guaranteeing economic and social security to older persons as well as providing them with opportunities to contiribute to national development. In the documents circulated during the conference and in the recommendations entitled 'Vienna International Plan of Action on Ageing' (United Nations 1982) the world assembly on ageing among other measures, sponsored the idea of active ageing as an important strategy for the adjustment of the ageing in modern societies.[16]

The Vienna International Plan of Action of Ageing lays great stress on creating conditions which enable the ageing to live with their close relatives as long as possible.

---

16. V. D'Souza 'The Concept of Active Ageing', *Indian Journal of Social Work*, 1993, 54 (13), 333-44.

Article 17 of the Vienna International Plan of Action points out humanitarian issues related to specific needs as health and nutrition, housing and environment, family, social welfare, income, security, employment and education of the elderly. From the development point of view, society should guarantee to all persons regardless to age, the right to belong, participate and contribute. The recognition of the interdependence between the development of ageing and that of society would make it evident that the social resources invested in the betterment of ageing instead of a drain on the economy are on the contrary a productive investment having both tangible and intangible benefits.[17]

Active ageing

It deals with the way in which ageing can contribute to development, focussing on the welfare of the aged themselves. Countering the disengagement theory the active ageing has some similarity with the activity theory but with a wider connotation. Unlike the activity theory active ageing implies attainment of certain objectives on the part of the elderly such as economic security, sense of purpose and meaning in life and integration in the community and society. Active ageing embraces a very broad perspective including the inter-relationship between humanitarian and development needs of the elderly and those of their society.[18]

United Nations 'logo' for International Year of Older Persons (IYOP) 1999

The United Nations official logo for the year of older persons: IYOP 1999 (1-10-1998 to 31-12-1999) is meant to represent vitality, diversity and interdependence as well as movement and progression. Vitality

---

17. *Indian Journal of Social Work,* 1993, 54(13), 333-44.
18. United Nations Activities, 'United Nations Logo for the International Year of Older Persons' Bulletin on Ageing, 1998, no. 1, p. 11.

refers to the increased ability of mind and spirit made possible by healthful lifestyles as people age. The combination of vitality and diversity is seen as heralding both 'a new age for old age' and the reality of 'old age in a new age'. The concentric lines draw attention to the independence and interdependence of the generations, which create a dynamic and reciprocal exchange and caring. This notion of reciprocity is reflected in the theme for the year 'towards a society for all ages'.[19]

Prospects for the aged

INFRASTRUCTURE

1. To strengthen or establish a national co-ordinating mechanism on ageing for developing and promoting implementation of the national strategy on ageing composed of ministeries, councils, departments, committees, advisory groups, representatives of the elderly, political or religious groups and task forces.
2. *Promote the establishment and effective functioning of organisations of older persons.* The expertise and energy of older persons could be harnessed through these organisations to promote self-help, make contributions to policy and implement programmes for all age groups, e.g., pensioners organisation, senior volunteers corps, etc.
3. Promote the expansion or establishment of international policies and programming to encourage mutual co-operation, support and exchange between youth and the elderly at the individual organisational levels.
4. Improve or establish standards with enforcement protocols for elderly care providers including in home, community based and residential settings to ensure quality services.

---

19. United Nations New, York 1997, Department for Policy Co-ordination and Sustainable Development, *Older persons in Countries with economies in Transition, Designing a Policy Response,* 126-31.

5. To integrate the issues of ageing into national development plans.
6. To strengthen or establish national education, training and research activities on ageing as a basis for understanding the elderly and their concerns.
7. Ensure that national data collections include information which is gender and age specific.
8. To produce and widely disseminate regular reports on the national ageing situation.

HEALTH AND NUTRITION

9. Launch a campaigning on 'Healthy Ageing for all' to stress a holistic approach to health and to decrease the risk of dependency in old age through an emphasis on avoidance of health damaging habits and practices.
10. To establish national indices of health and disability among the aged.

    To ensure that primary health care is available and accessible to the elderly.

    To encourage establishment of a technical aids supply system which will encompass funding and distribution of health accessories and equipment with special attention to eye glasses, hearing aids and teeth prostheses need for prevention and treatment of age related disorders.
11. Provide adequate nutrition especially to the elderly at risk including such groups as refugees, victims of disasters and those in isolation.
12. To strengthen or establish a public health programme ensuring accessibility to clean water and adequate sanitation for the elderly.

HOUSING AND LIVING ENVIRONMENT

13. Provide support for the elderly so that they may continue

living in their own homes as long as possible or choose alternative accomodation if their home is no longer suitable or desired. These supports may include in home, health and social services, home maintenance and rental assistance.

14. Provide barrier-free community integrated accomodation and public facilities for the elderly in cities, towns and villages, national housing policies should pay due respect to the requirements of ageing.
15. Promote community education on personal security in the home and community which will address accident prevention and security against crime and abuse.
16. To provide and enhance accessibility and mobility for the elderly to work, social and health services and leisure facilities.

FAMILY

17. To develop and enhance skills whereby men and women may fulfil their roles as family leaders, counsellors and care givers.
18. To promote, enhance and support family care giving, housing and rental subsidies for multi-generational families, provision of respite care, remuneration for unpaid long-term care giving.
19. Establish support groups for families with special problems and care giving needs such as those having to deal with dementia and physical disabilities.

EDUCATION AND MEDIA

20. Launching information education and communication campaings on ageing to promote positive images of ageing as a subject of general social relevance in which everyone pariticpates.

21. Incorporate information on ageing in primary, and secondary school curricula, as well as specialised information and courses on ageing in post-secondary level, health, political, religious, economic, architecture, planning and design studies.
22. Provide key roles for older persons as voluntary or paid resource persons in literacy programmes, public awareness, campaigns and in education programmes on cultural tradition and heritage, the environment, substance abuse and other areas.
23. Provide literacy education and continuing education for older persons.
24. Integrate the subject and activities of ageing into national events and meetings.
25. Disseminate and apply the United Nations principles for older persons.
26. Enact legislation to ensure equitable access for older persons to social welfare services.
27. To examine and determine the most equitable and efficient mix of public and private incentives which encourage the development and provision of services and opportunities for older persons.
28. Give recognition to services providers including informal care givers of older persons by providing training, adequate compensation and a positive public image.
29. Strengthen and establish community based continuing care programmes. These programmes should aim at developing supportive partnerships for care between the informal and formal sectors.

INCOME SECURITY/EMPLOYMENT

30. Suitable measures should be taken to ensure that elderly person get an appropriate minimum income, either in the

form of social security benefits or retirement benefits or through some other devices.

31. Government should facilitate the participation of elderly persons in the economic life of the society by providing them with suitable employment opportunities.

32. Older workers should be provided with satisfactory working condition taking into account their specific characterstics.

33. Older workers should be suitably protected against occupational diseases.

34. The transition from active working life to retirement should be gradual and not abrupt.

35. In deciding the working conditions of the older people, internationally adopted standards as set out by ILO should be adopted.

14

Deprivations of the Elderly in Slums

Joni C. Joseph

Introduction

SLUMS are fringe areas of urban settlements and are places of deprivations of various kinds. Old age also in modern times is becoming a fringe area on the life span of human beings and hence it faces lot of neglects. Naturally, old age in slums would be experiencing the disprivileges of both these factors. Further, in Indian social system the role of female members is subsidiary and getting lesser privileges. Hence, the deprivations of elderly females in slums might be greater than those of their male counterparts. In this background this paper enquires into the following issues:

(a) Deprivations of physical, social and psychological needs of the elderly in slum settlements and their relative severity.

(b) Influence of gender difference on the deprivations.

Deprivations of slum life

Slums have uniform characteristics everywhere. A satisfactory explanation of slum should portray the physical, social and psychological profiles of human life there. In fact, the profiles are sagas of deprivations.

Slum is an area meant primarily for residential use where deteriorated, overcrowded unsanitary of unsage structures situate (Newman, 1934). It is, in fact, a conglomerate of dilapidated physical structures built with sundry materials which are readily available but easily perishable. Hunter considers poverty, dilapidated housing, overcrowding, health problems and dirt are the physical characteristics of slums (Hunter 1964). Manjumdar also gives the same characteristics in his definition of slums (Majumdar 1983). We could extend the deprivations of slums by adding such factors as acute shortage of drinking water, lighting, drainage, toiled facilities and roads and pathways. These conditions of slums compel the inhabitants to follow the life patterns of lower animal species.

The social issues of slums are more severe than the physical problems. These relate to the social fabric of the society which is more complex and mysterious than physical degradation (Glazer 1970). Slums are places of concentration of lower class people, racial and caste segregation, crime, broken families and alienation. So slums have been perceived to be the result of structural inequalities in society (Jha 1986). Income inequality and consequent poverty loosen every other social ties, primary as well as secondary, existing among the members. As Lewis stated a culture of poverty (an integrated set of values, norms and behaviour characteristic of some of those who live in poverty conditions) socialise the slum dwellers and perpetuate it (Lewis 1965). The phenomenon infuses an attitude of indifference towards hygiene standard, education of the children and birth control. The socialisation, naturally, culminates in crimes and social disorganisation.

The psychic condition of slum community is characterised by lack of achievement motivation and emptiness (Gill 1994). The marginality of the community inculcates an insecurity feeling and anxiety towards future. Even if messages of development are pumped into the community they may not create the desired effect, rather cause the acceptance of an unorganised and unethical life.

Deprivations of old age

The proportion of people aged over 65 years (older people) is increasing rapidly the world over. In addition to the rising percentage of older people, the roles and status of them are decreasing in the present society. These processes together deprive them of their physical, social and psychological need satisfaction (Mishra 1989).

Poverty, destitution and disease are considered as the major problems of old age in developing countries (Nayar 1980). A psychological problem also threatens the older people, namely, decreasing opportunities for intergenerational interaction (Joseph 1986). This makes them feel lonely. The children, were the 'eyes', 'ears', 'hands' and 'feet' to the elderly (Simmons 1960). As such their physical weakness was not a problem. They were also given powerful position of decision-makers and advisers of their family and community. But the present society does not give opportunities for the aged to lead a comfortable, respectful and socially useful life. Their wisdom and experience lose significance in the proper functioning of the society. Ageing becomes more disturbing in society whose culture provokes irreverence to the aged and where the economic competition works to the disadvantages (Baron 1952).

As we know, in India the strong institutions of joint family, caste and community are getting disorganised and the esteemed position of the old is getting declined. Education and wealth are gaining prominence over such ascribed status as seniority based on age and caste membership. This creates many problems to the elderly.

Gender difference and the deprivations

Gender bias against females is very serious in Indian society. Neera Desai and Krishnaraj have with concrete evidences substantiated the discrimination faced by Indian women in work situation, educational matters, health care, family environment and even control over ones own body. Domestic violence is another area highlighted in their discussion (Desai and Krishnaraj 1987).

In city slums women suffer social and economic oppression more (Desai and Krishnaraj 1987). It has been identified that women are prevented from external contacts in a Delhi resettlement colony in order to keep them less assertive.

Deprivations of the elderly in slums

Survey of the literature shows that studies are very scarce which analyse deprivations of the elderly in slums. However, when we superimpose the conclusions of the above analyses we have sufficient basis to assume that the elderly suffer from various deprivations and they are discriminatory against the females. Accordingly this study was undertaken with the objectives mentioned above.

Methodology

Interview questionnaire administrated to 30 male and female persons each aged 65+ in a slum in Calicut city analysed the extent of their physical, social and psychological needs satisfaction using indices. The indices chosen for assessing deprivation of physical needs were availability of food, clothing, resting space, assistance for personal hygiene maintenance, attention during illness from others and arrangement for satisfying the needs at the appropriate time. Deprivations of social needs were analysed using indices, namely, participation in family decision-making, regards received from youths of the family, attachment of children of the family, regards received from neighbours, advice taken by the community members and obedience shown by them. Similarly, deprivations of psychological needs were assessed by such indices as feeling of loneliness, communication shortages, unfounded fear, feeling of despair, doubting others unnecessarily and anxiety towards future. Negative or positive responses as the case may be to below 2 indices were considered as low deprivations, 3 and 4 medium deprivations and 5 and 6 high deprivations. Gender difference was taken as the background variable in the analysis of the data. Association between attributes was tested using chi-square test of independence.

A brief description of the slum

There are 48 small and large slums in Calicut city. This study was conducted in one of the slums. The slum spreads out in 3.6 ha of low lying marshy land. There are 223 houses and 251 households in the slum. The population of the settlement is 2068 persons. The water supply is made by 6 public taps. Lighting facilities, pathways and drainages are very poor. Shortages in toilet facilities are also very serious. During rainy season the entire area floods dangerously.

Regarding the socio-cultural profile, the population consists of three religious groups namely, Hindus, Muslims and Christians.

Most of them belong to the backward sections of their respective religions. It is estimated that the households have been occupying the area ranging from 15-40 years. Few recent migrants from other slum areas are also present there. The main occupation of the female members is cleaning work of city households. The male members engage themselves in various jobs ranging from head load work to drug trafficking.

Analyses

DEPRIVATION OF PHYSICAL NEEDS

In the need hierarchy of human beings comes first the physical needs, namely, those for food, clothing, shelter, protection against disease, etc. Satisfaction of the needs at the proper time is also very important and this is the reason why enquiry was also made into this aspect assess the extent of the deprivation.

Table 1 shows that only 10 per cent feel the deprivation severely and 25 per cent moderately. However, it is very interesting to note that 65 per cent do feel that they were not deprived of their physical needs very severely. In this analysis we should be very cautious not to confuse the level of the satisfaction with that of the non-slum communities.

Table 1 : Gender difference and level of physical need satisfaction

Gender difference	*Need satisfaction*			*Total*
	Low (1)	*Moderate (2)*	*High (3)*	
Male (1)	2 (6.67%)	4 (13.33%)	24 (80%)	30 (100%)
Female (2)	4 (13.33%)	11 (36.67%)	15 (50%)	30 (100%)
Total	6 (10%)	15 (25%)	39 (65%)	60 (100%)

Chi-square = 5.94, Table value = 3.84, df = 1, $P \leq 0.05$

Note : Columns (1) and (2) were combined for calculating Chi-square value.

They are comparing availability of the facilities with their own standards. This can be explained by the details revealed in other analyses which are beyond the scope of this paper and are not given here. However, as an example it may be interesting to note that two meals a day fully satisfy the need for food of many of the respondents while for the non-slum dwellers it is quite unsatisfactory. Similarly, by and large, the elders take bath once in a week but they are highly satisfied with the arrangement. Hence, when we see that 65 per cent of the respondents are fully satisfied with the facilities we should not be under the impression that everything is well with the elderly. However, the reality is that they are satisfied with the matter and does not create any frustration for them. Here we have to remember the phenomenological insight that what is perceived is more important than the really real situation.

As seen from Table 1 the satisfaction is gender specific. While 80 per cent of the males are highly satisfied with the facilities available the figure in respect of the females is only 50 per cent. As we know, in Indian society females have been living in shortages compared to males. It is significant that the reflections have come from the gender which has more suffering capacities. Therefore, we could guess the real deprivations of the female members in the matter.

DEPRIVATION OF SOCIAL NEEDS

When we apply the Maslow Hierarchy principles of needs to this situation the old becomes contented only when their social needs namely acceptance in the family, neighbourhood, etc., are also satisfied. In order to understand how far their social needs are satisfied, the data collected pertaining to the topics described in the methodology were analysed as shown in Table 2.

Table 2 : Gender difference and level of social need satisfaction

Gender difference	*Need satisfaction*			*Total*
	Low (1)	*Moderate (2)*	*High (3)*	
Male(1)	4 (13.33%)	14 (46.67%)	12 (40%)	30 (100%)
Female (2)	9 (30%)	16 (53.33%)	5 (16.67%)	30 (100%)
Total	13 (21.67%)	30 (50%)	17 (28.33%)	60 (100%)

Chi-square = 4.01, Table value = 3.84, df = 1, $P \leq 0.05$

Note : Columns (1) and (2) were combined for calculating Chi-square value.

It is seen that the extent of social need satisfaction of the old is very low. Only 28.33 per cent have high satisfaction. 50 per cent are moderately satisfied while another 21.67 per cent have low satisfaction.

In this analysis also the influence of gender difference is seen, the need satisfaction of the females being lower. 40 per cent of the males have high social needs satisfaction while the females coming under the category are only 16.67 per cent. A large portion of the females come under the low satisfaction segment (30 per cent). It is a meagre portion of 13.33 per cent of the males who come under the category. The analysis clearly reveals that the social deprivations of elderly women in the slum are far higher than that of their male counterparts. The relationship is established statistically by the chi-square test.

DEPRIVATION OF THE PSYCHOLOGICAL NEEDS

Mental peace and tranquillity are the foundation of healthy human life. This is particularly true in the case of older person. In the study the state of psychological need satisfaction of the respondents was analysed under Table 3.

Table 3 : Gender difference and level of psychological need satisfaction

Gender difference	*Need satisfaction*			*Total*
	Low (1)	*Moderate (2)*	*High (3)*	
Male(1)	15 (50%)	8 (26.67%)	7 (23.33%)	30 (100%)
Female(2)	17 (56.67%)	11 (36.66%)	2 (6.67%)	30 (100%)
Total	32 (53.33%)	19 (31.67%)	9 (15%)	60 (100%)

Chi-square = 0.27, Table value = 3.84, df = 1, $p \leq 0.05$

Note : Columns (2) and (3) were combined for calculating Chi-square value.

Surprisingly we see that the psychological need satisfaction is extremely low. Only 15 per cent of the total respondents have high contentment in their psychological need satisfaction and majority

(53.33 per cent) lack this core basic need. This deprivation of the older persons in the slum are more than any other forms.

Coming to the influence of gender difference on the matter a very insightful result is seen. Contrary to the two previous analyses we see that there is no significant difference between the deprivation of psychological needs men and women (see the chi-square values). That is, the mental agony of the aged men and women in the slum is more or less the same.

COMPARISON BETWEEN THE COMPONENTS OF DEPRIVATION

Analyses 1, 2 and 3 indicate that the psychological need satisfaction of the elderly is comparatively the least. Physical need satisfaction occupes the other extremity and social need satisfaction lies in between these two poles. When we take the other way round we may say that psychological deprivation is the most severe factor threatening the elderly in the slum (Illustraion 1).

In order to reveal the deprivations in a descriptive manner few case analyses have been done in following section.

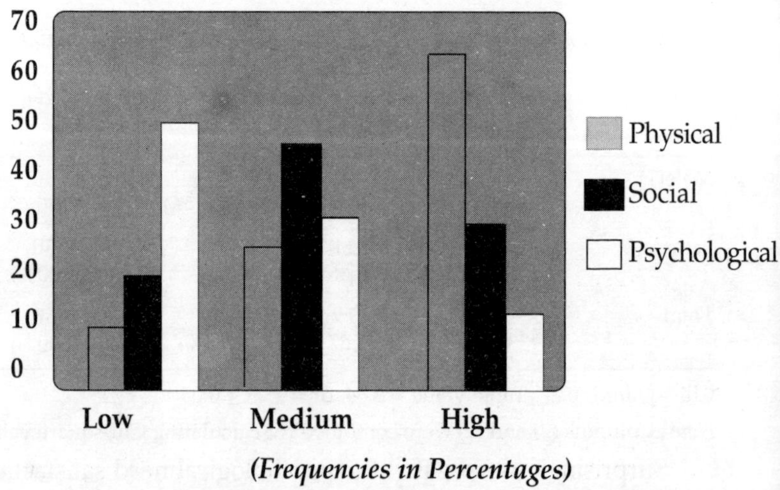

Illustration 1: Bar chart representing the level of satisfaction of physical, social and psychological needs

CASE ANALYSIS

Case Analysis 1

One of the cases analysed is that of a women aged 76 years. She has been residing in the slum for the last 13 years. She is a backward Hindu. She is illiterate. She refused to give the details of her marriage, husband and children. However, she is now living with her grand-children, two granddaughters and two grandsons who are also married. Her occupational history did not confine to any single job. She informed that she worked in several capacities. Now she is confined to the domestic atmosphere. She is seriously deprived of food, clean clothes, sleeping space, etc. She takes bath once in a while and that too at the mercy of her granddaughter. Whenever she is ill practically no one takes care of her.

Her social interaction is practically nil within the family and outside. The only interacting members are the great grandchildren who are not grown up.

Her loneliness and anxiety towards future are unfathomable because of the indifference of other members of her family. Even if she likes to speak something no one is ready to hear. She very much fears others who come over there because of the dangerous atmosphere of the settlement created by such visitors. She doubts strangers because, she says, it is not a safe place to live in. The general atmosphere of the settlement causes fear to the old irrespective of sex difference (this is discussed briefly in a later part of this paper). Finally, to a question, are you interested to leave the settlement she responded, 'yes, to the place where there is no sufferings and neglect from others'.

Case Analysis2

A second case which has been analysed was that of a man aged 70 years. He is a member of the Muslim community and an illiterate. His wife is 60 year old. He is the head of a family of 10 members. 5 of the members are not living with him. He was a cooly but now he is not even able to move around due to his acute filarial disease. The family now depends on the income of his wife and two sons who are attending to sundry jobs. His family migrated to the slum more than 15 years ago. He is getting the very best of physical comfort which can be expected in a slum. Since his wife is alive his social atmosphere also is lively. But his grown up sons are not very pleased with him. However, his psychological condition is very poor. The shame he feels due to his disease is very much. He is very much afraid of the culmination of the disease. He feels that his future is bleak. He is quite desperate. Another problem with him is that he fears to live in the slum as it is not a peaceful place according to him. He fears torture by outsiders who have various forms of connection with the slum dwellers.

Case Analysis3

A third case depict another problem of elderly slum dwellers. The woman is a 68 year old forward Hindu. She has been in the slum for the past 18 years. She is a widow who is educated up to the primary level. She is not attending to any job. She has two daughters and a son and all of them are married. She resides with her elder daughter. The economic condition of the household is very precarious as the whole family is to depend on the income of her daughter who is working as a sales girl. Her son-in-law is a problem to all of them as he is involved in drug trafficking and many times went under police custody. Due to their poor economic condition she is to satisfy with a one time food. Her daughter is giving her physical comfort to the extent possible. The social atmosphere is somewhat good as she is with her loving daughter. The problem she faces primarily is insecurity feeling in the settlement. The feeling is brought about by the involvement of her son-in-law in anti-social activities including drug trade. Whenever, a case of drug abuse comes up he becomes the target of the authorities. Her mental peace is lost due to him. She is very anxious about the future of her family. She becomes quite often desperate. She is skeptic about any stranger who comes to the slum for she feels that he/she shall cause harm to them including physical torture. She is quite anxious about her daughters safety. Slum is a dangerous settlement for girl children — she considers.

These cases reveal that the severe mental agony of the elderly has its root in the conditions of the slums. Nowadays Calicut slums have become more disturbed. They have become the nucleus of communal tension, drug trade, illicit liquor trade, trafficking in women and children and what else is possible. Whenever the authorities are activated raids are conducted in slums causing violation of persons of culprits and innocent persons alike. The peace and security feeling of the total settlement are destroyed. For an elderly person (both male and female) the incidents of frequent raid by police and taking custody of sons and daughters under charges of anti-social and immoral activities and communal conflicts are heart breaking. Since the elderly are migrants from other areas and the increasing problems are of comparatively recent origins they are not well adjusted with them. Most of them have severe aspiration for leaving the place but the big question before them is, where to go?

Conclusion

The study substantiates that elderly people in slums face deprivations of physical, social and psychological needs to various degrees. The deprivations of psychological needs are most sever. The deprivations except psychological ones are gender specific, the females being more a victims of them. The severity of the psychological deprivation has its root in the increasing confusions and chaos created by vested interests in slum settlements.

Sincere slum improvement activities could reduce the deprivations of the elderly as well as others. The slum areas are to be secluded by constructing strong compound walls with gates at appropriate locations which are guarded by security personnels. This will prevent the spread of slums. The increasing population of the slums should be transferred to resettlement units which may be established in the nearby area itself by acquiring land. The compound wall will enhance the security feeling of the dwellers. Moreover this will prevent free entry of strangers into the slum.

Care taking centres for elderly persons with adult education facilities *anganwadies*, PHCs and community centres are to be established at the periphery of the slums. Awareness inculcation should be another mode of improving the conditions of slums. For spreading the meassages of structured living strong motivating teams are to continuously function in slums. If sincere efforts are taken by the authorities slums can be made a better place to live in for all the sections including the elderly.

References

Barron, Milton L., *et al.*, 1952, 'Research on the Social Disorganisation of Retirement', *American Sociological Review*, 17 (August): 472-82.

Desai, Neera and Krishnaraj, M., 1990, *Women and Society in India*, Ajanta Publications.

Gill, Rajesh, 1994, *Slums as urban Villages*, Rawat Publishers, Jaipur.

Glazer, Nathan, 1970, *Cities in Trouble*, Quadrangle Books, Chicago.

Hunter, D.R., 1964, *The Slums : Challenges and Response*, The Free Press, New York.

Jha, S.S., 1986, *Structure of Urban Poverty : A Case of Bombay Slums*, Popular Prakasan, Bombay.

Joseph, Joni C., 1988, 'Interaction Between the Old and Young, *Social Welfare*, 25 (6): 17-19.

Lewis, Oscar, 1965, 'Further Observation on the Folk Urban Continuum and Urbanisation with Special Reference to Mexico City' in Hauser and Schnene (eds.), *The Study of Urbanisation*, John Wiley, New York.

Majumdar, T.K., 1983, *Urbanising Poor : A Sociological Study of Low Income Migrant Communities in the Metropolitan City of Delhi*, Lancers Publishers, New Delhi.

Mishra, Saraswathi, 1989, *Problems and Social Adjustment in Old Age: A Sociological Analysis*, Gian Publishing House, New Delhi.

Neyar, P.K.B., 1980, *A Study on the Working of Old Age Pension Scheme in Kerala*, Kerala University, Trivandrum.

Newman, Nernard J., 1934, 'Slums, *Encylopaedia of Social Sciences*, vol. 13, The MacMillan Company, New York.

Simmons, Leo W., 1960, 'Ageing in Pre-industrial Societies', pp. 62-91 in Tibbits, Clark (ed.), *Handbook of Social Gerontology*, University of Chicago. pp.62-91

15

Health Problems and Health Needs of the Aged in the Villages of Tamil Nadu

C. Karupiah

INDIA is developing country and the number of aged persons is bound to increase with better health and medical facilities, control of communicable diseases, reduction in death rate and decrease in birth rate. In spite of all these developments the population growth in India is not expected to decrease much in case of substantial decrease in growth the proportion of aged to total population would increase.

> The average life expectancy in India at birth was 32 years in 1951, which increased to 52, years by 1981. Improved health care practices and their expansion at the grassroots level further improved the life span of man in India as 58 years in 1985 which further expected to cross 60 by the end of 1989.
>
> — Bajpai 1998

The number of old people is increasing in all countries mainly due to two reasons, that is, falling death rate and increasing life span. In India, in 1911 only 1 per cent of the population was above 60 years of age, in 1981 it was 6.5 per cent and now more people survive to then 60s and 70s. Old age has become a major medical and social preoccupation. Age is often found to be associated with health problems. Age people require a wide range of preventive, curative, and rehabilitative care. They have special needs regarding food, nutrition, hygiene, exercise, immunisation, housing, transport and personal security.

Research in all areas of social and biological processes of ageing should receive new impetus. In the village the old do not have access to medical facilities. They do not receive minimum attention on their health, as they are growing older. The family members also neglects the health of the aged. This kind of situation aggravates the health problems of the aged. In order to study the status of the aged, a village was selected for on in-depth analysis.

A complete enumeration of all the 50 aged persons was done for the study (census method) in a village in Madurai district of Tamil Nadu State. 74 percent respondents were females and the remaining 26 percent of the respondents were males which strengthens the fact if women can survive the hazards of child bearing potential they live longer than males.

Out of total 50 respondents, 80 percent belonged to nuclear families and the remaining 20 percent represent life in joint families. This situation is due to urbanisation and industrialisation.

With regard to educational status, it was revealed that as many as 95 percent were illiterate, where as 5 percent were able to read and write. The low educational status indicates slow improvement in all other aspects of life including health.

Analysis of occupational status of the respondents revealed that 55 percent of the responded unable to do any work. In other words they were dependent upon the family members for their livelihood. The remaining 45 percent of the respondents were engaged in agricultural activities.

Adequate income is the most pervasive concern for those over 60 to maintain the status in their life. Majority of the respondents are living below poverty line. Only 6 percent of the respondents have income between Rs. 5000-10,000. The decrease in income poses problems of the aged.

Housing one of the primary needs of the human being. In rural area keeping the houses clean self-prevents health hazards. Housing is an important factor intimately connected with health. There is a chronic shortage of adequate housing. 96 percent of the respondent living in low quality and highly unsatisfactorily style the remaining

4 percent of the respondents were living in separate room in moderate houses. 58 percent of the respondents suffered from stomach problem, 5 percent were suffered from eye sight problem and deafness.

Advances in medical sciences and changes in the organisation of medical practice have enabled contemporary. Physicians to provide the highest quality of care for the ailing persons. But at the same time the cost of this care has reduced availability of this care to different kinds rural people. The low income families who are considerably more disease prone and who have need for medical attention because of the nature of the environment of the rural area, have less ability to pay for the need medical services.

Medical needs of the aged people are of very specialised nature. Old people also lack capability to cover the cost of their health care on account of high premium put upon the medical services. Primary Health Centre medical check-up is necessary for the aged people. 87 per cent of the respondents do not go in for the medical check-up. Remaining 13 percent of the respondents go for the medical check-up at the time of health problem.

To conclude in the rural areas problems of health arise due to low economic conditions. Rural people depend upon agricultural economy. A large number of them live under common shelter, majority of the people do not get proper food and they do not go for regular medical check-up.

References

Ageing and Society, *The Indian Journal of Gerontology*, vol. VI. no. III and IV, July-Sep. 1996 and October-December. 1996 p. 94.

Ageing and Society, *The Indian Journal of Gerontology*, vol. IV. no. I and II Jan-Mar. 1994, April-June 1994, pp. 64-5.

Bajpai P.K, *Social Work Perspectives on Health*, Raw Publication, New Delhi, 1998, pp. 225-9.

Dak T.M., *Sociology of Health India*, Raw Publications, New Delhi, 1991, p. 430.

Gupta Monica Das, *Women's Health in India*, Oxford University Press, Delhi, 1988, p. 299.

William, C., Cockerham, *Sociology*, Prentice Hall Internationl, Inc. USA, 1998, p. 43.

Section III
Institutional Care

16

Home Away from Home

A Survey of Old Age Homes in Kerala

S. Irudaya Rajan

Introduction

POPULATION ageing or ageing of the population is the ultimate consequences of demographic transition. The final stage of demographic transition means fewer births and deaths in any population. As Kerala is ahead from the rest of the country in the fertility transition by 25 years, the ageing scenario of Kerala is much more important. For instance, on an average, Kerala women ends up producing only two children throughout her reproductive span. A child born today in Kerala is expected to live above 70 years. As of 1998 Kerala Migration Study, Kerala's population is 31.4 millions with an annual growth rate of 1.1 percent (Zachariah, Mathew and Irudaya Rajan 1999).

Ageing is generally defined as population above 60 years of age. Demographers also define the elderly in four categories: young old (60-9 years), old old (70-9 years), oldest old (80-9 years) and the extreme old (90+ years).

Data sources and objectives

For the background materials, this paper utilises the 1991 census and 1998 Kerala Migration Survey data. The assessment of state level scenario old age homes in India is made on the basis of the survey conducted by the Madras Institute on ageing. Kerala Oldage Home Survey (KOLDS) and Kerala Oldage Home Imnates Survey

(KOLDINS) conducted by the author in 1999 will be used extensively to assess the profile of old age homes throughout the state and also to assess the inmates in all old age homes.

The objectives of this paper are as follows:

Assess the ageing scenario in Kerala by districts

Examine the socio-economic conditions of elderly in terms of pensioners, beggars and those elderly living in institutions.

- Map the old age home situation throughout the country.
- Understand the existing old age homes in Kerala.
- Assess the profile of inmates in all old age homes in Kerala.

Emerging ageing scenario

As per the 1991 census, there were 56.88 million elderly (60+) in India representing 6.8 percent of the country's population. The old old (70+) accounted for 21.07 million and the oldest old (80+) numbered around 6.37 million. Among elderly women, 54 percent of the young old, 67 percent of the old old and 70 percent of the oldest old are widows (Irudaya Rajan, Mishra and Sharma 1998). The statistics are quite different in Kerala compared to India (Irudaya Rajan and Zachariah 1998; Irudaya Rajan and Mishra 1997; Irudaya Rajan 1999).

According to the 1961 census, the number of elderly aged 60 and above was just 1 million which increased to 2.6 million in 1991 (a 160 percent increase). According to our projections, the number of elderly is expected to reach 7.2 millions by 2021 (a 180 percent increase) and 11.9 millions in 2051 (a 65 percent increase). The change in proportion of the elderly is even more dramatic. Their proportion was around 9 percent in 1991 but it is expected to increase to 20 percent in 2021 and 37 percent in 2051. The growth rate among elderly during 1981-91 is 3 percent and is likely to continue at the same level for the next few decades.

The old old population (70+) was just million in 1991. The pojection results indicate that the old old will reach 3.2 million by 2021 (a 222 percent increase) and 7.4 million by 2051 (a 130 percent increase). Their proportion, which was just 2 percent in 1961, doubled in 1991 and will again double in 2021, reaching 23 percent in 2051. Between 1961-91, the decadel growth rate among the oldest old hovered around 3 percent, and is expected to register a growth rate of around 4 percent in the next four decades.

The oldest old (80+) in Kerala is just 2,90,000 in 1991 and are expected to increase to 1 million in 2021 (a 258 percent increase) and further 3.3 million by 2051 (a 213 percent increase). The proportion of the oldest old in Kerala accounted for just 1 percent in 1991, which is expected to increase to 3 percent in 2021 and further to 10 percent in 2051. One of the main characteristics observed among the oldest old is their growth rate. The growth rate among the oldest old is higher than the young old and the old old in Kerala and is expected to be on the similiar line during the next half of the twenty-first century. In fact, among all the conventional age groups, the highest growth rate is registered among the old, especially the old old.

District level situation

Among the districts in Kerala, as of 1991 census, the highest number of elderly above 60 years is found in Thrissur district, followed by Ernakulam. The lowest is found in Waynad. However, eight districts in Kerala have registered over 200,000, sixty-plus population. If we consider the proportion of elderly, the highest proportion is reported for Pathanamthitta district for 60 plus, 70 plus, 80 plus, followed by Alappuzha and Kottayam districts. According to the 1991, only four districts in Kerala have reported one-tenth of its population as old. However, in 1998 as per the Kerala Migration Study, the number is doubled to 8 districts with Pathanamthitta still leading with 16 percent.

There are more number of female elderly compared to male elderly in all districts except Idukki in Kerala in 1991. In Kerala, the proportion of male elderly is 8.4 and for females, it is 9.4. In 1998, both males and females have crossed the 10 percent mark. In 1991, 3 districts have reported the proportion as above 10 for males and the number has gone to 9 districts in 1998. The same number for females are 5 districts in 1991 and 10 districts in 1998 respectively.

Non-workers among the aged

Indian census provides data on non-workers by categories such as household duties, beggars, dependants, pensioners, rentiers, and elderly living in institutions. In this paper, we shall discuss three categories of non-workers for Kerala by districts: elderly living in institutions, beggars and pensioners.

Elderly in Institutions (not only old age homes but also some other charitable institutions throughout the country, including those who live in jails) are reviewed to understand the institutionalised elderly observed in the census.

Elderly beggars are discussed with the view that these beggars when they become very old or sick, are picked from the streets by charitable, religious and other non-governmental organisations. The present elderly beggars are the potential candidates to become inmates of an old age home.

Pensioners among elderly are viewed to inform that they are regular income receivers from the past work. As some of the pay and stay old age homes emerging in the early 1990s in Kerala are looking for the inmates who have regular income. Some pensioners at old age, specially those who lose their life partners, and become single member household, would like to move to old age homes.

According to the 1991 census, 8,700 males and 7,450 females were enumerated as inmates in an institution. Among them, 1,590 males and 1,690 females were above 60 years. In other words, 18 percent of males and 23 percent of females were above 60 years among the persons live in institutions. There are more female elderly living in institutions compared to males. The district wise situation is different. In Kottayam, 70 percent of males in the institutions are elderly, followed by Pathanamthitta. In the case of females, the highest proportion of female elderly live in institutions at Alappuzha, followed by Kottayam and Kollam. Among the elderly in Kerala, 12 males and 13 females per 10,000 elderly live in institutions. Kottayam has reported the highest number for males and females.

There were more male beggars compared to females (4,580 and

3,260 respectively) in Kerala as of 1991. However, the beggars among older males and females were 1,680 and 1,190 respectively. Why there are more male elderly beggars then female elderly? Probably, older females can do some type of household work and may work as servants in old age. The highest number of male and female beggars was found in Thrissur district. The percentage of male and female elderly beggars to total beggars in Kerala was 37. However, the percentage varies between district to district. The highest proportion of male elderly beggars was found in Waynad (56) whereas the highest proportion of female elderly beggars was found in Ernakulam. The beggars per 10,000 elderly population in Kerala was 14 for males and 9 for females. Waynad takes the first position in this regard with 48 for males and 24 for females respectively.

One more interesting piece of information collected through census was the pensioners of all ages. As of 1991 census, Kerala has 230,660 male pensioners and 77,660 female pensioners. Among them, 150,910 male pensioners and 51,190 female pensioners were of aged 60 and above. As the retirement age in Kerala is only 55 years, the pensioners in Kerala will be around 3 lakh in Kerala. The highest number of male elderly pensioners was found in Thiruvananthapuram (20,180), followed by Ernakulam (19,510) and Thrissur (15,130). On the other hand, the highest number of female pensioners was enumerated in Thrissur (6,050), followed by Kozhikode (5,460) and Alappuzha (5,290). The lowest number of male pensioners was observed in Waynad (880) whereas the lowest female pensioners was found in Idukki (110). The pensioners per 10,000 elderly population of Kerala was 1,259 for males and 365 for females. The highest number (1,594) was found in Ernakulam for male elderly and the highest number (464) was observed in Kozhikode for females.

Old age homes in India: a state wise profile

Development of institutional care for the handicapped, infirm and aged persons in India has a long history. The first old age home in India is supposed to have been started in the early eighteenth century but information is available from 1,782. Today, the services are mainly provided by the non-government, private and voluntary, non-profit and particularly the religious charitable organisations. The central and state governments still play a very negligible role in providing care to the deprived sections of society.

According to the recent survey conducted by the Madras Institute of Ageing, there are 529 old age homes in India in 1995. The growth of old age homes occurred only after 1970s. For instance, India had only 96 old age homes around 1950, added another 94 in the next two decades (1951-70) and added 256 new old age homes throughout the country in the next twenty years. As of 1995, Kerala State leads with 102 old age homes, followed by Tamil Nadu with 94 and Maharashtra with 65. One out of 5 old age homes can be found in Kerala. South India (Kerala, Tamil Nadu, Karnataka and Andhra Pradesh) accounts for 275 old age homes. In other words, 52 percent of old age homes are located in south India.

As stated earlier, old age homes are run by various auspices: secular (non-religious organisations) religious groups (Hindu, Muslim, Christian), government and others. Throughout the country, non-religious organisations run 224 old age homes (or 42 percent), followed by Christians with 216 (40 percent) old age homes. Of the 216 old age homes maintained by Christians, 82 of them located in Kerala, followed by Tamil Nadu with 42 and Goa with 21. Though Hindu organisations manage 21 old age homes in India, they have none in Kerala. The governments initiated only 10 old age homes throughout the country. As of today, Muslims maintain only one old age home in India and it is located in Kozhikode district of Kerala. However, the Kerala scenario is different compared to other states. Among the 102 old age homes in Kerala, 82 are managed by Christians (80 percent), followed by non-religious organisation with 11.

As like any other institutions, there are separate old age homes for males, females as well as mixed exists in India. And some of the old age homes are meant for only aged persons, and some are for poor aged and destitute (mostly free) and some of them are aiming to help the sick and handicapped. There are 16 old age homes for males alone; 4 for aged, 13 for poor aged and destitute and 3 for sick and handicapped. However, the number for females is 87; 34 for aged, 42 for poor aged and destitute and 11 for sick and handicapped. The institutions which admit both male and female elderly members are exceptionally high. Among the 306 homes in this category, 141 exclusively for aged, 136 for poor aged and destitute and 29 for sick and handicapped. Kerala has 18 old age homes for females catering towards the need of poor aged and destitutes and 28 old age homes for both sexes for the same category.

As discusssed earlier, around 83 percent of old homes in the country are managed by secular (non-religious) and Christian organisations. How many of them accomodate the elderly at free of cost? How many old age homes exists on payment basis? How many homes exists for payment as well as free? Interestingly, three-fourth of old age homes managed by the Christian organisations offer free accomodation at their homes, against one-half of secular organisation who run old age homes. Number of homes run on payment basis is much higher among secular organisations (45) against Christian institutions (27). Almost equal number of both institutions (around 30) accomodate elderly on free as well as payment basis. Out of 529 old age homes, the above break-up is available only for 376 homes. Among them, 62 percent old age homes accomodate the elderly on free basis, and 20 percent each for payment as well as both (payment+free).

The Madras Institute of Ageing Survey also reported the number of inmates of 398 old age homes in India. As of 1995, 21,217 elderly live in institutions. Of them, 1,120 males live exclusively in male old age homes, 2,759 females in female's old age homes and the remaining elderly are found in the old age homes where males and female reside together. Of the 21,272 elderly persons, 22 percent reside in Kerala old age homes; 59 percent in south India.

With the above background in mind, let us assess the Kerala Old Age Home Survey and Kerala Old Age Home Inmates Survey, 1999.

Kerala Old Age Home Survey, 1999

Two surveys were conducted simultaneously throughout Kerala to study the profile of old age homes as well as inmates. Why we need such type of surveys? The State Planning Board in its latest economic review devotes only one paragraph on institutional care though the report runs into several hundred pages. The report says,

> The government and voluntary agencies extend assistance to the orphan children, disabled children, aged, infirm and other special categories like cured mental patients, leprosy patients and so on through various institutional measures. In Kerala at present institutional care is provided to about 54,344 persons, of which 44,728 are orphan children and 4,721 are aged and infirm.

In an appendix table of Economic Review, the details of the institutional care listed for elderly are as follows:

Name of Scheme	Nature of Care	Year of Starting	No. of persons benefitted
Care home		1957	100
Thiruvananthapuram	Welfare and Rehabilitation of the old age and ex-convicts		
Old age homes			
Kollam			
Kottayam			
Kannur			
Kasaragod	For providing physical social, psychological and economic support for the aged	1995-6	100
Pathanamthitta			
Ernakulam			
Thrissur			
Malappuram			
Kozhikode			

The economic review says that there are institutions run by voluntary organisations for the welfare of aged but provide no details about the functioning of such organisations.

In this context, it is felt to undertake a profile of old age homes as well as inmates of all old age homes in Kerala. According to the 1999 Kerala Old Age Home Survey (hereafter referred as KOLDS), the number of old age homes in Kerala is 134, including the nine old age introduced by the government during 1995-6 (State Planning Board, Economic Review). Of which, the highest number of 31 is found in Kottayam district, followed by Ernakulam (27) and Thrissur (25) (other district details, see Table). Kottayam, Ernakulam and Thrissur districts accounts for 62 percent of old age homes in Kerala. Suprisingly, Kasaragod, Waynad and Malappuram, there are no old age homes. Thus Waynad is the only district in Kerala where there are no old age homes. As most of the old age homes are run by Christian organisations in Kottayam, we just looked at the religious distribution of population specially at Kottayam. Among the fourteen districts of Kerala, Kottayam district has the highest Christian concentration with 46 percent of its total population. Half of the Kottayam population is Christians.

As per KOLDS, there were only 19 old age homes in 1950, added 17 homes in between 1950-69 (two decades) and in the next two decades (1970-89), Kerala added 60 new old age homes. During the last 8 years, 38 old age homes initiated in Kerala specially 9 by the government. Currently, at least 5 old age homes are coming up every year and it is likely to increase to 10 in the years to come. Among the 125 old age homes, 13 homes are run only for males and another 48 for females only. Almost 55 percent of old age homes accomodates both elderly men and women; another 36 admits only females. Almost of the half of the old age homes in Thrissur caters to the needs of elderly women only, followed by Ernakulam and Kottayam.

Who administers the old age homes in Kerala? Around 73 percent run by other Christian organisations throughout the state, followed by 13 percent by other non-governmental organisations. Government runs only 13 old age homes (remember, 9 old age homes were initiated in only 1995-6). The district like Kottayam (the highest number of old age homes in the country, second only to Greater Mumbai district of Maharashtra), 87 percent (27 out of 31 homes) old age homes are managed by the Christian organisations. The percentages are 63 and 72 respectively for Ernakulam and Thrissur districts.

The running of an old age home requires some manpower to look after the elderly. Some of the requirements are: food preparation, nursing, administration, watchmen and other activities to help the elderly. According to KOLDS, 881 persons are working in 125 old age homes (9 old age homes initiated by the government in 1995-6 need an official permission to conduct the study and permission is not granted immediately in different districts during the survey so the 9 homes will be covered at the final stage of the work). In other words, the each old age homes provided employment to 7 persons. However, 30 percent of them work in kitchen, 24 percent in nursing and another 30 percent in administration. Employment such as working in kitchen and looking after the administration require formal education. However, nursing specially geriatric care, needs very careful training as many of the elderly requires in an old age not only in an old age homes but also in the elderly living in households. Kerala should concentrate on special training to take care of elderly because there is a greater potential for employment opportunities. Some groups of elderly needs special care such as one elderly for one nurse. Groups are as follows: some of the oldest old (80+), extreme old (90+), centenerians, physically handicapped in old age (specially falls), bedridden elderly, mentally retarded, depressed elderly and dementia patients. Who are the normal care givers for elderly at home? Most case, it is women (wife or daughter-in-law (as parents normally reside with son) or daughter) who suffers most. As the elderly men of (80+) likely to have their wives who themselves are elderly (70+), they need a special care. Younger women who work outside the home is on the increase, they have to replaced by paid care givers. It is time, Kerala should exploit this opportunity to create more employment among women. As the growth of old age homes is on the increase, Kerala might create some employment opportunities for the younger generation in the name of older persons. How many? It requires further investigation. During the course of my visit to old age homes, I have found that many elderly help them in kitchen and other activities of the old age homes. District wise situation is presented in Table. As per KOLDS, 4,176 elderly persons live in 125 old age homes. Among them, 36 percent (1,496) are males and 64 percent (2,680) are females. If we add the nine old homes initiated by the governments, the total number in the old age home increased to 5,076 (as each of them managed around 100 persons). As Kottayam has the highest number of old age homes, followed by Ernakulam and Thrissur, more elderly persons are found in the same sequence. However, 27 percent of elderly males are reported in Kottayam district (401) followed by Kannur district (342).

Among females, Ernakulam leads with first rank (23 percent), following by Kottayam.

The survey also listed various facilities available in the old age homes so that the suitable policy can be adopted to improve the living conditions of the elderly in the institutions. The following five questions are asked from the management of the old age home?

1. Do you have a vehicle?
2. Do you have a telephone?
3. Do you have a library?
4. Do you have a recreation facilities?
5. Do you have a medical doctor at your disposal for emergency?

In Kerala, 72 percent of old age homes have telephones, 65 percent have a library, 82 percent have a recreation facilities, 84 percent have a medical doctor at their disposal and only 18 percent old age homes own a vehicle. Interestingly, Kottayam, Alappuzha and Pathanamthitta district reports 100 percent medical doctor facility but no old age homes in Pathanamthitta own a vehicle. Again, three-fourth of old age homes in Pathanamthitta, Ernakulam, Kottayam and Kozhikode, have telephone connection in old age homes. Recreation is cent percent in Pathanamthitta and Alappuzha.

Kerala Old Age Home Inmates Survey

As per KOLDS, 4,176 persons live in 125 old age homes of Kerala. However, Kerala Old Age Home Inmates Survey (referred as KOLDINS) could interview only 3,362 persons. Around 814 elderly could not be interviewed because some of them are mentally retarded psychiatric patients, mental patients, and some of them very sick and some of them have gone to see their children, relatives and friends during the survey period. The survey covered total of 3,362 persons. Some of the surveyed are not above 60 years of age. Many old age homes run by charitable and religious organisation accomodate very poor elderly, widows, beggars, mentally retarded and physically handicapped without an age limit. The KOLDINS was conducted among 347 persons who are below 50 years and 267 persons who are between 50 to 59 years. In the analysis, we have excluded the persons below 50 years of age. Thus, the discussion in this paper refers to persons above 50 years of age. Few details about the survey as follows:

	Male	*Female*	*Total*
Total elderly persons in old age homes	1,496	2,680	4,176
Not surveyed	310	504	814
Surveyed	1,186	2,176	3,362
Less than 50 years	97	250	347
50 + surveyed for analysis	1,089	1,926	3,015

Thus, the discussion follows in this paper confined to 3,105 elderly inmates in old age homes. The demographic, social, economic characteristics are presented in the Table. Of which, 36 percent (1,089) are males and 64 percent (1,926) are females. Among the elderly live in insitutions in Kerala, 32 percent of them young old (60-9), 36 percent of them old old (70-9), 19 percent of them oldest old (80-9) and 3 percent of them extreme old (90+). The female elderly are 77 percent higher than male elderly in the institutions. It is true for all the age groups under study. Among the young old, the sex ratio (males per 100 females) is 48, increased to 60 among old old, 62 among oldest old and 64 among extreme old.

In the married and divorced category, number of males are high whereas never married and widowed category, there are more females. Almost 44 percent of the elderly are not married and another 8 percent are belong to divorced and separated. 38 percent of them are widows or widowers. Among males, 41 percent of them belong to never married category followed by widowhood (26 percent). In the case of females, 46 percent of them are never married and another 44 percent of them are widows.

According to KOLDINS, 72 percent of elderly in institutions are Christians, followed by Hindus with 26 percent. Though the inmates of an institution were ready to report their religion, many of them (333 out of 3,015) during an informal talk as well as in the survey, did not want to reveal the caste identity. Among the reported elderly

(2,682), 13 percent of the elderly are Nairs, followed by Ezhawas with 7 percent scheduled castes and tribes with 2 percent.

Among the institutionalised elderly, 6 percent of them own house (7 percent for males and 6 percent for males) and 4 percent of them own land (5 percent for females and 3 percent for females). It is not the poor and destitute stay in old age homes, but some of them own land and house. One would expect the number of elderly with house and land is likely to increase in the home with the more private old homes to caters the needs of middle class or rich elderly.

We are interested know about the sponsorship or financial assistance of elderly who reside in the old age homes. Many of the old age homes are run on free basis, around 90 percent of the inmates reported they don't pay anything for stay. Interestingly, 7 percent of them are supported by their past savings (pensions), 2 percent of them supported by their own children and another 2 percent of them by relatives. As stated earlier, Kerala has 1,50,910 male pensioners and 51,190 female pensioners of aged 60 and above. Some of them at their extreme old age may move into old age homes thus increasing the demand for old age homes. Some of the free old age homes run by government and religious and charitable organisation, there are waiting lists. As one of the old age home in Trivandrum, which I visited, has a provision only for 20 widows. But the actual number of inmates are 25 and they have at least 10 members waiting. They can take any new entrants only if one of the inmates die.

Do you like the environment at old age home? This is one of the questions asked to all the inmates of all old age homes. 16 percent of them reported that they 'like very much' and another 82 percent of them stated the conditions are 'alright' and another 1 percent of them reported their stay and environment in old age home as 'bad'.

What are the push factors or reasons for joining an old age homes. The results are as follows: No one to take care at home: 67 percent; children are away: 1 percent; problems with children: 8 percent; own preference: 19 percent; and another 5 percent as other reasons. Most of the inmates in old age ended up there because none to take care of them at home. When you talk to those inmates who stated as own preference little more in detail, they also indirectly indicate children away and none to care at home as main reasons. Migration of children also play an important role in pushing their parents in old age to old age homes.

Children are supposed to be care giver in old age. The reasons for high fertility or preference for at least one son (avoiding females by foeticide and infanticide) is basically arise out of security in old age. Do the elderly living in the institutions have living adult children? 63 percent of them have no children (as stated earlier, some of them are not married). Some of the women have lost their husband and living children. However, 37 percent of inmates have living adult children. Of the 1,125 elderly live in old age homes who had children, 23 percent had one living child, another 23 percent had two children, 20 percent had 3 children and 34 percent had four and more children. The situation is quite different for males and females. Among females, 28 percent had one child and it is only 17 percent for females. The proportion is higher for males and with 4 and above children. The percentages for male and female elderly are 37 and 31 respectively.

More results on this aspect are worth reporting. The percentage of elderly who had one living son residing in old age home is 48 percent and the corresponding percent for one living daughter is 41. The results clearly indicates, even people have children (male or female), they are left along to live in the household or move into old age homes on their old age.

We have also asked the elderly to study of role of migration about their living children's place of residence. The place of residence is classified as follows: residing in the districts, other districts but within Kerala, other states of India, and abroad. For the elderly who had at least one child, 46 percent reside in the same district, 40 percent in the district within Kerala, 10 percent within India and another 5 percent live in abroad. Almost 55 percent of children are migrated from the district. Of the 1,125 elderly who had children in the survey, the total number of living children reported by them is 3,195. On an average, the elderly had 2.8 living children to support in their old age. Among the 3,195 children, 45 percent live in the same district, 42 percent in the other districts of Kerala, 9 percent within India and 4 percent in abroad.

Table 1 : Demographic profile of aged in kerala

	Number ('000)			*Proportion to total population*			*Growth rate (%)*		
	60+	*70+*	*80+*	*60+*	*70+*	*80+*	*60+*	*70+*	*80+*
1961	986	363	85	5.13	1.89	0.44	—	—	—
1971	1328	496	125	6.18	2.31	0.58	2.98	3.12	3.86
1981	1910	712	186	7.45	2.78	0.73	3.63	3.62	3.97
1991	2574	1001	290	8.85	3.44	1.00	2.98	3.41	4.44
2001	3487	1572	449	10.98	4.95	1.41	3.04	4.51	4.37
2011	4884	2260	708	14.37	6.65	2.08	3.37	3.63	4.55
2021	7205	3223	1039	20.44	9.14	2.95	3.89	3.55	3.84
2031	10001	4906	1538	28.24	13.85	4.34	3.28	4.20	3.92
2041	11584	6758	2401	33.59	19.59	6.96	1.47	3.20	4.45
2051	11861	7439	3256	36.61	22.96	10.05	0.24	0.96	3.05

Note: Compiled by the author for the periods 1961 to 1991 using the Indian Censuses; The figures for the years from 2001 to 2051 are extracted from the projections done at the Centre for Development Studies, by S. Irudaya Rajan and K. C. Zachariah (for details of the projections, see **Irudaya Rajan and K C Zachariah,1998**).

Table 2 : Proportion of elderly by districts, Kerala: The 1991 census and the KMS, 1998.

	The 1991 Census			*The 1998 KMS*		
	60+	*70+*	*80+*	*60+*	*70+*	*80+*
Kasaragod	7.06	2.60	0.65	8.35	2.71	0.50
Kannur	8.43	3.25	0.86	9.44	3.46	0.74
Waynad	6.20	2.19	0.58	7.47	3.08	0.62
Kozhikode	8.33	3.14	0.86	10.56	3.84	0.62
Malappuram	6.53	2.29	0.62	7.79	2.80	0.75
Palakkad	8.92	3.42	0.94	11.50	4.42	1.35
Thrissur	10.02	4.05	1.19	11.32	4.30	1.25
Ernakulam	9.40	3.86	1.21	12.67	4.96	0.98
Idukki	6.84	2.60	1.76	7.57	2.16	0.39
Kottayam	10.63	4.61	1.51	12.69	4.65	1.40
Alappuzha	11.08	4.19	1.17	13.44	5.68	1.13
Pathanamthitta	12.04	5.15	1.75	15.56	6.77	1.76
Kollam	8.89	3.40	1.04	11.38	4.42	0.93
Thiruvananthapuram	8.49	3.13	0.82	10.90	4.11	0.82
Kerala	8.85	3.44	1.00	10.88	4.14	0.97

Source: Calculated from the 1991 census and 1998 Kerala Migration Study.

Table 3 : Proportion of elderly by districts and Sex, Kerala: The 1991 census and the KMS, 1998.

	The 1991 Census (60+)		*The 1998 KMS (60+)*	
	Male	*Female*	*Male*	*Female*
Kasaragod	6 .97	7.14	8.03	8.63
Kannur	7.85	8.97	8.67	10.23
Waynad	6.10	6.30	7.36	7.58
Kozhikode	7.78	8.88	10.05	11.05
Malappuram	6.22	6.81	7.85	7.73
Palakkad	8.39	9.42	11.72	11.30
Thrissur	9.26	10.71	10.53	12.03
Ernakulam	8.66	10.15	12.09	13.26
Idukki	6.87	6.80	8.85	6.05
Kottayam	10.26	11.00	12.75	12.64
Alappuzha	10.35	11.77	13.86	13.04
Pathanamthitta	11.97	12.11	17.53	13.73
Kollam	8.51	9.26	10.74	11.99
Thiruvananthapuram	8.00	8.96	10.64	11.14
Kerala	8.37	9.32	10.73	11.03

Table 4 : Elderly in institutions by districts, Kerala, 1991

	The 1991 Census (60+)		*% of elderly live in Institutions to total institutional Popn.*		*Institutional elderly per 10,000 elderly Popn.*	
	Male	*Female*	*Male*	*Female*	*Male*	*Female*
Kasaragod	6.97	7.14	25.00	0.00	2.7	0.0
Kannur	7.85	8.97	14.91	16.67	19.7	5.8
Waynad	6.10	6.30	0.00	0.00	0.0	0.0
Kozhikode	7.78	8.88	7.85	6.45	14.8	3.4
Malappuram	6.22	6.81	11.11	8.33	1.1	0.9
Palakkad	8.39	9.42	26.67	16.67	4.1	2.6
Thrissur	9.26	10.71	18.10	23.02	17.3	21.0
Ernakulam	8.66	10.15	28.57	27.33	14.7	33.0
Idukki	6.87	6.80	0.00	10.53	0.0	5.6
Kottayam	10.26	11.00	68.88	30.00	32.0	26.9
Alappuzha	10.35	11.77	43.33	45.24	25.7	15.8
Pathanamthitta	11.97	12.11	50.00	25.93	10.2	18.9
Kollam	8.51	9.26	12.82	34.62	5.0	8.0
Thiruvanantha-puram	8.00	8.96	7.73	8.20	12.0	3.7
Kerala	8.37	9.32	18.28	22.68	12.3	12.7

Table 5 : Elderly beggars by districts, Kerala, 1991

	The 1991 Census (60+)		*% of elderly beggars to total beggars*		*Pensioners per 10,000 elderly popn.*	
	Male	*Female*	*Male*	*Female*	*Male*	*Female*
Kasaragod	6.97	7.14	22.73	12.50	13.5	5.2
Kannur	7.85	8.97	37.84	15.00	16.2	3.0
Waynad	6.10	6.30	55.56	50.00	47.7	24.2
Kozhikode	7.78	8.88	28.26	10.00	12.9	1.7
Malappuram	6.22	6.81	38.46	25.00	16.0	9.3
Palakkad	8.39	9.42	43.40	50.00	23.8	18.2
Thrissur	9.26	10.71	36.49	41.82	22.2	15.1
Ernakulam	8.66	10.15	42.11	53.85	6.5	4.9
Idukki	6.87	6.80	21.43	41.67	8.0	13.9
Kottayam	10.26	11.00	36.67	28.57	11.7	4.0
Alappuzha	10.35	11.77	37.50	50.00	8.9	5.0
Pathanamthitta	11.97	12.11	21.43	44.44	8.7	5.4
Kollam	8.51	9.26	40.74	33.33	10.9	7.8
Thiruvananthapuram	8.00	8.96	48.15	50.00	11.2	13.5
Kerala	8.37	9.32	36.68	36.50	14.0	8.7

Table 6 : Elderly pensioners by districts, Kerala, 1991

	The 1991 Census (60+)		*% of elderly pensioners to total pensioners*		*Pensioners per 10,000 elderly popn*	
	Male	*Female*	*Male*	*Female*	*Male*	*Female*
Kasaragod	6.97	7.14	67.23	64.71	747.0	142.8
Kannur	7.85	8.97	62.96	71.93	1322.1	437.1
Waynad	6.10	6.30	72.13	65.63	419.4	203.3
Kozhikode	7.78	8.88	68.00	70.45	1383.5	464.9
Malappuram	6.22	6.81	66.84	68.80	812.7	298.1
Palakkad	8.39	9.42	69.24	73.07	1318.6	452.3
Thrissur	9.26	10.71	67.67	65.05	1243.8	397.6
Ernakulam	8.66	10.15	73.13	61.83	1594.2	337.9
Idukki	6.87	6.80	59.68	5.82	490.3	30.6
Kottayam	10.26	11.00	62.25	59.65	1079.1	304.5
Alappuzha	10.35	11.77	62.42	70.44	1417.1	439.0
Pathanamthitta	11.97	12.11	57.37	58.66	1297.9	343.5
Kollam	8.51	9.26	62.19	63.67	1133.4	325.7
Thiruvananthapuram	8.00	8.96	64.08	61.25	1736.1	394.8
Kerala	8.37	9.32	65.43	64.63	1259.1	365.0

Table 7 : Old age homes in India, 1995

	Before 1950	*1951-70*	*1971-80*	*1981-90*	*1991-95*	*N.A.*	*Total*	*%*
Andhra Pradesh	6	4	14	20	2	5	46	10.0
Delhi	3	4	2	0	1	1	10	2.2
Goa	5	6	6	4	1	0	22	4.8
Gujarat	5	8	4	3	2	1	22	4.8
Karnataka	7	6	8	6	0	1	27	5.8
Kerala	24	19	28	18	2	10	92	19.9
Madhya Pradesh	2	2	4	6	0	0	14	3.0
Maharashtra	16	12	13	10	3	11	54	11.7
Tamil Nadu	16	14	20	34	6	4	90	19.4
Uttar Pradesh	1	5	1	4	0	4	11	2.4
West Bengal	5	7	9	13	0	19	34	7.3
Other States and Union Territories	6	7	11	18	0	10	41	8.9
All India	96	94	120	136	17	66	463	100.0
	20.7	20.3	25.9	29.4	3.7		100.0	

Soure: Tabulated by the author from the following publication:
Mdrass Institute on Ageing. 1995. Care for Elderly.

Table 8 : Old age homes in India by its auspices, 1995

	Secular	*Hindu*	*Muslim*	*Christian*	*Govt.*	*Others*	*Total*	*%*
Andhra Pradesh	34	1	0	11	0	5	51	9.6
Delhi	4	0	0	4	2	1	11	2.1
Goa	0	1	0	21	0	0	22	4.2
Gujarat	19	2	0	0	0	2	23	4.4
Karnataka	9	1	0	16	0	2	28	5.3
Kerala	11	0	1	82	1	7	102	19.3
Madhya Pradesh	6	2	0	6	0	0	14	2.6
Maharashtra	34	5	0	16	0	10	65	12.3
Tamil Nadu	45	5	0	42	0	2	94	17.7
Uttar Pradesh	6	1	0	5	0	3	15	2.8
West Bengal	29	1	0	5	0	18	53	10.0
Other States and Union Territories	27	2	0	8	7	7	51	9.7
All India	224	21	1	216	10	57	529	100.0
	42.0	4.2	0.2	40.8	1.9	10.8	100.0	

Note: Same as Table 1

Table 9 : Old age homes by sex and types of admission, 1995

	Male			*Female*			*Both*		
	A	*PA&D*	*S&H*	*A*	*PA&D*	*S&H*	*A*	*PA&D*	*S&H*
Andhra Pradesh	-	-	-	3	2	-	4	17	6
Delhi	-	-	-	1	2	-	-	-	-
Goa	1	-	-	8	0	1	12	-	-
Gujarat	1	-	-	1	-	-	15	-	2
Karnataka	-	-	-	-	1	-	10	13	1
Kerala	-	5	2	9	18	6	17	28	8
Madhya Pradesh	-	1	-	-	1	-	4	7	-
Maharashtra	1	1	-	4	3	1	13	18	2
Tamil Nadu	-	5	1	3	7	-	27	34	3
Uttar Pradesh	-	-	-	2	1	-	8	-	1
West Bengal	1	1	-	3	3	-	7	6	3
Other States and Union Territories	0	-	-		-4	3	24	13	3
All India	4	13	3	34	42	11	141	136	29

Note: A = Aged; PA&D = Poor aged and Destitute; S&H = Sick and Handicapped

Note: Same as Table 1.

Table 10 : Mode of services of old age homes by auspices, 1995

	Secular				*Christian*				*Total*			
	F	*P*	*B*	*N.A.*	*F*	*P*	*B*	*N.A.*	*F*	*P*	*B*	*N.A.*
Andhra Pradesh	15	1	5	-	10	-	-	-	22	1	5	4
Delhi	-	-	-	2	1	-	2	-	2	1	4	1
Goa	-	-	-	-	3	10	7	1	3	11	7	1
Gujarat	11	2	3	1	-	-	-	-	13	2	2	3
Karnataka	2	2	5	1	10	4	1	1	12	6	7	3
Kerala	1	4	3	-	73	7	4	-	74	10	6	7
Madhya Pradesh	3	-	2	-	5	-	-	1	8	-	3	1
Maharashtra	12	14	3	2	9	1	6	-	21	17	11	12
Tamil Nadu	17	13	5	-	31	1	7	2	44	15	12	4
Uttar Pradesh	2	-	2	2	-	3	2	-	2	4	4	4
West Bengal	9	6	3	1	3	1	1	-	11	7	3	12
Other States and Union Territories	14	3	3	1	7	-	-	-	22	3	1	6
All India	86	4534		10	153	27	30	5	234	77	65	58

Notes: F = Free; P = Paid; B = Both; N.A. = Not Available.

Note: Same as Table 1.

Table 11 : Number of elderly in old age homes, 1995

State	*Male*	*Female*	*Both*	*Total elderly*	*Total homes*	*N.A.*
Andhra Pradesh	-	140	1564	1704	32	5
Delhi	-	122	175	299	6	2
Goa	20	166	415	601	22	-
Gujarat	75	130	928	1133	18	3
Karnataka	-	43	2057	2101	27	1
Kerala	445	1211	3122	4778	90	9
Madhya Pradesh	10	15	509	534	12	1
Maharashtra	135	319	2294	2748	49	13
Tamil Nadu	260	140	3476	3876	70	6
Uttar Pradesh	-	23	345	368	11	4
West Bengal	175	295	862	1332	25	14
Other States and Union Territories	-	155	1588	1743	36	6
All India	1120	2759	17335	21217	398	65

Note: Same as Table 1.

Table 12 : Old age homes and inmates by districts, Kerala

	Old age homes		*Per cent of*	*Number and % of inmates*			
	Number	*%*	*Christians*	*Male*	*Female*	*Male*	*Female*
Kasaragod	1	0.7	6.64	0	0	0.0	0.0
Kannur	13	9.7	10.72	342	305	22.9	11.4
Waynad	0	0.0	23.39	0	0	0	0
Kozhikode	6	4.5	4.63	78	119	5.2	4.4
Malappuram	1	0.7	2.33	0	0	0	0
Palakkad	3	2.2	4.07	5	41	0.3	1.5
Thrissur	25	18.7	24.50	196	525	13.1	19.6
Ernakulam	27	20.1	37.83	197	617	13.2	23.2
Idukki	2	1.5	42.23	63	76	4.2	2.8
Kottayam	31	23.1	45.83	401	588	26.8	21.9
Alappuzha	2	1.5	21.70	24	23	1.6	0.9
Pathanamthitta	9	6.7	40.35	86	211	5.7	7.9
Kollam	4	3.0	17.00	28	70	1.9	2.6
Thiruvananthapuram	10	7.5	17.27	76	105	5.1	3.0
Kerala	134	100.0		1496	2680	100.0	100.0

17

Caring for the Aged

Emerging Alternatives

L. Packiam

Introduction

ONE of the biggest challenges that confronts the modern society today is the provision of adequate and effective care to the aged. The unprecedented advancement in medicine and standard of living has significantly brought down the mortality rate and substantially increased the average life span. Consequently, the census is witnessing a steep increase in the proportion of the old in the general population and this trend is bound to increase in the future. India is no exception to this demographic transition.

India in particular is expected to be among the top 10 countries globally in terms of the aged by 2020. It is estimated that India may account for one-seventh or 14.4 per cent of world's total population of the aged by 2020 as against one-eighth or 12.4 per cent in 1995. In absolute numbers, there could be 142 million elderly persons in India by 2020 as compared to 57 million in 1991 and 76 million in 2000.[1]

Old age as a problem

Caring for the old is a difficult task. This is because old age is

1. *Hindu*, April 9.

characterised by physical decline, gradual loss of eyesight and hearing power, loss of appetite, chronic illnesses and pains, all of which demand special medical and personal care. As David E.Biegel points out

> Ageing persons begin to experience substantial losses in body functioning, mental functioning, family and peer group support, income, self-image, self-esteem, control and power.[2]

The happy and worthwhile life at the old age will depend on how well a person had anticipated this inevitable stage in his life and had prepared himself to accept and adjust to the hard realities of powerlessness, dependence and loneliness. It will also depend on the innovative support systems for the elderly offered by the society.

Old age in the present Indian setting

This inevitable situation of looking at old age as nightmare both by the old and by the care takers of the old are the direct outcome of socio-economic transformation of the society. Industrialisation, urbanisation, modernisation, individualism and the materialism, disintegration of the joint family system, women going for the gainful employment, migration of children to other countries for better prospects, these and many other practice have drastically changed the attitude of society especially the family towards the aged.

The elderly parents are no more wanted in Indian families is not surprising in the present Indian situations where families are freely going for foeticide and infanticide purely for economic reasons. Today in the modern society where economic factor is the prime motivating factor and life guiding principle for many, lives and relationships will be sacrificed for one's pleasures, comfort and luxury, the old who have lost all their vigour — physical, mental and economic — can no longer expect respect and dignity.

---

2. David E. Beigel, *Buildings Support Networks for the Elderly: Theory and Applications*, Sage, New Delhi, 1984.

Alternative modes of old age care

To my knowledge at present there are three types of old age care.

A. HOME CARE

There can be no second opinion that Home is the best place for the old. It is a place which belongs to him and he belongs to it. All his loved ones, his children and grandchildren are there to look after him. Any old person would like to spend his old age only in his own home with which he has familiarity, attachment and strong sentiments. The importance of Home is stressed by Bent Kruger Smith. Home becomes a symbol of security for the old. To stay in one's own home means to hold on to selfhood, to maintain identity. For the person growing older giving up a home often symbolises losing the last hold on independence.[3]

Luckily most of the old people today in India are in this normal mode of old age care.

However, there may be certain factors which force people to opt out of this type of care. Ours is a partriarchal system where parents are supposed to live with their married sons. When things do not go smooth between daughter-in-law and old parents other types of care are sought after.

In our tradition parents are not to live with their married daughters. Actually this will be a good setting for the old because women are the major care takers in a home providing for food, nursing, etc. This is found only in few cases where son-in-law is willing to accept. Even if he accepts there may be objection from his own parents and relatives. In Korea a transition is taking place regarding who is to care for aged parents

Traditionally sons in Korea is held responsible for their older parents both finacially and emotionally. Nowadays however

---

3. Bert Kruger, Smith, *The pursuit of Dignity*, Beacon Press, Boston, 1977.

daughters are beginning to support their parents as well. The level of solidarity between elderly parents and their children especially their adult daughters are extremely high.[4]

B. HAVING INDEPENDENT HOME OF HIS OWN

Old age is usually characterised by the loss of the spouse. In such a situation the aged person may hire a servant or get the help of a relative to manage his home. Here he is his own master and need not adjust with others. But to opt for this he should be economically sound.The servant or relative must be willing to look after him in his sickness. He must also be trustworthy because sometimes servant may conspire against him, may attempt to robe and even kill him taking advantage of his vulnerable position.

C. INSTITUTIONAL CARE

The third type of care coming into prominence today is institutional care. The old person is admitted in the home for the aged and all his needs are met here. He spends his old age in the company of the old, who are similar to him in age, state of health, mental make-up, views of life, etc.

Old age homes are of two types — free and paid. In free homes the inmates need not pay any fees. Generally such homes are run by voulntary agencies belonging to Christian and Hindu organisations and secular trusts. Their chief motive is service. The paid homes charge a monthly fee from the inmates which ranges between Rs. 400 and Rs. 1000. They are also asked to pay a refundable deposit which ranges between Rs. 2,000 and Rs. 10,000. The deposit is charged so that on the death of the inmate the relatives may come if not for anything at least for the sake of money. Suppose they do not turn up the deposit is used to meet the funeral expenses.

---

4. Suh, H.K., 'A Study on the Relationship between the Elderly Parents and Their Adult Daughters based on Their Early Relationships', *1997 World Congress of Gerontology, Book of Abstracts*, Adelaide, 1997.

In India there are 700 free and paid old age homes according to the *Directory of the Old age Homes* published by Helpage India.

The following table gives state wise distribution of old age homes in India*

S.No.	State	No. of old age homes	S.No.	State	No. of old age homes
1.	Kerala	123	13.	Delhi	13
2.	Tamil Nadu	115	14.	Assam	8
3.	Andhra Pradesh	76	15.	Himachal Pradesh	6
4.	Maharashtra	66	16.	Haryana	5
5.	Karnataka	64	17.	Pondicherry	4
6.	Gujarat	55	18.	Rajasthan	3
7.	West Bengal	44	19.	Chandigarh	3
8.	Punjab	28	20.	Jammu & Kashmir	3
9.	Goa	25	21.	Meghalaya	3
10.	Orissa	24	22.	Bihar	1
11.	Uttar Pradesh	16	23.	Nagaland	1
12.	Madhya Pradesh	13	24.	Tripura	1
	Total	700			

* Directory of the Old Age Homes in India, Helpage India, New Delhi 1998.

Kerala tops the list followed by Tamil Nadu. In some states like Bihar and Uttar Pradesh old age homes are few in number. The reason for this is not known.

Generally in India old age homes have been established only to serve the destitute. Paid Homes is an entirely new concept.

Old age homes are not of homogeneous character. Some are meant exclusively for men, some exclusively for women, and some for both men and women. Generally old age homes are exclusively for old people but in some homes both destitute old and destitute children are taken care. In such homes there is possibility for mutual love and help between children and the old. Some old age homes are very small taking care of 5 to 10 inmates and some are quite big caring for 50 to 70 inmates. Inmates of smaller homes seem to be happier than the inmates of bigger homes.

Rules for admission also vary widely. In free homes normally the age of admission is 65 and above. But in paid homes they are admitted even at the age of 50. Some homes insist that at the time of admission they must not be bedridden and be capable of self-care. Once they become bedridden they will be send back. But in some other homes once they get admitted they will be looked after still they breath their last. In some free homes a strict conditions for admission is destitution. Hence, once they get admitted they cannot have any visitors but in some other homes destitution is not a condition and hence relatives are encouraged to visit them.

Homes run by nuns and priests get regular assistence. Mother Houses and a few other houses have financial backing and security. So providing for the physical needs of the old is satisfactory. But some are run by trusts and welfare clubs which solely depends upon donations and mere subscription from members. So living conditions in such homes are far from satisfactory.

Feeding 25 to 60 people without any financial support is not an easy thing. So for breakfast they are served rice-kanji, for lunch rice with one curry and for supper the same thing. The only redeeming feature is - thanks to the generosity and thoughtfulness of the public - on occasions of celebrations like birthdays, wedding anniversary good lunch is provided. In some homes such special feeding is for 15 to 20 days in a month. But when homes are far away from the city and less known such feeding also becomes a rare occasion.

Homes run by Voluntary Trusts do not have their own building and so spend the major portions of their meagre funds on rent. Finding a rented house for running an old age home is also a difficult task. Also many homes do not get any voluntary service by doctors and hence medical expenses of these homes are also very high. In such an economic situations these homes cannot afford to employ workers, leave alone trained workers. The only indispensable worker a home employs is the cook.

In these old age homes only a very few get old age pensions of

Rs. 150 per month. Those who gets this amount give it to the management. In a few well established homes a part of this money is given back to them as pocket money. Conventionally old age pension is not sanctioned for those who are staying in old age homes. The argument is that they have food and shelter and so they need no assistance but it should be remembered that they need some pocket money to meet their personal expenses and owning some amount though it is very little give them some satisfaction. Moreover there is no rule that inmates of old age homes are not eligible for pension. The only conditions are (1) that they must be above 65, (2) they must not have adult sons or son's sons.

The second condition looks meaningless, for the deserted poor destitute old man having a son or daughter does not make any difference.

In paid homes conditions are better. Unlike the free homes inmates do not permanently stay in these homes. They come to these homes on occasions of some unpleasantness and misunderstandings. They long to return to their houses. In a few months time things become normal and they do return. Paid homes look more like hostels. They maintain contacts with their families through letters and phone calls and attend family functions. When they stay in their children's homes they are obliged to do some work even when their children do not insist. Their children's problems and worries affect them and so for peace of mind and rest they prefer these homes. Moreover they have a choice. If they are not happy in one home they can switch-over to another home.

If they are pensioners they themselves pay the fees. Otherwise their family meets this expense. In these homes they long for affection, personal care and occasional visit by their children and grandchildren. But the family members think that if they send the monthly payment their duty is over. And this sort of rejection and neglect have driven many old persons to heart attacks, deaths and insanity.

Reasons for coming to these old age homes vary from persons to persons. Persons staying in free homes have long stories to narrate. Verbal abuse (most severe form of ill treatment), beating, denial of food. Such extreme form of rejection have driven them to take refuge in old age homes. For inmates of the paid homes even simple sign of rejection, lack of respect and recognition have been sufficient causes for opting for the old age homes.

We cannot blame sons, daughters, son-in-laws, daughter-in-laws alone for such state of affairs. The old people are also to be blamed. Finding fault with the youngsters, unwillingness to adjust, sticking on to their pride and self-righteousness, being very sensitive to unfavourable comments of others, exaggerating their problems, gossiping with neighbours, impatience, anger and aggression, too much interference in daily activities, too great expectations, false imaginations, continuing resentment towards daughter-in-law and her relations, not caring to be neat and clean, unwillingness to give up their power and authority are some of the reasons which make adjustment in their homes very difficult.

Whether it is free or paid home there is an inner sadness in them that they are not with their children and grandchildren. They exhibit a sense of alienation and also a longing for human communication and love. Some, shattered by their life experiences have become completely closed neither willing nor able to communicate sensibly. However in most of these homes the managers and care takers have service as their motive and try their best to help them lead a peaceful life in their last days.

Suggestions to improve functioning of old age homes

1. Economic support to be mobilised both from government and non-governmental agencies and general public.
2. A comprehensive list of old age homes in major cities with all particulars to be compiled and published to, facilitate the old people to choose the homes according to their conveniences and to help interested public to offer their contributions in material goods and services.
3. An association of the old age homes in major cities to be formed to facilitate exchange of information in various fields relating to the old.

4. Care to be taken to establish old age homes in the city or close to the city. When the homes are situated far away the old are totally isolated.

5. Efforts are to be taken up to instil in the minds of the young respect and concern for the old and motivate them to visit old age homes.

With more awareness created about the problems of the old, government implementing a favourable social policy for the old voluntary agencies intensifying their efforts for the cause of the old and a general change in the attitude of people towards the old will help to improve the lot of the aged to a great extent.

18

Institutional Care for the Aged

I. Sobha
Vijayalakshmi Ramamohan
M.S.N. Reddy

THE physical and cognitive frailties of the older impaired persons is indicative of their valuable status requiring the attention of researchers, planners, practitioners and policy analysts.

Rapid progress in science and technology as also path breaking inventions and medicines have secured for the aged a new lease of life. The elderly destitute are aged family members with minimum social security or economic support have access to institutional care — a facility which they did not have a few decades ago. The company of the same age group and similar thoughts, similar situations and similar experiences will lead to an affinity between the aged residing in the institutions. It is also possible that affections and interrelations will blind the aged living in these homes. However, in the Indian joint family context as also against the backdrop of traditional, cultural value assigned to family security — the pertinent question is how do the homes substitute for the Indian family security with reference to the living aged.

Objectives of the study

1. Description of the needs and problems of old age.
2. Enlistment of the supportive services required by the aged.
3. Survey of available services in institutions for the aged.

4. Medical facilities available for the aged in the institutions.
5. Outlining the expectations of the aged from institutions.

Methodology

The study was conducted in Chittoor District, Andhra Pradesh, the respondents were 60 women residents of the homes for the aged, selected on a random basis. The data was collected using a pretested schedule focussing on the major objectives outlined above. The collected data was pooled and subjected to simple statistical analysis. The results are presented herein.

Needs and problems of old aged

Family as a close kinship unit provides for social, economic health and psychological needs of the members, particularly the aged. It was primarily for this — that the family was treated as a social security for the needy, sick and aged. However, the changing trend in family life have forced the aged people to fend for themselves at this advanced age as also to delineate the health, economic, psychological and social needs such as depending on the government for old age pension. Dependency on family is a problem and a need because of the lower physical strength and lack of suitable occupations for their age. Deterioration physical health restricts mobility and causes a degree of impairment. Thus biological ageing and weak economic conditions lead to disabilities and health problems for the aged such as T.B., diabetes, blindness, cataract, asthma, pain in the joints, abdomen and orthopaedic disabilities, besides disabilities of the senses. By and large the aged people have a very limited range of routine activities such as sitting idle, worshipping, walking, taking care of children, utensil cleaning, sweeping and mopping the homes. More important of all these is the feeling of powerlessness which has been largely attributed to their inability to earn. All these encourages the aged people to cultivate the idea that their lives have lost all charm and they have become meaningless.

Minimal supportive service requirement for the aged

A perusal of the census data across the world indicates that most survivors among the married couple are women, who live longer than men. The older the widow grows the greater are the problems. The transitional problems include coping with grief on the passing away of the partner and the responsibility of making decisions and handling family affairs amidst for grief. The other accompanying problems are that of employment, housing, food security, health, emotional secutiry and companionship. The results of the data related to these aspects are projected in Table 1.

Table 1 : Supportive services required by the aged

Supportive services	*Frequency*	%
Food security	50	83.3
Economic security	10	16.7
Emotional security	40	66.7
Health security	30	50
Companionship	60	100

Among the five listed, companionship was of overriding concern to all respondents. This was followed by need for food security (83.3 percent), companionship and food security, when inadequate, led to lack of emotional security which was third in the list of the supportive services required by the aged. Health security was a neutral issue with (50 percent) of the respondents listing it as a required supportive service and the remaining 50 percent choosing not to do so. The most encouraging trend was observed in the case of economic security with only 16.7 percent of the respondents, opted for it as a requisite supportive service. However, this lost point may be also interpreted in the context of the reply given by the respondents, why do I need money at this age?

Availability of supportive services for the aged

Examining the available supportive services in the institutions has given results which are in consonance with the requirements of the aged as enlisted in Table 1. The pertinent data is projected in Table 2.

Table 2 : Supportive services available in Institutions

Supportive services	*Frequency*	*%*
Food security	60	100
Economic security	-	-
Emotional security	20	33.3
Health security	30	50
Companionship	50	83.3
Recreational facilities	50	83.3
Personal attendance	15	25

Food security, companionship, recreational facilities were readily available in all institutions. However, health security was just 50 percent. This is certainly not a healthy sign for the aged. The tendency to fall sick, recurrence of minor health problems and persistence of nagging illness require ready availability of medical and health facilities, which have been found to be lacking in the present study. Emotional security and personal attendance was also available though relatively at lower percentage. These two services together, if not provided in the requisite dimension can lead to other related problems, particularly the health status of the aged. Economic security has not been provided to the respondents in the present study.

Availability of medical facilities

Declining health due to physical degeneration, nutritionally inadequate diets, lack of exercise and limited sources of interaction can altogether precipitate health problems for aged. In this context information related to the medical services available in the institutions is presented in Table 3.

Table 3: Availability medical facilities

Medical facilities	*Frequency*	*%*
First Aid	50	83.3
Treatment of minor ailments	35	58.3
Referral services	25	41.7
Subsidised health care	20	33.3
Timely health care	15	25

A majority (83.3 percent) of the institutions had first aid facilities. What is more pertinent and important is that treatment of minor ailments was available only in 58 percent of the institutions. Further refferal services (41.7 percent), subsidised health care (33.3 percent) and timely health care (25 percent) was lacking in a majority of the institutions. These three factors can have serious repercussions on the health status of the women-affecting their longevity, mobility, emotional security and also their mental state of health. All this can further aggravate the gnawing sense of isolation, depression, and a feeling of unwantedness among the emotionally vulnerable aged.

Expectations of the aged from the institutions

Individuals join institutions for satisfying several or some of the securities which they miss in their homes or to secure such of the securities which are not available in their homes. In this study also the expectations of the aged from the institutions have been collected and this data is presented in Table 4.

Table 4: Expectations of the aged from insitutional care

Expectations	*Frequency*	%
Minimum basic needs	60	100
Personal attendance	50	83.3
Recreational facilities	60	100
Emotional security	45	75
Minimum comforts for stay	60	100
Economic security	20	33.3

All respondents have expressed varying levels of dissatisfaction with the supportive services and care provided by the institutions where they reside. The prime expectations included satisfaction of minimum basic needs (100 percent) and minimum comforts for their stay (100 percent). Further personal care through regular attendance to the needs (83.3 percent) and emotional security (75 percent), were the other two expectations. The surprise package in the list of the expectations included recreational facilities (100 percent) which included sight seeing, visits to religious places and reading, music and watching T.V. Economic security was also on the list of expectations though by a small percentage of respondents (33.3 percent).

The aged individuals have to be provided adequate socio-economic securities which happen to be the main preoccupation during old age. The institutional living for the aged to a certain extent provided scope for sharing of the bottled up emotional securities. This itself is a tension releasing mechanism for the aged. Interactions with the aged respondents has also indicated that the respondents were quite satisfied with the care provided by the institutions. In fact, they appeared to have become more open and free in the institutions when compared to their family residential life.

Institutional care offers particularly the disabled old people a sheltered home, a common place for lunch. It offers a place for recreation and a platform for overcoming, bouts of depression and a source for sharing feelings, thoughts and companionship. For many elderly who are in similar situations the home becomes a place for support, encouragement and a chance for finding friends. Over and above all these a home offers a secure place for elderly to overcome loneliness and health care facilities. The old age homes provide a quiet and peaceful atmosphere for reminiscing.

Ageing is not only a biological, but also a psychological process, effecting major changes in the role and status of the aged individual. Sound mental and physical health, healthy socio-economic status and continuation of personal independence are important goals for the aged. However, retirement spells reduced income, diminished physical responsibility and a general decline in health and vigour. All of these creates low morale and withdrawl symptoms from the society since the aged are isolated, static and self-centred existence. The psychological problem of having to cope with mental ageing and decreased ability to handle technical, skill related activities, create emotional problems for aged. Reduced family support and attention are both responsible for feelings of emptiness, loneliness and anxiety, leading to instability which is avoidable. Breakdown in social values or familiar support and personal problems in coping with the changing social support scenario, causes infringement of the basic rights of the aged leading to feeling of isolation and insecurity feeling of the aged.

All these issues have been raised at different levels in this paper. What is required for professionals, policy planners, administrators, medical and social personnel to co-ordinate their activities so as to help the aged to deal with the multiple problems which accompany old age. It could be best for every individual to remember that youth and adults have to ultimately be transformed to old age.

References

James William, Coleman and Donald; R. Cressey, *Social Problems*, Harper & Row Publishers, New York, 1987.

Mahajan, A., *Problems of the Aged in Unorganised Sector*, Mittal Publications, Delhi, 1987.

Marcia, G., Ory and Alfred, P., Duncker, in *Home care for order people, Health and Supportive Services*, Sage Publications, 1992.

Paul Chowdhary, P., *Hand Book of Social Welfare*, Atma Ram & Sons, Delhi, 1993.

Peter, G. Coleman, *Ageing and Reminiscence Processes Social and Clinical Implications*, John Wiley & Sons, New York, 1986.

19

Comparative Study of Elderly Care by Families and Institutions in Kerala, India

Jacob John Kattakayam

INDIA'S elderly population is growing very fast that the projection shows that there will be 71 million old population by 2001 and 113 million elderly in 2016. India currently ranks fourth among the world's countries in terms of the absolute size in its elderly population. By the year 2000, India will become second in rank next to China.

Growth of elderly population in India

In India, birth rates and death rates were very high till 1951 which kept the persons above 60 at a low level. However, from 1951 onwards the old population started growing steadily. In India, the growth rate of the elderly population defined as people who are above the age of 60 years, has been 3.1 percent compared to 2.1 per annum in the general population in the last decade (Bhat 1992: 440-8). Due to the success of the family planning programmes and the increase in the literacy rate, a steady decline in the birth rate has decreased the number of young persons and increased the aged in the population structure. In 1971 the elderly population of India was 5.6 percent and it has increased to 6.3 percent in 1981 and 7 percent in 1991. According to the Committee on Population Projections the elderly population in India is likely to reach 7.8 percent by 2001. Compared to any developed country, the population of India's elderly is less, but in absolute number it is very large. There were 24.7 million persons above the age of 60 in 1961 and 42.1 million in 1981 and is expected to reach about 77 million in 2001 (Chanana and Talwar 1987: 23-38).

Though aged are commonly understood as elderly population they are defined as the people whose growth has arrived at a relatively steady state (Gilbert 1997: 173). In India elderly population are defined by the Central Government as people above 60 years to attain the status of the senior citizenship. But the retirement age which is another criteria for defining the aged varies from one Government to another. In India the old age is associated with the people who are having grey hair and wrinkled skin.

Family care for the elderly

The obligation of the Indian family system to look after the elderly, continues from traditional days to the present day. The traditional family bonds and solidarity have not completely eroded. The elderly are by and large looked after by their children and near relatives. But the Western winds of change and the rapid industrialisation and consequent urbanisation have initiated the disintegration of the joint family system which provided family support both the young and the old.

> The aged in the traditional societies enjoyed unparalleled sense of honour, legitimate authority in the family or community, had decision-making responsibilities in the economic and political activities of the family and were treated as repositories of experience and wisdom.
>
> — Singh, 1997: 3

Today, the structural and functional changes in the family brought the aged to its periphery, though they prefer family for their living. Thus, the family is still the strong institution in India for the old people. The members of the family usually share with the elderly, love, affection, respect and care.

In India most of the aged are not having any income of their own as these people's occupation during their active life was agriculture or agriculture related occupations. The major segment of the aged live in villages where poverty and unemployment are widespread. The tendency in India is that the younger generation migrate to cities leaving the old in the villages with their close kin or under the institutional care. A great majority of the elderly live with their married or unmarried children banking upon their support, though it may not guarantee fulfilment of hopes.

The magnitude of the problems of the aged in India arises from the rapid social changes and its impact on families. Till recently these problems were handled as socio-economic problems but now gerontological studies have started in India and this paper is a consequence of that. The study makes an attempt to understand how elderly people are cared by the families and institutions in Kerala.

Situation in Kerala

Kerala and Punjab are having large number of old population in its demographic structure (Table 1). Kerala is characterised by heavy outmigration and high literacy rate, remarkable achievement in family planning and health education. As a result, the birth rate and the death rate have decreased. According to the 1991 census Kerala had 2.5 million persons above the age of 60, i.e., 7.9 percent of the total population of the state. The total population of Kerala is projected to increase from 27.6 million in 1986 to 45 million in 2026. In this period, the young population is projected to increase from 8.8 to about 10 million, working age population 16.6 to 26.8 million and the elderly population from 2.2 million to 8.3 million. To put it briefly in the next forty years the population increase in Kerala will be 1.6 times but there will be a four-fold increase in the elderly population (UN 1991).

A special feature of Kerala in that the proportion of females in the 60 plus population is higher than that of males while in the country the position is the opposite. Traditionally Kerala is a matriarchal society where women enjoy social, economic and political power. Majority of the old in Kerala are active in various

Table 1 : Elderly population in the selected states of India 1981

Major States	*% of old population (60 yrs and above)*
Andhra Pradesh	6.43
Bihar	6.27
Gujarat	5.60
Haryana	6.28
Karnataka	6.26
Kerala	7.55
Madhya Pradesh	5.98
Maharashtra	6.35
Orissa	6.22
Punjab	7.70
Rajasthan	5.34
Tamil Nadu	6.51
Uttar Pradesh	6.49
West Bengal	5.40
India as a whole	6.27

Source: Census of India 1981 Series-1. India Paper 5 of 1984, Controller of Publications. New Delhi. (Registrar General and census Commissioner for India).

sectors of life which are socially inherited having no specified age for retirement. However, due to decreasing employment opportunities income of the old is marginal, which is the main cause of dependency. Though the old are taken care by the family a shift in the care giving system is seen recently. At least a few live under the institutional care. Kerala is having the maximum number of old age institutions and according to 1997 reports there are 77 such institutions in Kerala. These homes varies widely in respect to management and economic policies. The present study was initiated with the following objectives. The respondents from the institutions are referred as aged living in the homes and the others in families are referred as those living in the households.

- To study the socio-economic background of the aged in the various institutions.
- To study the status of the old in 'Homes' and 'Households' in terms of economy and health.
- To analyse the aged's attitude towards family.

Methodology

The area of investigation were districts of Thiruvananthapuram, Ernakulam and Calicut located at the southern, central and northern parts of Kerala giving equal representation to the major religions of the country and the state namely Hindus, Christians and Muslims. 100 respondents were selected from the families who are above 60 years either living in rural or urban areas. Representation was given to the two genders and various classes. Likewise 100 respondents were selected from the homes taking into consideration the same variables as in the households.

The data were collected mainly through pretested interview schedules. In certain cases, unstructured interviews were also used to elicit the data. The data collected were analysed using many variables such as class, age, gender, occupation and regional background according to the context.

Results of the study

SOCIO-ECONOMIC BACKGROUND OF THE AGED

The socio-economic background of the old reveals that it is the urban middle-class and upper-class who prefer institutional care. Another feature of the elders who are in homes is that most of them choose homes after the death of their spouses. In the sample it is found that 68 percent of the elders who stay in the homes do not have their spouse alive whereas 78 percent of the elders of the households have their spouse alive.

A large number of the elderly selected for the study are from the urban areas and it is also observed that 67 percent of the aged in the homes do not have an independent income whereas 67 percent of the aged residing in the various households have an independent income. From the views of the respondents 16 percent of the aged have very good health and 48 percent of the aged have good health. The rest said that they have frequent health problems.

Table 2 : Socio-economic background of the respondents

Region	*Homes*	*Households*
Rural	22	50
Urban	78	50
Marital status		
Spouse alive	32	73
Spouse dead/No spouse	68	27
Age		
60-75	55	63
75+	45	37
Income		
Independent	33	67
Dependent	67	33
Religion		
Hindus	37	52
Christians	49	37
Muslims	14	11
Literacy		
Literate	83	65
Illiterate	17	35
Sex Male	59	58
Female	41	42

Non-institutionalised versus institutionalised

Among the aged who are in the homes there are two categories (1) those entering homes out of sheer poverty and (2) those who pay for their living. The old age homes have a protected environment, regular daily routine, medical care and occasions to meet with peer groups. In contrast, the old living in households do not have these advantages, in spite of their rich socio-economic background. Both the upper-class and the lower-class aged living in the homes feel that they are living alone. 89.83 percent of the men in the homes feel that they are insecure where as only 37.93 percent of the men living in families feel that they are insecure. 70.73 percent of the women feel that they are insecure in the homes.

Table 3 : Feeling of insecurity by the aged in homes & households

Nobody	*Homes*		*Households*		*Total*
	M	*F*	*M*	*F*	
Feeling insecure	53 (89.83%)	29 (70.73%)	22 (37.93%)	13 (30.95%)	117
No insecurity	6 (10.16%)	12 (29.26%)	36 (62.06%)	29 (63.04%)	83
Total	59	41	58	42	200
Miss the family	55 (93.22%)	39 (95.12%)	4 (6.89%)	2 (4.76%)	100
Do not miss	4 (6.7%)	2 (4.87%)	54 (93.1%)	40 (95.23%)	100
Total	**59**	**41**	**58**	**42**	**200**

Those living in families do not have peer group due to the shifting of the residence by the aged or by their caretakers. The aged in the families shave to yield to the special demands and requirements of children and usually they feel that they are marginalised. But in the present study the old and the adults have compromised in many situations that the old do not feel marginalised. When the old is involved in the family affairs, the old and the other members of the family gain too much especially mental satisfaction and thereby a peaceful atmosphere. This environment is totally absent in the homes. Nearly 95 percent of the old in the homes feel that they miss their families very much.

Status of the aged in the homes and the households

Status is determined by age, gender, marital status, education, economic background, etc. It is observed that the aged living in the families with their husbands or wives having their own income have a higher status in the families than widows or widowers having no income. Those who own property have a higher status in the families. This is because their kin know very well that the property owned by aged will be inherited by them. The aged who are having a bank balance are also respected in the families. Any way more than 60 per cent of the aged residing in the homes say that they do not have any status. It was found that the old are engaged in the family in many ways. Most of them help in the day-to-day affairs of the family. Helping in home management is found to be the most favourite activity of the old.

Table 4 : The way the old are engaged in the family

	M	*W*	*Total*
Home management	50 (84.75%)	32 (78.04%)	82
Helping in kitchen	10 (16.94%)	39 (95.12%)	49
Helping children	26 (44.06%)	36 (87.80%)	62
Spiritual culture	42 (54.24%)	31 (75.60%)	63

84.75 percent of the men and 78.04 percent of the women do this whereas kitchen work is done mainly by the old women. In other activities both men and women take interest though only 44.06 percent of the men look after the children. 54.24 percent of the men and 75.60 percent of the women help the family members in the spiritual activities.

In the matter of interpersonal relationship within the family, the person who loves the respondents most was the spouse and vice versa. As far as their liking is concerned it is the spouse, the eldest son, and their grandchildren and then the daughters. The choice is based on care giving, especially the money.

Another indicator of the status of the old in the family is their role in decision-making. This study observed that the decision-making power of the elderly are very little because in most of the households where this study is carried out the aged are not fully involved in the family matters. It was found that only a few people (20.0 percent) participate in the decision-making process. Of these 7 percent participate in the day-to-day decision, 5 percent participate in long-term decision and 8 percent take all kinds of decision.

While the old are not totally by-passed in family decision they are increasingly driven to a secondary position. However, the old do not have any regrets and they still think that they are important in the family, 42 percent of those who have kinship ties stated that their physical support was critical in the family, 12 percent felt their financial contribution was necessary for the family exchequer. 21.0 percent stated their role in kitchen help is important and another 30.0 percent felt that they are important in all the above and several other matters. In fact, neither the old nor the young felt that the aged contribution as insignificant or useless. But only 60 percent of the old felt that their work has been appreciated by the family members. All except 4.5 percent felt that his work has been appreciated by the family members.

Economic problems of the aged

Most of the aged under study had economic problems as only 33.0 percent of the aged in homes and 6 percent in households have independent income. It was found that even these people were supported with additional income as their income is too low for self-support. 80.0 percent of the people who are having independent income has only less than Rs. 250 a month. Their income are from the land or retirement benefits or savings or money given by their kin.

Only 48 percent were satisfied with the quantity and quality of food and the rest have some problems about their food. In clothing, the condition is better. Unlike the expenditure on food, spending on clothing is occasional. Moreover cloth is more a subjective item than food, its need increases proportionate to one's self-estimation. However, 24 percent of the respondents are not satisfied with their clothing needs. As regards medicine only 11.0 percent are not satisfied.

Health problems of the elderly

The present study found that as many as 75.0 percent of the respondents are in need of medical care. Of these, the majority are those who lost their spouse, living alone and those who are in the homes. The intake of medicine ranges from occasional to regular. A steady deterioration in the health condition of the aged has been observed. 65 percent have poor eyesight, 25 percent have hearing problems, 40 percent have sleeplessness, 25 percent problems in the memory power, 50 percent have pains in the joints and 20 percent of them have nervous problems. Health problems are more among the destitute and lower income groups. The study analysed the health status of the elderly for the past two years and found that there is a steady deterioration of the health status among the aged. The health care of the elderly in homes are better than the households. The regular or periodical check-up in the homes gives a physical and psychological well-being of the elderly.

The health problems of the old mostly arise either due to negligence or due to economic conditions. Kerala has a well developed health care and delivery system. Medical services are within the reach of even remote villages. But the concepts of geriatric illness and geriatric care have not become popular. Doctors either treat old age diseases like other diseases or like terminal decease. Traditional concept on ageing makes the aged carry their diseases to their graves. To remedy this situation, paramedical services, the services of health/social workers and subsidised medical care are necessary. They should replace the present system of free medicines to the poor which results in lack of critical medicines in government hospitals.

Attitude of the aged towards the family

Unlike the institutionalised old, the non-institutionalised old seem to be reconciled to their age and treatment received from the family. It was found that all the aged living in families spent their income on their family like children's education and marriage, etc. It is also found earlier (Table 4) that many of the old are engaged in taking care of children, management of the houses and helping in the kitchen. More than 90.0 percent of the respondents are helping their families either physically or financially or both in spite their socio-economic background. This trend indicates that the aged like to involve themselves in the household activities. When asked whether they would like to help their kinsmen more if they had money, 60 percent of the respondents living alone, 52 per cent of the destitutes living in families and 47 percent of the affluent groups replied in the affirmative. Financial assistance to the family may be possible remedy to overcome the resistance of the families to keeping the old with them.

Participation of the old in familial, community and social activities

Absence of elderly in many cases is not due to lack of interest but lack of ability, poor health and absence of income. Unfortunately, there are very few forums for mobilising the services of the old. The old cannot participate on equal terms with the young in many of the existing social and community clubs. In major cities of Kerala, there are senior citizen clubs but they are not more than a monthly meeting or a get-together. Kerala villages have scattered dwellings and it is difficult for the old to come to a common forum and mix together because of distance. Hence organisations have to be designed to bring the old together and to mobilise their talents.

The need for strengthening the family

From the above, one can easily infer that the main support system of the elderly is the family. Those who are deprived from the family also say that they love to be with their families than being in the homes. Therefore the family should be overhauled to suit the aged especially in the line of care giving.

1. The family could be given a special allowance to enhance its income. Along with this, income tax subsidy or exemption may be given to tax paying families which maintain old persons. The government can consider the family income and provide accordingly.
2. The destitute old age pension scheme may be expanded to cover all deserving people and the amount of pension may be raised to cope with the inflation. At present the pension is too low that it is not enough for their maintenance.
3. For urban residents community recreation could be planned. Most of the aged in the present study feel that

there is no outlet for them.

4. Health insurance of the aged is another important item. Fully or partly paid group insurance could be set-up in the urban and rural areas. The scheme benefits aged as well as society as health status will improve.
5. In housing shemes and land allotment, priority may be given to old person or his family as this will become an incentive in taking care of the old.

Role of voluntary organisations

The voluntary agencies confine themselves in setting up of homes either free and paid. Paid homes are scarce. Since the demand for the service is increasing, this has to be taken care of on a priority basis. Non-government organisations can also run Day Centres and Day Care Centres along with counselling centres equipped with workers and paramedical staff.

Table 5 : Respondents' liking towards the kins

Respondents	*Homes*		*Households*	
	M	*F*	*M*	*F*
Spouse	48 (81.35%)	36 (87.8%)	50 (86.20%)	41 (97.61%)
Sons	(43) (72.88%)	33 (80.48%)	45 (77.58%)	38 (90.47%)
Daughters	32 (54.23%)	40 (97.56%)	27 (46.55%)	39 (81.25%)
Grandchildren	47 (79.66%)	37 (90.24%)	23 (39.65%)	40 (95.23%)
Other relatives	10 (16.94%)	4 (9.75%)	5 (8.62%)	12 (28.57%)
Others	4 (6.79%)	3 (7.31%)	3 (5.17%)	6 (14.28%)

Conclusion

Old age is a new problem in India as in the past societies old was looked after by the joint families. Today, increasing life expectancy coupled with the increasing demands of life marginalise the old from the family, giving a mental dilemma for the old as well as for the young regarding their status and position in the family *vis-a-vis* the society. This study infer that elders consider family as the main support system though many aged are forced to institutional care giving system. Comparing the aged who live in the homes and the households, the aged who live in the households are more healthy and happy than those in the households. For those who stay in the homes the company of the peer groups do not give much satisfaction as they feel that they miss their families very much. Though both the groups have deprivations, the aged who stay in the homes have more deprivation than those who stay in the families.

Reference

Bhat, P.N. Marie, 1992, 'Changing demography of the elderly in India', *Current Science*, 63 (8), 440-8.

Chanana, H.B., and P.P. Talwar, 1987, 'Ageing in India: Its socio-economic and health implications', *Asia-Pacific Population Journal*, vol. 2, no. 3, September, pp. 23-38.

Gilbert, G. Jeanne, 1991, *Understanding of the old age*, The Towald Press Co., New York, p. 173.

Rajan, Irudaya S., 1989, 'Ageing in Kerala: One more population problem', *Asia-Pacific Population Journal*, vol. 4, no. 2, p. 19.

Singh, Yogendra, 1997, 'Changing Trends in the Indian Family and the adjustment of the aged', *Research and Development Journal*, vol.3, no. 2, p. 32.

United Nations, 1975, *Poverty, Unemployment and Development Policy*, New York.

United Nations, 1991, 'Economics and Social Aspects of Population, Ageing in Kerala', *International Economic and Social Affairs of the United Nations*, CICRED, Paris.

Section IV
Gender Perspective and the Old

20

Are the Elderly Women the Most Deprived among the Deprived?

A Micro level Investigation in Rural Tamil Nadu

N. Audinarayana
J. Sheela
N. Kavitha

Introduction

DURING the twenty-first century the world is going to face a typical demographic problem, viz., ageing, that is, a conspicuous increase in the number of older persons (aged 60 years and above). For instance, in the more developed countries, where the process of ageing is ahead, the percentage of population aged 60 years or older is about 19 during 1999, which may likely to increase to about 33 per cent by 2050. However, because of the rapid demographic transition in less developed countries such percentage is likely to increase from 8 to 21 during the same time. In India also though the corresponding increase is expected to be from 8 to 21, in absolute numbers the increase is from 75 millions to 324 millions, next to China (439.6 millions in AD 2050). Another interesting feature of ageing is that the population of older persons will be larger than the population of children (0-14) for the first time in human history (United Nations 1999).

In Indian context, the process of population ageing has a special concern because it occurs at a low level of economic development in comparison to the experience of the West and some other Asian countries. Since there is going to be a large size and share of older population in India, several socio-economic and health problems may arise in future. These will cause severe economic burden both at the individual level as well as at the national level. Further, there is sense that the ability and/or willingness of families to support the elderly is declining and that the elderly themselves have suffered a loss of status in the course of economic and social change (Martin 1990).

The increasing importance of the studies on ageing and senior citizens has been emphasised by a series of national and international conferences and seminars. In India, over the past two decades a number of studies have focussed on one or the other issues of ageing (De Souza 1981; Desai 1982; Bhatia 1983; Sahayam 1988; Nair 1989; Reddy 1990; National Sample Survey Organisation 1991; Chandra, *et al.* 1993; Chakrabarti 1993; Mahanta 1993; Singh, *et al.* 1994; Asharaf 1995; Audinarayana, *et al.* 1996; Nair and Santhosh 1997; Irudaya Rajan, *et al.* 1999). The need for more studies on the elderly people is being felt by social scientists (Sharma and Dak 1987; Vatuk 1991; Gore 1992; Mahadevan and Sumangala 1992; Vijayakumar 1995; Irudaya Rajan, *et al.* 1999) as well as policy-makers on the ground that many more issues remained unexplored. This is because the studies hitherto conducted were mostly dealt with the retired government employees, inmates of institutions and middleclass urbanites. Of course, some studies have focussed on the ageing issues of Indian rural elderly, but the information is little in comparison with the bulk of elderly living in rural areas. Besides these, a few studies have attempted to analyse the socio-economic characteristics of the aged controlling for their gender background. Almost all these have concluded that the female aged are the most deprived among the deprived (Bose and Saxena 1964; Kaur, *et al.* 1987; Sahayam 1988; Nair 1989; Vijayakumar 1991; Chakrabarti 1993; Mahanta 1993; Singh, *et al.* 1994; Asharaf 1995; Nair and Santhosh 1997; Irudaya Rajan,*et al.* 1999). Under these circumstances, this paper presents the gender differentials in the demographic and socio-economic profile of the rural elderly based on an empirical study conducted in Coimbatore district, Tamil Nadu.

Data and methodology

Data used for this paper had been collected from 415 households with at least one elderly person — 60 years and above — belonging to four villages of Palldam block, Coimbatore district, Tamil Nadu State. Information on the demographic and socio-economic profile was gathered for 558 elderly persons. Cross-tabular analysis was carried out to observe the gender differentials in their demographic and socio-economic profile. Chi-square test was used to test the association between the gender background and the demographic as well as and socio-economic characteristics of the elderly.

THE SETTING

The study villages are approximately 25-30 km away from Coimbatore city (popularly known as the Textile City or the Southern Manchester of India). Hindus are predominantly residing in these villages. Gounders, the agricultural community, followed by the Chettiars (the weaving community) and Kurumbars (the sheep rearing community) are the major caste groups residing in the study area.

Agriculture is the major avenue for livelihood of the people in these villages. Weaving (both handlooms and powerlooms) and sheep rearing are the next main income generating activities. A wind mill project and a medium-size spinning mill also provides employment for some of the villagers. All the villages can be reached by town bus service (short-distance bus service from the nearest town/city), though the frequency is comparatively less. Two of the villages have subcentres (besides a Registered Medical Practitioner in one of the villages) provide the basic medical and health facilities to the villagers. Overall, the socio-economic development of these villages is at a moderate level.

Results and discussion

AGE STRUCTURE AND SEX RATIO

Age and sex are the two basic ascribed characteristics of population. Generally, with advancing age the share of elderly population will decrease because of higher prevalence of morbidity and mortality among them. Among the sample elderly (Table 1), 32 percent belong to 60-4 age group (young-old) followed by 23 percent and 20 percent respectively to 65-9 and 70-4 years. The rest 14 percent and 10 percent respectively belong to old-old (75-9 and 80+years) age groups. The mean age of the sample elderly is 69.18 years. Gender differentials across the age distribution are negligible though the concentration of females is slightly higher among the 60-4 and 65-9 age groups as against their male couterparts. This has also been reflected in average age of the females (68.80 years) as against males (69.61 years).

Table 1 Age structure and sex ratio of the elderly

Age group	*Males*		*Females*		*Total*		*Sex ratio*
	%	*No.*	*%*	*No.*	*%*	*No.*	*(F/M*1000)*
60-64	29.72	77	34.78	104	32.44	181	1351
65-69	21.23	55	24.08	72	22.76	127	1309
70-74	23.55	61	17.73	53	20.43	114	869
75-79	16.22	42	12.71	38	14.33	80	905
80 +	9.27	24	10.70	32	10.04	56	1333
Total	100.00	259	100.00	299	100.00	558	1154

With regard to the sex ratio of the elderly sample population (Table 1), in general, it is favourable to females, i.e., 1154 females per 1,000 males. However, it is more favourable to females in case of young-old and very old-old elderly. The general trend in sex ratio is in conformity with many less developed countries (UN 1994) and also in selected states of India (NSSO 1991) where women tend to outlive men in older age groups. Some possible explanations are: men generally exposed to greater occupational and other hazards (including drinking alcohol, cigarette smoking, etc.) and sex differentials in mis-reporting of age. On the other hand, in recent times there is evidence that the biological basis of better longevity for females is seen even in India as indicated by the available data. For instance, among India's elderly it is estimated that the extension of life at the expectation of life at age 60 years for men and women during 1980-5 was 14.6 years respectively, which may likely to increase to 15.8 and 17.2 years respectively by 2001-5 (Gulati and Rajan 1999).

MARITAL STATUS

Marital status is one of the prime social characteristics of the elderly population. In India, depending upon the marital status of the elderly, especially that of women, their position and status within the family as well as in the society will be determined. Generally, widowed women receive less respect and care from the family members so also by the members of the society at large. On the whole, nearly two-thirds of the sample elderly (66 per cent) are currently married at the time of survey and the rest (34 per cent) are widowed. One elder woman has reported that she is living with her widowed mother by separating herself with her husband (panel 1 of Table 2). However, it is conspicuous to note that more than 50 per cent of the elderly women (53 per cent) are widows as against one-eighth of their men counterparts (13 per cent). On the other hand, a greater proportion of the elderly is in currently married status. These sex differentials in marital status of the elderly are statistically highly significant (Chi-Square = 99.14; p< 001). Women marrying older men and negligible number of re-marriages among women than men are the prominent reasons for such differentials. The high incidence of widowhood could be one of the important factors for the low status of many elderly females. In the Indian context, at least three major reasons have been identified for the greater incidence of widowhood among women than among their men counterparts. They are: (i) women generally marry male persons older by age (with large age difference), (ii) negligible number of re-marriages among women as compared to men because of less social and cultural support and (iii) as noticed earlier, the life expectancy of women would be higher than men.

Table 2 Gender differentials in the Socio-economic profile of the elderly

Socio-economic characteristics	*Male*		*Female*		*Total*	
	%	*No*	%	*No*	%	*No*
Married	87.28	226	47.16	141	65.77	367
Widowed	12.74	33	52.84	158	34.23	191
	Chi-square = 99.14; p<.001					
2. *Educational status*						
Illiterate	69.88	181	93.65	280	82.62	461
Primary school	22.39	58	5.69	17	13.44	75
Middle school +	7.72	20	0.67	2	3.94	22
	Chi-square = 55.82; p<.001					
3. *Occupational status*						
Non-working	35.91	93	64.21	192	51.08	285
Agri. coolies	25.48	66	19.40	58	22.22	124
Weaving coolies	10.04	26	6.35	19	8.06	45
Cultivators	11.20	29	3.34	10	6.99	39
Own weaving	3.47	9	4.68	14	4.12	23
Artisans & others	13.90	36	2.01	6	7.53	42
	Chi-square = 65.23; p<.001					
4. *Monthly income*						
Not earning	34.36	89	58.86	176	47.49	265
Rs. 300 or less	16.60	49	19.73	59	18.28	102
Rs. 301-600	18.92	49	15.05	45	16.85	94
Rs. 601 and above	30.12	78	6.35	19	17.38	97
	Chi-square = 64.59; p<.001					
Total	100.00	259	100.00	299	100.00	558

EDUCATIONAL STATUS

Education plays its role as an important determinant of the life-pattern and social status of the aged. In rural Indian context, where higher education is absent, it is expected that the level of education will be less among the older people particularly among the women. Data shown in panel 2 of Table 2 reveal that, in general, a greater percentage of the elderly (83 percent) are illiterates, 13 percent educated up to primary school level and only 4 percent of the elderly educated beyond primary (middle school and above) school level. Obviously the age-old negligence to female education seems to be evident by the fact that the percentage of illiteracy is more among aged women (94 percent) than among men (70 percent). On the contrary, only 6 percent of elderly women as against 30 percent of men received some formal education. The gender differentials in educational status are observed to be statistically highly significant (Chi-Square = 55.82; p<. 001).

OCCUPATIONAL STATUS

Occupational status is one of the major socio-economic characteristics of population. Though old age meant for leisure and relaxation majority of the elderly, especially in less developed countries, will continue to work after age 60 years. For instance, while only 23 percent of men aged 60 years or older were still economically active (by 1999) in more developed regions compared with 52 percent of men in less developed regions (UN 1999). India is no exception to this pattern. According to 1991 census, in India the workforce participation rate was as high as 60 for men whereas such rate was only 11 in the case of women. The corresponding ranges for Tamil Nadu State were 57 and 18 respectively. Further, the rates were substantially higher in rural areas as compared to urban areas, ince the absorption of older labour force is somewhat easy in agricultural and related activities (Registrar General, India 1999). Some of the major reasons for such high activity rate among older men are: (i) limited coverage of retirement schemes and lack of social security policies, (ii) more intensive poverty and therefore difficulty to support themselves as well as dependents, (iii) less number of children to support (economic) in old age and (iv) weakening filial relationship because of social change and modernisation.

An analysis of occupational status of the elderly (panel 3 of Table 2) reveals that slightly more than half of them (51 percent) are not working either for wages or salary, 30 percent are working as coolies (22 percent in agricultural and related work and 8 per cent in weaving), 7 percent engaged in (own) cultivation, 4 percent in (own) weaving and the rest (7.5 percent) as artisans, petty shop owners and others (brokers in sale/purchase of house and/or house sites/cows/sheep, etc.). Gender differentials in occupational status are noteworthy. A large number of elderly women (64 percent) are not working (housewives) as against 36 per cent of men. On the contrary, the percentage of elderly men engaged in various income generating activities is higher as compared to their women counterparts, except in the case of (own) weaving. The gender differentials in occupational status are observed to be highly significant (Chi-Square = 65.23; p <.001). Gender differentials in work participation rates mainly arise because of the role of men as breadwinners in Indian society.

MONTHLY INCOME

Economic condition of the older people in India will always be at much lower side, i.e., live in severe poverty conditions. This is mainly because the earnings during their working life generally at lower side and therefore the per capita income will be very less. Even those who had saved a little during their adult ages for the future also experience poverty in old age due to continuing inflation, expenditure on medicines, marriages and other rites to be performed. Of course, elderly women will be in much worst position as far as economic conditions are considered.

In the present context, monthly income of the elderly is calculated based on the their wages, pension and regular income received from the savings, rent and from care givers. From Table 2 (panel 4) it is evident that slightly less than half of the elderly (47 percent) do not have independent source of income, whereas 18 percent earn Rs. 300 or less per month and 17 percent each earn a monthly income of Rs. 301-600 and Rs. 601 and above, respectively. The average monthly income of the elderly is Rs. 411. Sex differentials with regard to their monthly income are observed to be very large (Chi-Square = 64.59; p <.001). For example, while the percentage of non-earners and earning less monthly income is higher among elderly women, the per cent of elderly who are earning middle and higher levels of monthly income is large among men. This has been further reflected in their average monthly income, viz., Rs. 622 for men and Rs. 228

for women. Thus, it is clear that the rural elderly women are the poorer among the poor.

TYPE OF FAMILY

In India, during the past elderly members were use to reside in the family comprising of two or more generations. Such family use to provide certain amount of social security and social insurance for the aged, besides emotional support. However, with the result of urbanisation, industrialisation and Westernisation such families are transformed into either stem-families or nuclear families wherein the status of the elderly will be deplorable. Moreover, in the recent past, the cost of upbringing young children is more with little income and thereby neglecting the elderly has become quite common. This has lead to establishing a separate family (living alone) by the elderly (especially women) or at times even motivate them to join the old age home. In the study area too (panel 1 of Table 3), majority of the elderly used to live in nuclear type of families, i.e., couple with or without unmarried children (49 percent), closely followed by various types of stem-families (basic, residual, eroded, etc.), viz., families in which two couples of two successive generations with or without children of the second generation living together. Some elderly reside as single person family (14 percent). Differentials in type of family be the elderly across their gender background noticed to be highly significant (Chi-Square = 51.58; p <.001). While the percentage of elderly living in nuclear family is higher among men (64 percent), a greater proportion of the elderly women prefer to live in stem-family (42 percent) closely followed by nuclear family. Another interesting fact noticed here is that elderly women as against men tend to live substantially in large number as a single member family. This analysis shows that nowadays more and more elderly women (that too widowed) prefer to live alone. This may be because of not getting support from son(s), son(s) living in nearby towns for work, hesitant to live with married daughter and adjustment problems/strained relations with daughter(s)-in-law.

Table 3 : Gender differentials in family structure and related aspects of the elderly

Family structure and related aspects	*Male*		*Female*		*Total*	
	%	No	%	No	%	No
1. *Type of family*						
Single person family	5.41	14	21.07	63	13.80	77
Nuclear family	64.09	166	36.45	109	49.28	275
Stem family	30.50	79	42.47	127	36.92	206
	Chi-square = 51.53; p<.001					
2. *Size of the household*						
Single person	5.41	14	21.07	63	13.80	77
Small (2-3 persons)	62.16	161	46.15	138	53.58	299
Medium (4-5 persons)	18.53	48	21.07	63	19.89	111
Large (6 + persons)	13.90	36	11.71	35	12.72	71
	Chi-square = 32.29; p<.001					
3. *Living arrangements*						
Living alone	5.41	14	21.07	63	13.80	77
Living with spouse	48.65	126	28.42	85	37.81	211
Living with unmarried son(s)	12.35	32	8.36	25	10.22	57
Living with married son(s)	23.17	60	26.76	80	25.09	140
Living with unmarried daughter(s)	2.32	6	3.68	11	3.05	17
Living with married daughter(s)	3.09	8	5.02	15	4.12	23
Living with grandson(s)	3.09	8	3.01	9	3.05	17
Living with others	1.93	5	3.68	11	2.87	16
	Chi-square = 48.80; p<.001					
Total	100.00	259	100.00	299	100.00	558

SIZE OF THE HOUSEHOLD

The size of the household in which the elderly persons live is also a good indicator of their familial well-being. For the purpose of discussion, the households are divided into four size categories, viz., single (1 member), small (2-3 members), medium (4-5 members) and large (6 members and above) households. Data given in panel 2 of Table 3 reveal that more than half of the elderly persons (54 percent) are live in small-sized households, one-fifth in medium (20 percent) and one-eighth (13 percent) in large-sized households. A sizeable proportion of the elderly (14 percent) live alone, i.e., single member households. Gender differentials in the size of the household lived in by the elderly are highly significant (Chi-Square = 32.29; $p < .001$). While a greater proportion of the elderly men live in small households (62 percent) as against elderly women (46 percent); the percentage of elderly residing in single member households is conspicuously higher among the women (21 percent) than among the men (5 percent). By and large, the findings suggest that the family support and care for elderly women seem to be comparatively less that their men counterparts.

LIVING ARRANGEMENTS

In India, the cultural values give high respect to the elderly and the familial ties are quite strong especially in rural areas. Till recently family used to take care of the elderly and act as the principle source of support and security in old age. Further, culturally, more emphasis and value is placed on co-residence with son(s). In the study area, majority of the elderly (38 percent) living with their spouse only, closely followed by married sons (25 percent). Some of the elderly persons are living alone (14 percent) closely followed by unmarried sons (10 percent). Very few elderly are residing with married (4 percent) and unmarried (3 percent) daughters, grandson(s) (3 percent) and with others (3 percent) such as siblings, other relatives, house owners, etc. Gender differentials in living arrangements are observed to be highly significant (Chi-Square = 48.80; $p < .001$). For instance, the per cent of living alone is conspicuously higher among the elderly women (21 percent) as against their men counterparts (5 percent). On the contrary, the per cent of elderly men living with spouse is substantially higher among men (49 percent) as compared to the elderly women (28 percent). Further, the percent of elderly women residing with married sons, married and widowed daughters, and with others is comparatively higher than the elderly men, which is natural phenomenon in the absence (death) of husband.

Summary and implications

Demographically, elderly females in rural Tamil Nadu, by and large, are at advantage side. For example, elderly women are slightly younger (average age being 68.80 years) as against their men counterparts (69.61 years). The sex ratio for the elderly is favourable to women (1,154 females per 1,000 males). On the other hand, they are seriously at disadvantage in terms of socio-economic aspects. A large number of elderly females are in the status of widowhood, illiterates, non-working and belong to lower and/or no income brackets. Familial status of the elderly females too is not in a better position as compared to their male counterparts. For instance, a large number of females are residing in stem-family type and as single person households and thereby reside in small size households mostly with spouse or sons(s). All these findings lead to the conclusion that the aged females are the most deprived among the deprived.

Based on the findings it may be suggested that first of all women, particularly widows, should be taken care in terms of familial and economic fronts. Younger generation especially son(s) may be motivated and encouraged to take care of the aged persons in a family environment with due respect. Government may evolve strategies to help elderly to be economically active in their later ages that will make them active in life and economically independent. Suitable social security policies may be envisaged by the government to suit the different groups of elderly persons (like men/women, young-old/old-old, rural/urban, etc.). Such measures will be more meaningful than the charity/old-age pension given to them. Of course, efforts may also be taken to increase the amount of old-age pension to a reasonable level (say Rs. 300) and be provided to only the needy elderly like destitutes and/or in the state of frail.

References

Asharaf, A., 1995, 'Profile of Elderly: A Study on Western Suburb of Bombay', *Ageing and Society: The Indian Journal of Gerontology*, 5 (3 & 4): 33-8.

Audinarayana, N., N. Revathy, J. Sheela and N. Kavitha, 1996, 'Living Arrangements of the elderly Women in Rural Tamil Nadu:

Patterns, Differentials and Determinants', Paper presented in the *International Congress on Ageing of the International Sociological Association,*August 19-21.

Bhatia, J.S., 1983, *Ageing and Society; A Sociological Study of Retired Public Servants*, Udaipur: The Arya Book Centre.

Bose, A.B. and P.C. Saxena, 1964, 'Some Characteristics of the aged population in rural society', *The Journal of Family Welfare*, 10 (3): 33-9.

Chakrabarthi, Prafulla, 1993, 'Perception of old-age problems in rural Nadia', *Ageing and Society: The Indian Journal of Gerontology*, 3 (4): 1-24.

Chandra, Suparna, Debkumar Shome and P. Chakrabarthi, 1993, 'Are the old really obsolete? — An Explaratory Study', *Man in India*, 73 (3): 215-28.

De Souza, A., 1981, *The Social Organisation of Ageing among the Urban Poor*, New Delhi: Sage Publications.

Desai, K.G., 1982, *Ageing in India*, Bombay: TISS.

Gore, M.S., 1992, 'Ageing of the Human Being', *The Indian Journal of Social Work*, 53 (2) 212-19.

Gulati, Leela and S. Irudaya Rajan, 1999, 'The Added Years Elderly in India and Kerala', *Economic and Political Weekly*, 34 (44): 46-53.

Irudaya Rajan, S., U.S. Mishra and P. Sankara Sarma, 1999, *India's Elderly: Burden or Challenge*? New Delhi: Sage Publications.

Kaur, Malkit, R.P. Grover and Kusum Aggarwal, 1987, 'Socio-economic profile of the rural aged', in *Ageing in India: Challenge for the Society*, M.L. Sharma and T.M. Dak (eds.), Delhi: Ajanta Publications, pp. 67-75.

Mahadevan, K. and P. Sumangala, 1992, 'Approaches to the study of Elderly Population', in *The Elderly Population in Developed and Developing World: Policies, Programmes and Perspectives*, P. Krishnan and K. Mahadevan (eds.), Delhi: B.R. Publishing Corporation, pp. 483-504.

Mahanta, K.C., 1993, 'Socio-economic Status of the Aged: A Case Study', *Man in India*, 73(3): 201-13.

Martin, Linda G., 1990, 'The Status of South Asia's growing Elderly Population', *Journal of Cross-cultural Gerontology*, 5 (2): 93-117.

Nair, P.S., 1989, 'Socio-economic and Health Problems of the Aged in Rural Karnataka, India', in *Population Transition in India*, vol. 2, Asish Bose, *et al.* (eds.), Delhi: B.R. Publishers, pp. 63-70.

Nair P.S. and S. Santhosh, 1997, 'Population Ageing in India: A Study of Trichur District, Kerala', in *Demographic Transition: The Third World*

Scenario, Ajazuddin Ahmad, *et al.* (eds.), New Delhi: Ravat Publications, pp. 278-89.

National Sample Survey Organisation, New Delhi, 1991, 'Socio-economic profile of the Aged Persons: NSS 42nd Round (July 1986-June 1987)', *Sarvekshana*, 15 (2): 103-22.

Reddy, P.J., 1990, 'Family, Kin Life and Care of the Urban Elderly', *Journal of Social Research*, 32-3 (1 & 2) 32-45.

Registrar General, India, 1999, *Ageing population of India: Analysis of the 1991 Census Data*, New Delhi: Office of the Registrar General and Census Commissioner.

Sahayam, M. Deva, 1988, 'Aged Females: the most deprived among the deprived', *The Indian Journal of Social Work*, 49 (3): 261-9.

Sharma, M.L. and T.M. Dak, 1987, *Ageing in India: Challenges for the Society*, Delhi: Ajanta Publications.

Singh, C., *et al.*, 1994, 'Social Profile of the Aged in a rural Population', *Indian Journal of Community Medicine*, 19 (1): 23-5.

United Nations, 1999, *Population Ageing 1999*, United Nations, Department of Economic and Social Affairs.

Vatuk, Sylvia, 1991, 'Gerontology in India: The State of the Art', *Journal of Cross cultural Gerontology*, 6 (2): 259-71.

Vijayakumar, S, 1991, *Family Life and Socio-Economic Problems of the Aged*, Delhi: Ashish Publishing House.

Vijayakumar, S., 1995, *Challanges Before the Elderly: An Indian Scenario*, New Delhi: M.D. Publications Pvt. Ltd.

21

Status of the Aged Women in Modern India

Priorities for Action

G. Sandhya Rani
B. Suguna

AGEING is a universal fact and no society can escape it. The term 'old age' conjures up images of frustration and pity; sickness and poverty; despair and senility; warmth and responsibility. If the term 'ageing' is used descriptively, it refers to a sequence of changes across a life span of an individual. It is a biological process and experienced by the mankind in all times. Though ageing is a multidimensional process, old age is the closing period in an individuals life. It is a period when people 'move away' from their more desirable periods or times of 'usefulness'. Old age is generally characterised by certain physical and psychological changes.

There are individual differences in the effects of ageing. Poor adjustment is a characteristic of age. Old age is judged by different criteria in terms of physical appearance and activities. They have to adjust to decreasing physical strength, reduced income, death of spouse and the social roles in a flexible way.

However, concern for the aged is a relatively new phenomenon, which has developed due to significantly large increase in the number and proportion of the aged persons in the society. In traditional Indian society aged people enjoyed better status and authority in the family when joint family system was prevalent. In mythology and religious scriptures, irrespective of region and religion the moral and material support to the aged has been regarded as the highest virtue of human beings. But, the problems of senior citizens in India are bound to differ from the problems of old persons in the West and other developed and developing societies. The social institutions, mechanism of cultural milieu, customs and traditions, religious and community controls as also the individual and group psychology of the people in various countries differ substantially.

According to the U.N. classification, Indian society would progress from a mature society (elderly population between 4 and 7 per cent to the total population) to an 'ageing society' (the aged accounting for more than 7 per cent of the total population), by the turn of the century. The major determinants of ageing — the life expentency at birth, the crude birth rates and the crude death rates are more favourable towards the growing population.

Though this indicates a healthy trend, in terms of achievements in medical sciences, the fact to be realised is that the changing social trends are not in favour of the elderly today and tomorrow.

At present India is passing through a phase of rapid social transformation and sustained economic development. Many important changes have been taking place in the social profiles of the people. The rapid industrialisation has led to the migration of villagers to urban areas in search of jobs has been associated with shortage of housing facilities in the cities which reflected on the existence of joint family system. Fascinating modern life tempted people's mobility and have changed their lifestyles and values, which have adversely affected the traditional respects as well as sympathy and care for the aged. Today the old people are no more heads of families. Increasing literacy rate among women accompanied by their employment in offices and factories leave no time for them to take care of the old people at home. Further the high cost of living and changing priorities in turn affected the intra-family distribution of income in favour of younger generation. As a result the vulnerability of the old people has been increasing and leading towards social disorganisation and individual insecurity.

Ageing — A global view

'The world assembly on ageing', adopted as its main focus of concern, the population aged 69 (or) over. For statistical analysis 60 is a convenient age. Considering population aged 60 or over as a monolithic group conceals two important factors. The age and gender discrimination, and the number of very old people defined as those who are 80 years (or) over. Globally speaking in 1985, the number of very old had more than tripled to 45 million. It is also expected that growth rates of the age group 80 (or) over will be more rapid in developing regions. In most countries females are much more likely to survive to older ages than males.

India's ageing population

According to a recent report of United Nations, India would become an ageing society by the turn of the century, where the aged would account for more than 7 per cent of the total population. The expectation of life at birth in India has increased from 41 years in 1961 to 61 years in 1991 and India now has the world's largest population over 60. The decadal growth rate of population in the age group 60 (or) over was higher than that of the general population.

The plight of elderly people has deteriorated as urbanisation, economic progress and altered social values have led to cracks in Indian traditional family system. The joint family system in India has often been used to illustrate the status of the aged in the society. Education of the children, changes in the marriage institution, importance given to conjugal relations and emancipation of women have brought changes in the joint family system and consequently challenged the authority of the aged people. Very often old people are slower to accept changes, new traditions than the young. As a result, the old are looked upon as obsolete or old fashioned.

Old age is a phase of human life cycle, and timing of this phase, its impact on role relationship and the meaning attached to it vary in different societies and even in different sub-groups of a society. In the process of ageing the last phase is considered as decline and death and in this phase majority of the aged face economic, social, psychological and health problems which of course vary from male to female. Recent advancements in medicine and public health have made illness less fatal. This combined with better standard of living has resulted in a substantial increase in the proportion of the older people in the population. According to 1981 census, the sex ratio in the age group 60 (or) over was 961 as compared to 933 in the population. Approximately half of the older population are women. Most of them have no economic support and social security. Further at this age, they generally retire from official services. Some lost their life partners. Hence, they have to depend upon their children for all kinds of support.

Women are the one who are greatly affected by the so-called 'old age'. Women live more years when compared to males. But their miserable status makes them to appear more aged than actually what they are. 'World Health Organisation Report' states that the percentage of the aged women who are 60 + is going to be doubled within two decades. But so far no specific study has been done to elevate their status. The present distinctive feature of the elderly throughout the world is the preponderance of women over men. This could be due to the significantly higher female life expectancy.

The situation is not so cheerful in the developing nations like India. While the incidence of these age related conditions is dropping in the developed world, it is increasing in developing nations.

It is evident from Indian history that women once enjoyed unique status even to the extent of being worshipped as goddess. During pre-Vedic period woman enjoyed equal rights on par with men in almost all social, political and religious pursuits. But a deterioration in the status of women started in post-Vedic period and continued thereafter. Women's rights were ignored in spiritual and political matters. She lost economic freedom. Though many attempts were made to raise the position of women in post-Independence era they did not change the miserable status of women due to blind superstitions, age old traditional and social practices. Education, modernisation and women empowerment went only to the limited segments of the younger generation.

Women were terribly looked down first as women, second as aged women. So these women constitute a special concern group in the general population. Sex ratio is one of the important factors having considerable impact over population ageing.

People in the developing countries are often heard to say that children are the security of parents in old age. Most of the parents as a right expect their children to care for there in their old age. In India especially sons are the major source of old age security.

Therefore, in this paper an attempt has been made to discuss about the status of the aged women in modern India and also tried to highlight certain priority areas where action can be taken. In this context, it is true that there is lot of difference between the problems of the aged men and the aged women.

Ageing is an inevitable stage of life. In every stage of life since birth people are facing many problems. Hence, it is not true that only old age is problematic. But it can be taken as that the problems that are required to face in old age may be more severe than the ones that we required to face when we are young or in middle age. At the same time it is also possible that we are less prepared to face the problems in old age and hence we think that they are very severe. However, we have to admit that old age has certain specific problems especially in the case of aged women.

Social problems

Woman is one who is greatly affected by old age. Generally men after their retirement from official service spend their time in leisure whereas women have no retirement in her life. She devotes all her time and strength to her family till her death. As long as husband is alive, she is looked after with great respect by the other family members. But when she loose her husband it can be said that she has lost all the respect, care and security. She is deprived of economic independence and has to obey to the orders of her children, grandchildren and loose the opportunity of acting on her own.

Psychological problems

These are the results of social problems faced by women during old age. Psychological problems like loneliness, fear of death, short temper, inferiority complex, feeling of insecurity are some problems mostly confronted by old women.

Health problems

Health is an important factor during ageing. Physical changes occur with ageing are usually in the direction of deterioration of overall health status. Apart from this, geriatric problems like nervous breakdown, general weakness, asthma, rheumatism, diabetes, indigestion, loss of sight, loss of hearing are found to be frequent among the old women. At 60-70 the daily amount of sleep is reduced by an hour or two. Majority of women suffer from insomnia which leads to loss of enthusiasm in performing regular duties and develops a kind of passiveness which leads to mental depression.

Economic problems

Most of the old women are economically dependent. As all their property is inherited by their sons, they will be deprived of any source from which they can draw money. As they are pennyless they have to depend on others for fulfilling their daily requirements. Old women need money due to their increased need for medical assistance. Thus, the health problems contribute to the financial problem.

Housing problem

Decent housing is especially important to the elderly women because they spend much of their time at home. Good ventilation facilities reduce the intensity and frequency of some common health problems. But most of the old women are living in substandard houses due to lack of money and support from others.

Apart from the above there are other problems which are responsible to the miserable conditions of old women in India. The status of the aged widows is still more pathetic. Nearly 16,000 widows are living as orphans in the streets of Mathura, Brindavan and Varanasi.

Therefore, it is inhuman and uncivilisation to treat the aged women as burden to family and society. Usually, nobody obeys them, nobody invites them to participate in any decision-making activities and in the absence of spouse they become isolated and later get alienated from society. However, the pendulum of social thought has changed and Indian society is now looking forward to a process of ageing which is economically productive and socially constructive.

In fact, old age is not a curse and old people are not useless to society. Their needs are simple and wants are very few. Now, when they are in the evening of their lives, it is our responsibility to give them back a little of what they have struggled to give us. Hence, it is a civic responsibility to assist them by extending necessary support through various channels. The priority areas identified to support the aged women are.

FAMILY

Whatever may be the rate of development that has taken place in the outside world, irrespective of that old people especially women prefer to live with their children and grandchildren. They usually wish to play with their grandchildren and share their experiences. They don't care for wealth or even too much of our time. They only want our companionship. Emotional involvement, thought sharing and a little amount of solace from family members helps them to rejuvenate their strengths and leads them towards a happy living. In fact, living alone is very dangerous during old age. As family is the strongest social unit, aged women must be provided with happiest atmosphere by all the family members. The affectionate talk, touch and association of kith and kin makes them to forget all fears of future and helps them to spend their lives in a quite healthy environment. Moral support extended by family members is of a great relief for the aged women who have already experienced and tired with the ups and downs of a long journey towards old age.

COMMUNITY

As citizens of this civilised society the responsibility lies on all the human beings to help old women to have a comfortable living. They are not waste or unproductive substances of the society. But in majority of cases in India the plight of old women is very miserable. On the overall working force of women the percentage of women in organised sector is very less and nearly 90 per cent of women are working in unorganised sector. Therefore, they are deprived of enjoying any monitory benefits, like pensions, etc. Lack of economic independency make them depend either on their children or on relatives during old age for livelihood. In the absence of support from any source they have to depend on their own efforts to earn money. As they are physically unable to do any hard work their status slowly degrades to the position of beggars. It is very common in India that most of old women wandering and begging on roads, platforms and bus stations.

Therefore, it is necessary to help women to help themselves. By making them to involve in income generating activities (which can be easily understood and accepted by them) we can make them confident to face old age and related problems. Non-governmental organisations can also take an active role to provide an alternative living arrangements to the aged women. Income generating projects to the needy aged women must be designed and executed properly.

Psychological support

During old age usually people loose their courage. The society has made old age a curse for those aged women who are deprived of any support from children. They may be provided necessary psychological support to face old age with dignity and courage. Arranging meetings in counselling centres and community halls helps them to accept old age with cheer.

Financial support

Economic dependency among the aged women is more common in developing countries. In a country like ours majority of women are illiterates and dependants on their husband and children for livelihood. When an aged woman loose her husband, her economic status, her position in the family and her involvement and power to take decisions, etc., are immediately withdrawn from her hands. Hence, for those women who are able to work, necessary help can be provided to earn their livelihood. Self-employment schemes for the aged women will help a lot in this context.

Further, government is giving Rs. 75 as pension to old people. The benefits of it are not fully enjoyed by the actual beneficiaries. Moreover, though about 11 percent of the elderly population is utilising the retirement benefits, it may not be sufficient as they grow older and older. Necessary action must be initiated in this regard, to help the old people especially women. Even the process of identification of the original beneficiaries is also not done properly.

Medical care

Nowadays medical care has become highly expensive. During old age women usually suffer from a number of health problems like hypertension, artherities, loss of hearing and eyesight, diabetes, respiratory problems and cardiac diseases.

As they are deprived of money, they have to depend on others for medical assistance. Children usually neglect to take their mothers and grandmothers to the doctors. As a result majority of women are dying without timely medical assistance especially in rural areas. Necessary health assistance may be provided to them either through government hospitals or through non-governmental agencies. Services of the health personnel may be made available by constructing special wards in hospitals. Free medical camps can also be arranged particularly in rural and semi-urban areas for identifying and providing necessary help.

Counselling centres

Counselling is an effective method to help aged women. It helps them to lead their future life gracefully and accept death with courage. Therefore, counselling centres must be established and run successfully. Both government and non-governmental organisations must take initiative to establish more number of conselling centres and provide all kinds of help with regard to their fears, tensions, conflicts in the family, economic problems, health assistance, guidance, etc., to the needy aged persons particularly women.

Old age homes

The establishment of old age homes is a new phenomenon in Indian context. In the background of various problems and structural changes that have taken place in the social set-up of India, old age homes have become important. Old age homes besides providing shelter also help old women to lead their last stages of life without any fear of struggling for existence. The establishment of old age homes, in fact, showed a solution to the various problems of aged women in our country. They have actually shouldered the responsibility of taking care of elderly during old age. Some of these old age homes are exclusively run for women under the supervision and monitoring of voluntary organisations. Apart from providing shelter and food, old age homes are also imparting training to the healthy and interested women in income generating activities like garment making, book-binding, yarn spinning and weaving, carpet weaving, soft toys making, pickle and papad-making, etc. The concept of rehabilitation through income generation is purely based on the principle that the elderly women should be enabled to live with human pride while maintaining their position and respect in their families and society.

Thus old age homes working with pure service motto are extending really a wonderful help to the elderly women belong to poor and weaker sections of the society. A number of studies made on the establishment and maintenance of old age homes reveal that nearly 70 to 80 per cent of women inmates expressed a feeling of happiness and social security. As the problems at old age are more or less the same for almost all the women joining old age homes, they feel themselves as the birds of the same nest and leading a life with full co-operation, satisfaction and concern towards other inmates.

The Vienna International Plan of Action has urged the governments throughout the world to explore alternative approaches for the care of the elderly not only to alleviate problems but also to contribute positively to the well-being of the elderly, the family and the community. The assembly also brough out a declaration 'add life to years' meaning that old age must be full of life and not merely prolonging of life.

The UN general assembly has called for a set of global targets on ageing for the year 2001 and declared 1999 as the International Years of Old Persons with a special slogan 'a society of all ages' emphasising the importance of interdependency of the generations.

Neither the community not the family alone would be able to provide a harromious atmosphere to the elderly and when the economic pressure on each of these institutions, increases hundreds of thousands of the elderly will be neglected. Hence, long-term plans are needed.

Areas that need attention

1. Research has to be carried out to examine the feasibility of providing retirement benefits and family allowances for which there is no provision in the existing low and welfare scheme.
2. Specific policies have to be formulated to suggest the most appropriate strategy for development of retirement benefits — whether it should be through the employees liability scheme or social insurance scheme or social assistance scheme.
3. Qualitative research is needed to clarify the impact of economic and demographic changes on the role of the family as care giver to the elderly. Specific attention must be paid to the problems of the aged women.
4. New job markets for the aged women have to be generated by analysing the existing labour market structure.
5. Geriatric needs and the services could be assessed through

multidisciplinary assessment of physical impairment, assessment of depression and cognition and socio-economic assessment.

6. A national committee on ageing with autonomous status should be set-up representing each state, comprising elders, youth, academicians, researchers and policy-makers.
7. Specific and appropriate social security measures, including legal security should be spelt out through proper amendments.
8. Specific strategies should be developed to create/promote awareness among the general public on the problems of ageing and how to tackle them.
9. Community-based supportive services for the elderly should be developed in partnership with their family members, utilising the local bodies.
10. Where the tradition of respect for the elders is under threat owing to cultural changes, efforts should be made to reinforce it, especially among the youth.
11. Priority should be given to elderly women, especially widows, in all intervention programmes.
12. Paramedical staff and physicians at primary health centres should be trained in geriatric services.

Conclusion

As a result of modern science and technology in recent years the Indian society is undergoing transformation in various dimensions. Social institutions, especially, family has undergone rapid qualitative change. The rapid growth in industrial sector and urbanisation affected the lifestyles and value system in the society. As a result of revolution in medical field, greying population has become as one of the most significant characteristics of the twentieth century. India is not at all an exception to this. In India the percentage of aged women is also gradually increasing. Through the Seventh and Eighth Five Year Plans, the Government of India has launched several schemes for the aged, so far little has been achieved. In fact, the living conditions of the aged women are miserable. As women outlive men, specific welfare interventions have to be worked out. The policies programmes formulated for old women must pay attention to their physical, economical and psychological needs. Special emphasis should be given to the programmes that assist the family in its traditional role of supporting the elderly women. The younger generation should react with a sense of responsibility towards the multiple problems of the aged women and help them to feel happy and enthusiastic during their last stages of life. Their services and contributions can also be used for the development of the society. Their experience and outlook help a lot in solving many problems and it is time to formulate a new action plan particularly for the welfare of aged women. Then only we will achieve the objective of the 'United Nations International Year of the Older Persons 1999'.

Reference

Biswas, S.K., 'Ageing in contemporary India', *Indian Anthropological Society*, Calcutta, 1987.

Doughlas, C. Kimmel, *Adulthood and Ageing*, John Willey & Sons Inc., New York.

Krishnan, P. and Mahadevan, K., *The elderly population in developed and developing world, policies*, problems, perspectives, B.R. Pulishing Corporation, Delhi, 1992.

Napolean, Wolenski, *Ecology of Ageing*, Kamala Raj Enterprises, New Delhi, 2000.

Patil, R.N. and Jenu, B, *Aged in India, Socio-demographic dimensions*, Ashish Publishing House, New Delhi, 1989.

Prakash, I.J., *Quality of ageing*, Association of Gerontology, Varanasi, 1991.

Ramachandran, C.R. and Shah, B, *Public Health implications of ageing in India*, Indian Council of Medical Research, New Delhi, 1994.

Kumar, Vinod, *Ageing: Indian perspective and global scenario*, All India Institute of Medical Sciences, New Delhi, 1996.

22

Mystique of Ageing

Constraints on the Autonomy of the Elderly Widows

B. Dharmalingam
K.R. Murugan

Introduction

THE International year of older persons is coming to a close, with twentieth century. Being on the threshold of the next millenium — the twenty-first century, where human values and human dignity are praised to the heights, it is shocking to know that the revered senior citizens often suffer abuse, neglect, and as in any group, women suffer worse than men.

The century has seen a dramatic increase in people's life expectancy and profound changes in the age structure of societies. The proportion of the elderly in the Indian population has been rising steadily over the last four decades. And the gender difference is sharply evident in the old age groups, with women far outnumbering men. The increasing life expectancy of women with the substantial age difference between marriage partners and the differing proportion of old men and women who marry, have given rise to a larger proportion of widows and, given social context, their problems are even more complex. The census shows that in 1991, while a large majority of the elderly male (80.7 percent) lived with a married status, only 44.2 percent of the elderly female carried this status. Table 1 shows that a majority of the elderly women (54 percent) were widowed. However, there is a growing number of elderly widows who will be victims of tripple neglect and discrimination on account of gender, age and widowhood.

Table 1 Marital status for 60+, 1991

Marital status	*Male*	*Female*	***Total***
Never married(million)	1.0(3.4%)	0.4(1.4%)	1.4(2.5%)
Married (million)	23.7(80.7%)	12.1(44.2%)	35.8(63.1%)
Widowed(million)	4.5 (15.5%)	14.8 (54.0%)	19.3 (34%)
Divorced/Separated (million)	93190(0.3%)	1,09,420(0.4%)	2,02,610(0.4%)
Total 60+ population (million)	29.4(6.7% of all males)	27.3(6.8% of all females)	56.7(6.8% of total)

Source: *Census of India, 1991* cited in India: Ministry of Human Resource Development, 1997: 12.

Family life cycle and widowhood

Feminists have consistently seen the family as the centre of women's oppression even though the form and content of the familial structure and ideology would vary cross culturally. A woman's status, role and self-image varies with her stage in the family life cycle. The family life cycle is a succession of stages that the family passes through from its formation of dissolution. Each demographic event marriage, parenthood, migration, death and widowhood makes a stage in the life cycle. The family life cycle covers the changes in size; composition and functions of the family over its lifetime (Young 1980). The family is said to come into existence with marriage of a couple and ceases to exist with the death of the surviving spouses. Widowhood, is a possible event in the life cycle of every person who stays married. Table 2 gives an idea of the time frame of events in the family: what path does the average Indian family take? What is its expected duration? And what is the duration of widowhood?

Demographic trends of elderly widows

While there is not much of a difference in proportion of the elderly

Table 2: Family life cycle and widowhood in India, 1971, 1981

	India	
	1971	*1981*
Mean age at marriage of men	22	23.4
Mean age at marriage of women	17	18.7
Life expectation of husband at the time of marriage	43.7	44.1
Expected duration of married life	37.1	37.9
Expected duration of widowhood for husband	6.7	6.2
Expected duration of widowhood for wife	11.9	11.5
Expected duration of family life	55.6	55.6

Source: Gulati Leela, 1992, *Dimensions of female Ageing and Widowhood.*

Notes: The expected duration of widowhood is defined as the sum of two duration of widowhood for husband and wife. The expected duration of family life cycle is defined in the following: E (FLC)=EM (duration of marriage) + EW (Widowhood).

among the respective male-female populations, (male 6.7 percent, female 6.8 percent Table 1) in 1991 men outnumber women among the aged (29.4 million, female 27.3 million — Table 1). For every 100 elderly men there were only 94 women in 1991. But the incidence of widowhood increases rather sharply for women with advancing age. While only 15.5 percent of the men found themselves widowers, 54 per cent of the women were widows, which is about 4 times higher than that of men. This was more sharp for those over 70 years; 77 percent women as against 22 percent of them. Thus, the overlap between the incidence of widowhood and ageing is rather striking among women's serious economic and social implication.

Table 3 : Incidence of widowhood by sex and age

	INDIA			
Incidence of widowhood	*1961*	*1971*	*1981*	*1991*
All men	3.7	2.9	2.4	1.9
All women	10.8	8.9	8.1	6.5
Men (60+)	27.5	22.4	19.4	15.5
Women (60+)	75.4	69.2	64.3	54.0
Widowers (60+) as a proportion of all widowers	40.7	45.3	51.1	53.9
Widows (60+) as a proportion of all widows	40.4	46.8	52.8	56.3

Source: Computed from *Census of India, 1961, 1971, 1981, 1991* reports for Social and Cultural tables, age and marital status.

Table 4 : Percentage of distribution of population by sex and 60+ age groups

Age group	*1971*			*1981*			*1991*		
(Years)	*Persons*	*Male*	*Female*	*Persons*	*Male*	*Female*	*Persons*	*Male*	*Female*
60-64	2.6	2.6	2.6	2.7	2.7	2.7	2.7	2.8	2.7
65-69	1.3	1.3	1.3	1.4	1.4	1.5	1.5	1.5	1.6
70+	2.1	2.0	2.1	2.4	2.3	2.4	2.5	2.5	2.5
60+	6.0	6.0	6.0	6.5	6.4	6.3	6.7	6.8	6.8

Source:Selected Socio-economic statistics, India, Central StatisticalOrganisation, GUI, New Delhi,1998, p. 10.

In 1951, when the life expectancy at birth for Indian women was only 32.5 years, 1/3 of women were likely to have lost their own mothers prior to the birth of their first child and nearly half of the women probably had lost at least one of the parents. Since, with the expectation of life at birth going up to nearly 60 years, 90 per cent of the women will survive to become grandmothers.

From Table 2, it can be seen that the expected duration of family life cycle is 55 years between 1971 and 1981. There is a slight decline in the expected duration of widowhood for husband and wife. However, the expected duration of widowhood for the wife remains almost twice as large as that for the husband.

Feminisation of widowhood

Widowhood has a female face. Widowhood and gender are strongly linked. Feminisation of widowhood is not merely that widows are now more in number than the widowers, but widowhood takes all the characteristics of widows, namely discrimination, dependence, oppression, health problems, etc.

Feminisation also involves seggregation by sex in widowhood, i.e., widowhood is gendered. Patriarchy as an ideological construct interacts with capitalist processes and reinforces specific constraints on women physically as well as mentally which permeates the understanding that women are principally housewives and mothers and subsidiary workers even after the death of their spouse and in which men dominate, oppress and exploit women.

This social system and cultural attitudes are expected over the life cycle. But as females continue to age/widowhood, their contribution as producers or reproducers is often considered to end.

They suffer a loss in status when parental care giving/ nurturance gives way to parental dependency. The mother-in-law – daughter-in-law syndrome, which leads to situations of tension and conflict more in the later age. It makes the widows to receive a very little support from the family. As a result they are very often subjected to discrimination, oppression and exploitation of various kinds, Moreover, the elderly widows will be dominated by gynaecological disorders (accumulated during their reproductive years) apart from the clinical disorders commonly associated with ageing. Dandekar's (1996) analysis of NSS data of 42nd round shows that although women live longer than men, elderly women always suffered from poorer health as compared to men of the same age.

Constraints on the autonomy of the elderly widows

Autonomy, sense of personal control and feelings of self-esteem are important components for late life adjustment. One does not come by such a condition in old age accident. Socialisation practices, early life experiences, economic conditions shape a person's sense of independence and self-confidence in old age. But, it is the patriarchy, which controls throughout their lives, shape many of the problems faced by women in old age (Hooyman 1987). The feminist theories show that the system of patriarchy subordinates women since birth by reinforcing specific constraints on women physically as well as mentally. This social construction of relations of power based on sexual differences is extended, through metaphors to all spheres of social life to signify situations of inequitable power relations or dominance and subordination (Scott 1986). With age, women get more and more marginalised in societies especially after the death of the husband. The growing marginalisation of elderly widows in the context of socio-economic and demographic changes made the researcher to examine the conditions of elderly widows with reference to their identity and also examine the constraints on the sense of autonomy.

The present study consists of 30 elderly widows belonging to all income groups. Samples were randomly selected in and around Karaikudi town and administered with a pre-tested interview schedule. Among the respondents nearly one-third of them (33 percent) are illiterates. No respondents had education above school level in all categories. Except a few (7 percent) almost all of them live with their children. These few are living by themselves in single households because of not having any children. Among the others, 73 percent live with their sons while 20 percent with their daughters 23 percent of the elderly widows are actively involved in work as wage labour in agriculture and domestic work for low wages. Others (77 percent) totally dependent on family members for financial support. It is inferred that illiteracy and a lack of remunerative occupation which may lead to neglect and abuse even by their sons and daughters-in-law.

Economic dependency seems to be a greater constraint to the autonomy of the women particularly elderly widows. It is found that only 14 percent of the elderly widows own land and house in their names. 86 percent of them don't have any properties. The elderly women who generally do not have the ownership right to family house or property tend to continue the house-hold duties in order to prove their usefulness to their family. Here, patriarchy works so systematically that although women continue to work throughout their old age, they are the poorest of the poor in this age. As a result, most of the women do not have the security of maintenance and housing in old age, especially after the death of the husband.

Recreation is one of the important issue which make its contribution to an individual's mental and physical health. But more than half of them (53 percent) do not involve in any one of the recreational activities. 24 percent watch T.V. occasionally and 13 percent spending their time with grandchildren and chating with neighbours. Most of the elderly widows feel that their grandchildren are not permitted to talk freely with them by in-laws. Some of them feel that the teenaged children also least bother about them and occasionally talk with them.

It is inferred that the teenaged children with their modern lifestyle have no time for their old grand parents. There is a big generation gap between them and the grand parents should appreciate the present-day lifestyles of the younger generation.

Most of them say that they receive adequate food, clothing, shelter and health care but they feel that they cannot get the things as their wish and in time. They wish that the family members and others should have a feeling of being wanted and respected.

Decision-making is a mental process based on conscious reasoning and maturation. In this case, only 33.3 percent are consulted by their children in the family matters while 43.3 percent are never consulted and 23.3 percent occasionally share their ideas. Majority of the widows feel alienated while their family members will not give due attention towards them. They also feel deprived of not having any discussion with them when their sons and in-laws decide to buy any property or in conducting any family functions.

The loss of the spouse may be more damaging to the physical and psychological well-being of women as they face not only emotional problems but also socio-economic and cultural problems. Before the death of their spouse the elderly women were the custodians of the rituals and religious ceremonies. They played a dominant role in running the house. But, after getting widowed they could not involve in such activities. It is proved in this study that 67 per cent of the respondents feel ill in the same manner.

Due to the reduction in income and due to the death of their spouse half of them (50 percent) have a feeling of loneliness and insecure in life while others cope up with the changing conditions. But almost all of them accept it that the demise of their husband is a great loss more than the other incidences.

Almost all the respondents feel that the loss of wife restricts certain social interactional patterns. Often they are ignored or rejected by the husband's relatives. Doubtless, this adversely affects their sense of worth and self-esteem.

Conclusion

The elderly widows are now more in number and face 'triple jeopardy' that of being old, being female and being widow. It is the partriarchy, which controls and marginalise them to the periphery of the lives through discrimination, dependence, oppression. Hence, the partriarchy as an ideological construct interacts with capitalist processes and specific constraints on the autonomy of the elderly widows physically as well as mentally.

References

Census of India, 1991, Ministry of Human Development, New Delhi, 1997

Dandekar, K., *The elderly in India*, Sage Publications, New Delhi: 1996.

Gulati, Leela, *Women and family in India — Continuity and change*, Department of Human Development and Family Studies, MS University of Baroda, Baroda, 1994.

Selected Socio-economic Statistics, India, Central Statistical Organisation, Government of India, and 1998.

Walby, Hooyman, N.R., 'Older Women and Social work curricula', in D.S. Burden and N. Gottilieb (eds.), *The Women Client: Providing Women Services in a changing world.* Tavistock Publications, New York, 1987, pp. 263-79

.Young, C., 'The family cycle approach in demography', in *Beginning Population Studies*, Development Studies Centre, Australia National University, Canberra, 1980.

Section V
Old Age Policies

23

Old Age Programmes and Policies in India

R. Mangayarkarasu

INDIA is passing through a phase of rapid socio-economic transformation. Sustained development service after Independence has brought in its wake many important changes in the socio-economic profile of the people. The rapid urbanisation has been associated with shortage of housing accommodation in the cities and the high rental acts as a severe constraint on the joint family system. In fact, the joint family system is gradually breaking down giving way to nuclear family.

The factors of urbanisation, modernisation, scientific advancement, mobility, self-centred approach, individuality, freedom of thought, generation gap, identity crisis, sceptical tendencies, approaching any problem including intensely personal ones, with an open mind by the youth and conflicting values between generations have introduced changes in the lifestyle and value system of the people which have adversely affected traditional ethos as well as harmonious attitude of empathy on the care of the aged.

Migration of the younger people due to employment from village to town, town to city and city to metropolitan city increases the vulnerability of the old who stay behind, particularly for families which do not have independent production assets like land, live-stock or household industry and are dependent primarily on their labour. Increasing literacy amongst women accompanied by their employment outside the home in offices and in factories leave no time for people to take care of the old at home. Besides, there is now greater investment by the family on education for upbringing of children. The high cost of living and changing priorities affect the joint family system, thus putting hardships to the older generation.

Life expectancy of the people has been increasing due to advance medical facilities and therefore, the number of old people is on the rise. According to 1981 census the population of the aged persons (60+) was 4.45 crores. By 1991, this population has increased to 5.48 crore as per Registrar General's Projections. The proportion of the old people to the total population has increased and is expected to increase further in future.

The idea of social security was started during the post-Vedic period. Kautilya in his *Arthashastra* has laid down various rules for the regulation of guilds, whose main purpose was collective security for life, prosperity and freedom from want and mercy. The observation by Shukracharya (AD 750-850) in his pioneering work *Shukraniti* had shown many references regarding sickness benefits, pensionary and old age benefits, family pension and maintenance allowances.

Article 41 of the Constitution of India enjoins on the state to make effective provision within the limits of its economic capacity and development for public assistance in case of unemployment, old age, sickness and disablement. The responsibility for providing relief to the disabled and unemployable is provided in List II, i.e., state list of the Seventh Schedule of the Constitution of India. Social security and social insurance, employment and unemployment find a mention in the concurrent list of Seventh Schedule. Thus, the Constitution specially vests the responsibility for social security and social insurance and public assistance in cases of unemployment, disablement, etc., including objections towards the old with the state and the central government. In pursuance of these commitments of the state towards the welfare of the aged, the state governments have been providing old age pension, maintaining old age homes for the destitute aged and providing grants-in-aid to voluntary organisations maintaining such homes.

The International Labour Organisation (ILO) defines social security services as one that provides the citizens with benefits designed to prevent or cure diseases, or to support them during their inability to earn and to restore them to gainful activity. Some of the contingencies covered in the social security system are sickness, maternity, occupational risks, invalidity unemployment, old age, retirement and medical care.

The ultimate objective of a comprehensive social security scheme is to provide protection to the entire population of the country.

Accordingly, the Government of India, is implementing the old age programme in the following categories providing physical, social, emotional, psychological and economic aids to the aged (60 years and above) with a view to help them to continue to be usefully active members of the community. The following schemes are envisaged and to provide

- Old age homes
- Day care centres
- Medicare service
- Foster care/adoption services
- Non-institutional services for the aged.

Old age homes

The schemes are being implemented through organisations/ institutions, statutory bodies like Panchayat Raj institutions, Red Cross Societies, municipal bodies including charitable trusts and other registered bodies set-up by the industrialists/business houses, etc., which have a performance record in welfare work (especially those which are already providing services for the aged). The Ministry of Welfare administers the scheme and provides grant-in-aid on the basis of applications received through the state government. The old age home will be the residential unit for at least 25 poor/destitute aged persons of 60 years and above.

The prime question is old age home — For whom?

Poor or rich or Middle-Class.

If old age homes are the wayout, many of them will turn out to be dumping homes. Love loyalty and affection will become a casuality. Middle-class values will get totally eroded.

Running old age homes should never be the sole responsibility of the NGO's. Even financial institutions like banks, religious and charitable bodies may also come forward to fulfil this obligation to society.

Day care centres for the aged

Assistance to the voluntary organisations will be given for maintenance of day care centres for the aged in urban/slum/rural/tribal areas having 50 aged persons.

The aim of this programme is to keep the aged integrated in their respective families and to supplement the activities of the family in looking after the needs of the aged. Both groups of the aged, viz., well-to-do and the poor in the age group of 60 years and above should benefit from the programme.

A day care centre for the aged will aim not only to provide services to its members but also to work a focal point of services to the elderly in the area.

Mobile medicare services for the aged

Under this programme mobile medicare services are maintained for consultation, treatment, etc., for health care of the aged persons. Since the family finds it hard to take the aged persons to medical centres at distant places, there is no doubt that the need for assistance for geriatric disabilities is more acute among the poverty-stricken elderly population of our country.

Under this programme, grant will be provided to voluntary organisation which are possessing experience and expertise in providing medicare services to the aged in rural/urban slum areas.

The suggestion at this juncture is that this scheme may be initiated in close co-ordination with primary health centres for its viability.

Foster care/adoption services for the aged

Under this programme services are provided to homeless and lonely aged persons living in distressed conditions due to poverty. The aged will be placed with the willing families, keeping in mind the local culture and values. Willing and capable families with small children will be identified and then matched with needs of the aged. A foster unit is intended for 25 aged persons only.

According to Seventh Schedule of the Constitution of India, the Tamil Nadu State Government is implementing the Old Age Pension Scheme in the following five categories to provide social security to the destitute persons who have no means of livelihood and support from their relatives. This scheme is an important one to bestow social security on the old age persons.

In keeping with the growing number of the aged in the total population a recommendation is required to be made in the interests of the elderly. The actual number of inmates in the foster care centres may be increased.

1. Old Age Pension (General) Scheme (implemented from 1st April, 1962).
2. Old Age Pension (Destitute Physically Handicapped) Scheme (implemented from 1st November, 1974).
3. Old Age Pension (Destitute Widows) Scheme (implemented from 15st June, 1975).
4. Old Age Pension (Destitute Agricultural Labourers) Scheme (implementd from 15th March 1981).
5. Old Age Pension (Destitute Deserted Wive) Scheme (implemented from 25th April, 1986).

OLD.AGE PENSION SCHEME (GENERAL)

This scheme pays pension to all the old citizens who are destitutes and are not having livelihood assistance. This scheme has been introduced and is being implemented from 1st April, 1962. The destitute fishermen and weavers were also benefitted by this scheme.

The minimum age limit to receive the old age pension scheme is 60 years in the case of persons who are not getting earnings due to leprosy, insanity, paralysis or loss of limb. For other persons the minmum age limit is 65 years. The government had ordered on 27th April, 1998, that the age proof certificate need not be submitted in the case of persons who seem to be older and in doubtful cases it is sufficient to submit a copy of the village or town panchayat resolution regarding the details of their economic condition, age and residence.

From 1st April, 1962, the destitute old persons were paid monthly an amount of Rs. 20. This amount was enhanced every now and then. Rs. 100 paid up to 31st March, 1998 was enhanced from 1st April, 1998 to Rs. 150 per month. The amount of Rs. 150 hither-to-being paid monthly to the 65 years old pensioners under the old age pension scheme includes the central government's contribution of Rs. 75.

Old age pension is being paid to all eligible applications without any ceiling. A sum of Rs. 141.19 crore has been earmarked for the year 1999-2000.

The coverage of the scheme may be widened to include the neglected categories like artisans and craftsmen.

One of the relevant questions arising at this hour is how far are we to judge the economic condition of the target groups?

OLD AGE PENSION (DESTITUTE PHYSICALLY HANDICAPPED) SCHEME

The scheme has been extended to benefit the destitute physically handicapped persons. It has been in existence since 1st November, 1974. The destitute physically handicapped persons whose disability is 50 per cent and above are eligible to come under this scheme. Initially the age limit for the beneficiaries was 55 and then from 6th October, 1995 it was relaxed to 45. In each district, a committee consisting the District Collector, District Medical Officer and District Social Welfare Officer has been formed from 19th December, 1980. The said committee has been enpowered to examine the applications received from the physcially handicapped persons requesting for pension and recommend for the grant of pension irrespective of age with reference to the scale of their severe disability. According to the recommendations the assistance is being paid to the physically handicapped. The assistance has been extended to the benefit of the leprosy patients also. The government has ordered on 27th April, 1998 that the physically handicapped persons who have lost both their legs need not submit medical certificate.

Accident victims who are rendered physically handicapped should also be included in the list to reap the benefits of the scheme.

OLD AGE PENSION SCHEME (DESTITUTE WIDOW)

The scheme has been extended from 1st June, 1975 with a view to benefit the destitute widows also. Initially under this scheme the minium age limit of the beneficiaries to get benefit was fixed at 45 years and then as per government order this has been lowered to 40 with effect from 24th July, 1978. Further the age limit of the beneficiaries to get benefit under this scheme has been ordered to be removed with effect from 25th April, 1990. The government has ordered on 2nd June, 1998 to grant assistance under this scheme subject to eligibility to the destitue widows who have not remarried, though they have legal heirs of 18 years old. Instead of getting the reports regarding the pension given to the widows from village administrative officers and revenue inspectors it is ordered on 27th April, 1998 to get a copy of resolution of village panchayat/town panchayat.

OLD AGE PENSION (DESTITUTE AGRICULTURE LABOURERS) SCHEME

This scheme has been extended with a view to benefit the destitute agricultural labourers from the year 1981. To these persons the minimum age limit is fixed as 60 years. The conditions prescribed for the Old Age Pension (General) Scheme are all applicable to these persons also.

OLD AGE PENSION (DESTITUTE DESERTED WIVES) SCHEME

The scheme of granting pension to the 30 years old destitute deserted wives is being implemented from 25th April, 1986. Those who do not have any link with their husband for more than 5 years and obtained legal separation from the competent court of law are eligible to get assistance under this scheme. It had been ordered on 2nd June, 1998 that the deserted destitute wives who are having 18 years old legal heirs are also eligible to get assistance under this scheme. Instead of getting the reports regarding the pension given to the destitute deserted wives from village administrative officers and revenue inspectors it is ordered on 27th April, 1998 to get a copy of the resolution of village panchayat/town panchayat.

Procedure for sanction old age pension

Under the above scheme, the power to sanction pension was delegated to Revenue Divisional Officers. Then the above power was delegated to the Tahsildar (Distress Relief Scheme) from 1989. Hence, the delay in sanctioning pension has been avoided.

The pension amount paid under the scheme is being sent by the Special Tahsildars to the address of the pensioners. The money-order commission amount is borne by the state government. With a view to reduce the work load in writing the bills and to avoid mistakes thereon, the government has permitted to prepare the money-order forms through computers and send the amount at an early date.

Other assistance given to the old age pensioners

Free supply of dhoties/sarees: From 1979, twice in a year, on the occasions of *Pongal* and Independence Day the old age pensioners are supplied with one handloom *dhoti* for each male and one handloom *sari* for each female free of cost. From the year 1992-93 onwards in addition to the presentation on the Independence Day, free *dhoti/sari* is being continuously given on *Deepavali* and *Pongal*.

Supply of free nutritious meal and rice to the old age pensioners: All the old age pensioners are supplied daily with midday nutritious meal in nutritious meal centres.

(a) The old age pensioners who had not taken midday

nutritious meal in nutritious meal centres were supplied one kg of free rice for every week. At present it has been ordered on 26th September, 97 to supply 4 kg of rice once in a month.

(b) The old age pensioners who were taking midday nutritious meal in nutritious meal centres are being supplied 1/2 kg of free rice per week. At present it has been ordered to supply 2 kg of rice once in every month.

The governments at centre and state have taken considerable efforts in alleviating the grief, depression, seperation and turmoil of the senior citizens arising out of the disintegration of the joint family system. Enormous amount of money is being spent by the governments by giving food and shelter to the older people. The schemes may solve the problem of physical starvation. Emotional starvation, feeling of loneliness, craving for affection and consideration, etc., are yet to be solved. In the earlier decades the social structure of the family was community centred, culture oriented and socially interwoven. The technological advancement, urban ward migration, enpowerment, youth seeking greener pastures, the cost of living, globalisation, shrinking of national boundaries, etc., made the family system to disintegrate. These conditions cannot be reversed under any circumstances. In the days to come the social isolation and providing external care for the aged through homes will be mounting enormous pressure on the socialisation of the people. The only remedy is not through the funding of government but through the value orientation of youngsters towards the care for elderly.

In this situation a radical change should be brought out on enriching the entire curriculum framework from the elementary level to university level towards value conceptualisation orientation, sensitisation on the care for the aged. Above all, total change of mind alone can bring generations to co-exist.

References

Bhattacharya, S.K., 1989, 'The problem of Aged', *Employment News*, September 22-9.

Desai, K.G., (ed.), 1982, *Ageing in India*, Tata Institute of Social Sciences, Bombay.

Mahanta, K.C., 1993, 'Socio-economic status of the Aged: A case study', *Man in India*, 73 (3): 201-13.

Sharma, M.L., and T.M. Dak, 1987, *Ageing in India: Challenges for the society*, Ajanta Publications: Delhi.

Social Welfare Policy Note 1999-2000, *Social Welfare and Nutritious Meal Programme*, Government of Tamil Nadu, 1999.

24

National Policy for the Welfare of the Aged in India

N. Saraswathy

A general plan of action for the elderly persons has to take into account (a) rapid demographic changes taking place in the country in favour of the increasing number (1901: 1.2 crore/1951: 3.2 crore/2001: 6.6 crore/2025: 14.6 crore) and proportion of persons above the age of 60, (b) declining labour-participation rates of elderly in economy, (c) increasing financial strains on account of early retirement trends, slow economic growth, spiraling medical costs and inflation, (d) a slow, but, marked withdrawal of family support due to weakening of joint family ties and migration of children to cities and developed regions, and (e) the special biological, social and emotional needs associated with the old age.

Policy formulation concerning the aged persons should also draw on developments in the international field beginning with the World Assembly on Ageing (1982), the Vienna International Plan of Action (1982) and its two subsequent reviews in 1985 and 1989, the United Nations Principles for Older Persons (1991) and finally the Global Targets on Ageing for the Decade 1991-2001 adopted by the U.N. General Assembly (1992).

As instrument of government policy, the plan of action for the aged persons has to take into consideration the broad constraints of resources of developing country and the limited income-base of the taxpayers/persons paying insurance premium. It is also required to take cognisance of the fact that, unlike the developed countries, aged population in India has a high proportion of destitute elderly living primarily in rural areas and working in the unorganised sector of economy without any reasonable prospect of pension of job security. It can, however, draw its strength from the strong family ties and the overall respect the aged persons still command in Indian society as a reservoir of socially useful talent and experience. It can also build up a framework on the basis of the promise shown by the voluntary organisations in providing health, shelter and daycare services to the aged persons. It can improve upon the initiatives taken by the State Governments and Union Territories in introducing old age pension scheme for the destitute elderly.

Seen in this light, the objectives of the Old Age Policy may be follows:

(i) Providing increasing employment options and evolving mechanisms for assisting elder persons seeking work after retirement.

(ii) Providing (a) family support, (b) mutual benefit socieities, (c) income security through personal savings policies, (d) social insurance, (e) occupational pensions, (f) provident funds, and (g) public and private social assistance.

(iii) Social and economic support to the old age persons living without families (on account of childlessness, death of spouses, migration of children, destitution, etc.).

(iv) Re-evaluating healthcare priorities and providing access to health services.

(v) Reorienting housing and area planning to suit the special needs of the elderly.

A review of current approaches and programmes reveals the status of the existing legal, economic and policy framework and the areas requiring focussed attention. Very briefly, the current approaches and programmes can be discussed in this paper.

Legislative framework

Article 41 of the Constitution recognises the needs of the elderly and enjoys upon the state the responsibility of making effective provision for public assistance in case of unemployment, old age, sickness and disablement and in other cases of undeserved want.

While welfare of the aged is a state subject, the nodal responsibility at the centre is assigned to the Ministry of Welfare.

Under the section 20(1) of the Hindu Adoption and Maintenance Act, 1956 an aged and infirm parent, if unable to maintain himself or herself, is entitled to maintenance. Muslim law also imposes an obligation to maintain needy parents, subject to certain circumstances. *Independent of the personal Law*, the Code of Criminal Procedure 1973 (section 125(1) (d)) makes it incumbent for a *person* having sufficient means to maintain his father or mother who is unable to maintain himself or herself and on getting proof of neglect or refusal, a first class magistrate may order such a person to make a monthly allowance not exceeding Rs. 500.

Social security Acts

(a) The Workmen's Compensation Act, 1923.

(b) The Employee's State Insurance Act, 1948.

(c) The Employees' Provident Funds and Miscellaneous. Provisions Act, 1952.

(d) The Maternity Benefit Act, 1961.

(e) The payment of garatuity Act, 1972.

(f) The Pensions Act, 1871.

Tax concessions to elderly persons under

(a) Income Tax (Amendment Acts), and

(b) Finance Acts passed each year in favour of

  (i) Pensioners (reduction allowed on pension) and

  (ii) Taxpayers (below the age of 70 years on health insurance).

Old Age Pension Scheme for the Destitute Elderly

All the State Governments and Union Territories are implementing old age pension schemes to the destitute/poor elderly. There are schemes drawn up for the purpose by each State/Union Territory according to their financial resources and they do not have a statutory sanction. They cannot be claimed as a matter of right. The first old age pension scheme was started in U.P., in 1957. Rate of pension, eligibility criteria, domicile conditions and coverage vary from State to State. The quantum of pension ranges from Rs. 50 to Rs. 100 per month. In Tamil Nadu, old age pensioners are eligible for free meals at the nutrition meal programme centres. In 1987-8, Rs. 227 crore were spent by the States/Union Territories to give pension to 49 lakh beneficiaries.

Old age homes in the State Sector

Another scheme in the State Sector which is catering to the needs of a large number of destitute aged is that of homes for the aged. Some States provide grant to voluntary organisations for maintenance of aged in these homes. At some places the old age pension due to the inmates is paid to the voluntary organisations for the upkeep of the aged. Besides, there are homes run by voluntary organisations without government assistance.

Assistance to voluntary organisations

Since 1983-4, the Ministry of Welfare is providing general grant-in-aid for assistance to voluntary organisations in the field of social welfare for (i) rendering welfare services to the aged and (ii) for constructing homes for the aged.

A scheme called welfare of the aged has been launched under the Eighth Five Year Plan (1992-7) marking the entry of the aged in Indian planning.

Welfare of the aged (under the Eighth Plan)

The scheme aims at encouraging voluntary organisations/ organisations of the elderly to provide old age homes, day care centres, medicare and non-institutional services for the aged by assisting through grant-in-aid.

Under the Old Age Home Programme, assistance will be available under the scheme for both maintenance and construction. Old age homes are expected to be residential units of the aged persons of 60 years and above. Old age homes are expected to take care of the physical and psychological well-being of its inmates with the help of trained social workers/counsellors and medical staff. Assistance for the building construction/extension of old age homes is also available under the programme for the grant of construction.

In addition to the old age homes, the scheme aims at providing assistance to voluntary organisations for setting up day care centres for the Aged. A day care centre should at least have 150 aged persons in its list so that even after drop-out and absenteeism, its daily attendance does not fall below 50. Day care centres should aim at gainful utilisation of the spare time of the elderly living in the neighbourhood and should appoint a part-time qualified physician for medical check-up and a full-time trained social worker. A day care centre is required to establish links with the medical, welfare and local institutions and services available in the area.

Under the Mobile Medicare Service Programme of the scheme, grants are available to voluntary organisations possessing experience and expertise in medicare services to the aged. Likewise, programmes can also be taken under the scheme for setting up or maintaining a foster care unit of 25 aged persons.

National Housing Policy

National Housing Policy has give due recognition to the special needs of the aged and the handicapped and has recommended construction of dwelling units with designs formulated to meet the specialised requirements of these categories. A large number of housing finance schemes have been formulated to subsidies the cost of housing for the priority groups. Government employees are encouraged to get house building loans at consessional rates during their service career.

Health care system

Providing a minimum package of primary health and medical services through the expansion of health care infrastructure has been country's first priority. Being an integral part of the overall population, the aged in rural, tribal and urban slum areas have been benefited by the expansion of health care infrastructure. In addition to these activities, voluntary organisations are being assisted to run special programmes for the health of the aged. Health insurance schemes such as Bhavishya Arogya and Mediclaim (by the General Insurance Corporation of India) also exist. Central Government Health Scheme facilities are now available to the retired central government pensioners.

Travel concessions and facilities

The Indian Railways provide 20 per cent concession in second class railway fare to every person aged 65 years and above for travel beyond 500 km. Free wheel-chairs are provided at all important and 'junction' stations to the aged and priority is given in the allotment of lower berths to passengers above 60 years of age. At large computerised reservation offices, a separate reservation counter is earmarked for the aged and handicapped persons. Some State Transport Corporation have provided for seat reservation in their buses for the aged persons. In most state transport buses entry for the aged is allowed from the exit door. Karnataka State Road Transport Corporation gives 50 per cent travel concession to the citizens aged over 60 years in city/sub-urban services during restricted hours.

The Inter Ministerial Committee set-up to formulate policy for the aged welfare was set-up by the government under the Chairmanship of Secretary (Welfare) with the representatives from Ministry of Labour, Department of Pensions, Ministry of Urban Development, Ministry of Rural Development, Ministry of Human Resource Development, Health Directorate, Department of Economic Affairs, Railway Board and Planning Commission. The terms of reference of this committee were:

(i) To examine the recommendations of the Round Table discussions of care of elderly sponsored by the Indian Council of Medical Research and other medical and family planning bodies and suggest ways and means of implementing them.

(ii) To consider the draft national policy on care of the elderly suggested by the Round Table discussions and suggest a policy frame for adoption.

(iii) To suggest programmes for the care and protection of the elderly in keeping with the changing socio-economic conditions as also for utilisation of their services and experiences with a view to supplement the income as also channellise their energies in community support activities.

After discussions and receipt of comments from the ministries and the institutions concerned, the following conclusions were arrived at:

1. Particular attention should be paid, in social security and social programmes, to the circumstances of the elderly women whose income is generally lower than men's and whose continuous employment has been broken up by maternity and family responsibilities. Structural inequalities of assets, savings, credit and income coupled with a narrow definition of what constitutes values ensures that women's work which is largely in the national and subsistence sectors remains under valued and uncounted.

   An important effect of the differential in life expectancy between men and women is that a high proportion of older women than men are widowed. Lone ageing increases with age and apart from serious economic dislocation and lack of effective kinship support, it has negative efforts upon physical and mental health.

2. Attempt should be made to facilitate participation of older persons in the economic life of the society by creating

conditions conducive to employment on a part-time or honorary basis in the unorganised sectors.

3. Measures should be taken to assist older persons to find or return to independent employment by creating new employment possibilities and facilitating training or retraining. The right of older workers to employment should be based on ability to perform the work rather than chronological age.

4. As for the aged persons who have acquired technical experience and expertise (having served the related field in the past), the aged may like to constitute voluntary employment bureau. The bureau may register the names of aged persons having specialised knowledge and experience. The bureau can undertake the job of maintaining contact with the employers, identifying the jobs suitable for the aged and place the aged in service.

5. Despite the significant unemployment problems facing the country (in particular with regard to young people) the retirement age for employees should not be lowered except on a voluntary basis.

6. Organisational framework and programmes at the Central and State level as recommended by the working group on special social problems for the Eighth Five Year Plan should be accepted for implementation including setting up of (i) National Board for Senior Citizens, (ii) National Institute for Senior Citizen, (iii) Formulation of policies and special programmes for schemes such as construction of homes for the elderly, maintenance of destitute elderly in homes, day care centres to improve the quality of life of elderly, foster care services for them, etc.

7. Constitute of Committee for Welfare of Senior Citizens at the State level.

8. As a basic human right, education must be available without discrimination to all. Realising that population of the 60

plus both for males (34.6 percent) and females (7.7 percent) is much lower than into the general population, educational policies should reflect the principle of the right to education of the aged through appropriate allocation of resources and through suitable education programmes devised for them. The need for continuing adult education at all levels should be recognised and encouraged.

9. Education departments need to be involved for ensuring that through curricular at school and college levels. The young are sensitised with the changing needs of the aged and their importance as integral parts of family and community. Non-formal channels and the mass media should be used to develop programme.

10. The financial and other social support should be provided through governmental and non-governmental programmes to the facilities, specially those belonging to the lower income group to help them to continue to maintain their elders.

11. The present policy of providing pensions only to destitute elderly is not conducive to the maintenance of the social structure. Prevention of destitution of the elderly by creating conditions conducive to the continuation of the elderly within the family fold is more important.

12. The aged should be encouraged to form their own voluntary organisations and co-operatives. These co-operative organisations should be helped by the government on priority basis under their programmes of grant-in-aid for undertaking social services.

13. Certain measures like preferential allocation of land for Group Housing Societies for the elderly, Housing Building Advances, repair and renovation advances at low rates, preference of ground floors to the elderly, etc., need to be integrated into the National Housing Policy and guidelines of the State Housing Board and Urban Development Departments. Welfare of the aged should be the focus of attention in the Urban Bank services programme of the

Urban Development Department.

14. A number of senior citizens are being asked to serve the public cause in their individual capacities. They may provide on the spot assistance to victims of crime and accidents and provide useful information for crime detection and prevention. They could escort individuals to police stations and hospitals and could intervene to check petty crimes like eve-teasing, chain-snatching which are so common these days. The Municipal Committees and Corporations in urban areas may like to register scuh persons and provide them identity cards.

15. Local bodies should construct group houses with common service to cater to the very specific needs of the elderly of all categories, viz., destitute, economically weak and those belonging to middle income group.

16. Flats and cottages should be built and rented out to senior citizens. The Tenancy Contract or Sale Agreement would be valid only for the lifetime of the elderly. L.I.C., Unit Trust of India, Housing and Urban Development Corporation, etc., should invest fund in the construction of senior citizens villages within 100 to 150 km away from the main cities. Necessary infrastructure facilities of transport, health and other services should be provided. Services of the senior citizens living in the villages should be linked with the development of the area. Arrangements should also be made to provide built up houses at affordable rents. The houses/ apartments should be specially designed provision support, guards, railings, lightings, etc., for convenient movement of the aged.

17. Special attention should be paid to evolve programmes and policy incentives for the unorganised sectors and the society which are not covered by the regular pension and other retirement benefits. These policies should be suitably formulated to attract people while they are still protective to plan for their future.

18. Elderly persons have to be provided recreational activities of their interest. This should be achieved by setting up of day care centres where the elderly may interact with the peers, articulate their needs, express their interests and participate in voluntary work. The opportunity to meet persons with commonality of interests and discuss common problems will lead to alleviation of emotional problems of the aged. It is recommended that the programme of day care centre for the elderly may be enlarged and day care centres set-up all over the country.

19. To cope with the emergent medical and psycho-social problems, greater emphasis needs to be given on geriatric medicine — both in teaching and in practice. For a detailed periodic medical examination of the elderly, comprehensive/total geriatric assessment. Units should be organised and incorporated with the primary health centres after due modification and training of their staffing pattern. These units may also be located in acture/long-term care hospitals.

    There should be separate geriatric OPDs in hospitals and least 5 percent beds be reserved for them.

    Big cities should be transit hospitals for the aged.

    In hospitals and dispensaries special counters and days in the week can be assigned to attend to their needs so that they are spared the exhaustion of standing in long queues in overcrowded hospitals.

20. Facilities of education and training should be available for doctors, paramedical staff and social workers from voluntary and government circles, to impart training in geriatrics and gerontology covering all aspects of old age aliments. Families should also be oriented on the health and nutrition needs of the elderly and ways to meet them through specially brought out information booklets the mass media.

25

Old Age Programmes and Policies in India

A case of Elders in Indian Railways

M.S. Kitchlu

THERE is a common saying that we know a thing well until we are asked to define it. The demand to define something in almost all cases is an exasperating demand. What is old age? It is the biblical one hundred and twenty or the four score and more years of Lear? The government considers a person old enough to retire at the age of 58. (You have reprieve of two years if you serve the Central Government.) The sociological expression of the phrase seems to carry a sense of disapproval and one sociologist thinks of defining them old by what they are not:

> They are not a deviant group or one small special section of the population. They are ordinary people who happen to have reached a particular age.
>
> — *The Elderly in Modern Society*, p. 8

He says that the most commonly accepted definition of the elderly is 'those over retirement age', i.e., 60 for a women and 65 for a man.

Who are the old?

Why is the study of old people important sociologically? The elderly are particularly interesting to study. Not only they are one of the largest of what are labelled 'special groups' but they are also the group to which in due time most people would belong. Unlike deviant groups such as offenders, or people with particular physical characteristics such as the disabled, the elderly present a cross-section of ordinary people whose sole common denominator is their age. Because they are such a large group and because most people will in time reach old age it is a matter of self-interest to consider their role in, and contribution to, society as well as their problems. Social gerontology is, debatably, one of the new segments of sociology, and one of the important angles of its interest in old people relates to the position of the old people in their time. This is something important in our consideration of the old people . . . and measures for them because it is something that determines our attitude to the old people as a separate group demanding special attention.

Social gerontologists are dealing with the historical period in which people live, the passage of time and its effects on people, the social meanings of the passage of time, and the perception of time within particular cultural settings.

To the extent that social gerontology studies 'old folks', it is attempting to see the effects of time, and since we are all vitally affected by the passage of time, we are, of course, interested in the findings. Ultimately, we are personally interested in how the passage of time affects us, and in a personal sense the study of social gerontology is really the study of ourselves. Students of ageing soon learn that we study older people not as a strange cult or a foreign culture but as future versions of ourselves as we move through time. The inevitable conclusion we reach is that older people are not 'them' but 'us'.

These are, however, general considerations. The fact is that for planning for the old people we have to take certain practical parameters, and that we could put our theoretical debates to use only in the practical handling (counselling, etc.) of such people. We get nowhere with statements like you are 'As old as you feel'.

Similarly, there is no point in talking about what old people are. Are they fountains of wisdom, bridges between generations, or in Shakespearean idiom, pitiable creatures' sans everything'? The general conceptions in this regard are misleading and contradictory. If one points out the traditional picture of the sagely wisdom of old people, another talks of imbecility that comes with age. (Recently, I came across a terrible description of somebody as having been 'precautious in nothing except imbecility'.) People who wax sentimental about the past speak of their elders who maintained wonderful health to their dying day but we see people who are sick and old, helpless if they did not have some companion. Sociological investigation shows that asssumptions (as usual) are contrary to facts. Psychiatrists like Keddie and geriatricians like Hodkinson feel that most old people suffer only from treatable diseases though the general idea is that old people are 'sick'.

Are the old to be a segregated group?

Our ideas of old age and what the old require keep changing, like everything else. Remaining youthful is today's obsession, and there is a lot in our advertisements which tell us how to 'remain young' at least at the surface level, cosmetically. There is little realisation that ageing is a process that has special characteristics only like any other stage in a life cycle has its own special characteristics.

It is unhealthy to think of old age and the aged as a generation or a race apart. If the old have their peculiar problems, adolescents have their own unique problems, and so do the middle-aged. When we tell our students some ancient crudities, like the habit that some tribes had of eating their elders and of throwing the old down feeding them to dogs, we sharply distinguish between tribes and civilisations. On the other hand, we say, 'civilised societies' the old were revered.

Our own sensitivity to the old is the product of our situation in history. Victor S. D' Souza and others have seen the modern condition in this way:

> An old person in the pre-industrical society was not at a disadvantage even when faced with the disability of old age. Status flowed from their inherent qualities which were divinely ordained. The older people filled positions of leadership because old age as such endowed people with leadership qualities of knowledge wisdom and virtue. The industrial economy depends upon effcient skills and modern

knolwedge which are the achieved attributes of individuals.

In the 1950s and 1960s the disengagement theory flourished. Sociologists thought of the ageing individual as one who recognised the inevitability of death, and started a process of advance adjustment to it. Such as individual is one who happily withdraws from a variety of roles as citizen, worker, parent, and turns in on himself. But this opinion (possibly stemming from Victorian conceptions) is discredited now.

Though middle-age is seen as a time for revaluation of self, ideas about ageing are less distinct. The disengagement theory of the 1950-60s not only felt ageing and disengagement to be normal but the best thing for society and the individual. It was this last assumption which has been discarded by modern gerontologists who had seen all too frequently the evidence of withdrawal and isolation and now took the view that the best thing for the individual and society was for the elderly and the aged to remain involved with life and living while they came to terms with the natural process of disengagement in their own time and in their own way.

A reference to these considerations is relevant in a discussion of the work that the government does for the old people because the way a society sees ageing has implications for social policy, as pointed out.

It is important to raise these questions about how society sees ageing because they have implications for social policy. The assumptions that 'the elderly' are a social problem, that they have similar aspirations and that they all need certain services are all questionable. Hugh Faulkner, in a letter to *The Times* (5-12-1972) said there is a frightening attitude creeping into the actions of some people caring for the elderly. While most bring true compassion and understanding to their work there are a vociferous few who regard those over retirement age as just a massive group of people who have to be coped with in the efficient manner.

In planning for the happiness and welfare of old people, we have to keep in mind the fact that neither the young nor the old should be made to feel that they are doing something special. When the aged are made to feel that they are 'required to adopt a somewhat passive role and to express a sense of gratitude for what is provided' they naturally feel a sense of alienation — they begin to feel that this is a 'youth-centred' society, that this is no country for the old.

There are two different kinds of old people. There are those who have some means of supporting themselves at least finacially; they have a pension or their savings and the only way in which they depend on other people is their emotional dependence or dependence forced on them by their health. Another category of old people consists of people who are destitutes in every way. To these people, help is intelligible only in terms of less dependence or even independence.

Another form of that the old feel in their special condition is the feeling that they are unwanted and that they have no place in the life of the community. 'If people feel that they have no role and they also feel dependent this may engender a sense of stigma' (The Elderly in Modern Society' p157) such people even want to establish the fact that they could be at the giving end, too.

All these are important considerations when we think of the old people and provisions for them. But this paper proposes to consider specially the programmes and principles in India relating to the old. The following points are made keeping in mind what has been said above.

The welfare state and principles relating to sections of the populations

THE HISTORY OF THE SCHEMES FOR THE AGED

Why is old age talked of so much at this time of the day? Old people have always been with all societies. If they could be assimilated without too much ado so long, why is there so much talk about them now? As far as the West is concerned, it is said that 'The elderly became a widely recognised and widely discussed 'social problem' for the first time in the late nineteenth century, i.e., from around the

1870s, not only in Britain but in many other countries. As late as 1982, the government of India could see the problem without too much excitement: In India the elderly have been traditionally assigned a place of honour and respect as exemplified by religion, social values and norms, and the social and economic organisation of society....

The obligation in the Indian family system to look after the elderly, to honour and respect them, continues to be discharged even today. There are, however, some emerging stresses and strains which in varying degrees, tend to increase the vulnerability of the old.

Pat Thane points out that the striking increase in the population of the old took place (in the West) after the First World War (due to obvious reasons). He relates the phenomenon of urgent concern with the old with three related processes in the last quarter of the ninetheenth century. First, it was realised that poverty is not just the result of individual improvidence but a complex of problems, secondly due to international industrial competition, employers desired to optimise productivity by maximising worker efficiency, and so workers found it difficult to retain their job as long as their health permitted. This led gradually to the notion of retirement around the age of 65. Thirdly, in particular localities there was a visible concentration of old people.

In England these were the reasons that prompted philanthropists, labour movement and employers to press for state pensions for the active aged. Some employers began providing occupational pensions. The state began running institutions where the 'deserving' could be given medical and other assistance. The beginnings of the old age pension in England is described thus:

> State pensions were introduced, after long discussion, in 1908, though with the utmost economy. They were very low. They were paid only the to the very old (to those aged 70 or above)... They were means tested, and people of previously bad character were excluded. They were non-contributory, financed directly from the exchequer.

This is how the idea, first, of state help for the aged, and second, for retirement benefits for the erstwhile regularly employed came into public consideration. Retirement of ageing workers for the sake of increasing employment for the younger people was thus the result of post-War conditions for England and many other Western countries. The idea was readily accepted in countries like ours which followed British models willingly.

However, the concept of pensions for people who have retired of old age has expanded with the years, and today pensioners enjoy many benefits. They are no longer insulted with meagre sums. As welfare state, government departments try to expand pension benefits in such a way that all the important aspects of an old person are attended to. In a way, these pension benefits, are extensions of benefits current employees enjoy. It is heartening to note that more and more sections of organised employees are brought under pension schemes. For instance, till recently bank employees did not have a pension scheme. Now they have been brought under contributory pension schemes. Not only that, a recent order has brought relief to people who retired before the pension scheme came into effect. This has brought relief to numerous very old people. More than the quantum of the pension, it is the gesture and the spirit behind it to these old people.

The great limitation of a state programme, however well-intentioned it be, is that it has its legal limitations, its formal limits. The state plan cannot go into individual cases. Its principles can be based only on generalities and precedents. It cannot afford to go into indiviudal cases.

The Welfare State has also got its financial limits. What it doles out cannot be much, given the conditions of a country like ours. Especially when a segment of the population for which the state plans happen to be an unorganised segment, the plans and the quantum are bound to be low. In the case of the people, for instance, the government of India wants to do something for the old in general, and the quantum of that help is certainly on the minimal level. The allowance given to old destitutes is indeed very small; its only merit is that something is better than nothing. But to the old people who come under the category of people who have retired from service in any department of the government get a far better treatment because their old age rests on the basis of a life-long employment in the department. Retirement benefits are also meant as things to help old people, but since they are given to organised segments of society, they are far better. Though this argument might appear harsh, the basic fact is that people who have retired are drawing on the present resources of a department which they served in the past: they get something from the income they do not now help in producing.

The Government of India's paper on the aged (1982) makes it clear that the Constitution of India makes certain mandatory provisions providing the framework for the steps to be taken for the elders of the population.

The Constitution of India recognises the duty of the State towards the elderly. According to Article 41:

> The State shall, within the limits of economic capacity and development, make effective provision for securing the right to work, to education, and to public assistance in cases of unemployment, old age, sickness and disablement, and in other cases of undeserved.

This provision in one of the directive principles of State Policy, which are considered fundamental in the governance of the country and 'it shall be the duty of the State to apply these principles in making laws' (Article 37). Section 125 of the Code of Criminal Procedure, 1973, requires every person having sufficient means to maintain his father or mother who are unable to maintain themselves. The Hindu Adoptions and Maintenance Act, 1956, lays down that it is the obligation of a person to maintain his or her aged or infirm parent (section 20 (3)).

The report says that several committees appointed by the government have gone into the question of helping the aged and many of their recommendations have been accepted by the government and have been acted upon. For instance:

The Study Group on Income and Wages (1978) recognised

> the needs of old persons not covered by pensions or other retirement benefits and suggested that there should be some standardisation of the criteria adopted by different states for giving old age pensions (non-contributory) to the destitute old.

The report concedes the

> Retired employees of the government and organised sectors of industry are comparatively better off as regards old age benefits. In government service retired employees are eligible for pension, gratuity, leave encashment and provident fund.
> -p.8
>
> The system of pensions to government employees was initiated by the enactment of the Pensions Act of 1871. Pension rules have been liberalised from time to time, and today pensions cover the dependent family members, family pension to the dependents of the deceased, which now makes special provisions for the seriously handicapped children of retired employees. The government also sees to it that the lives of the employees are insured. The employees, in their turn, make a contribution to the general provident fund the provisions of which are well enough known. Retired government employees can take up employment after superannuation. If they do it within two years of retirement they have to take the formal permission of the government to do so. Private enterprises are also under obligation to make provisions for retirement benfits to their employees.

Special mention is made in the report of the needs in health, housing, etc., for the aged people.

The Indian Railways

This paper looks into the arrangements the Indian Railways have made for the old age of its employees, as a case study. This department is the one that generates the largest income for the government, and it is also the department that employs the largest number of people: it has a workforce of 16.18 lakh as regular employees and nearly 2 lakh as casual labourers.

The employment strata in this department fall under the following pattern:

Group D (workshop and artisan staff)	5.16 lakh	32.17%
Running staff	1.02 lakh	6.36%
Group C	8.52 lakh	52.66%
Other categories	9.86	61.47%
Officers	0.16	0.82%

The ratio of officers to other employees works out to 1:141.

This huge structure, for the sake of effective administration, has been divided into nine zones and these nine zones are further divided into 59 divisions. The Madurai Division is one of the seven divisions in Southern Railways. It covers eleven districts of Tamil Nadu and two districts in Kerala. It caters to 40 per cent of the population in Tamil Nadu and 16 percent in Kerala. It has 11,459 employees in the categories of groups C and D, spread over fifteen departments, and they are controlled by 62 gazetted officials.

The pattern is mentioned here to suggest the structure in the other divisions and zones of the department because all the zones and divisions are governed by the same norms and rules.

Apart from the benefits mentioned in the governments report of 1982, many fresh benifits have been granted to the current and retired employees of the department (as is the case with other departments of the government). The following are the measures relating to the retired employees consequent upon the implementation of the recommendations of the Fifth Pay Commission (as on 12 November 1999).

1. *Revision of pension to ensure minimum of 50 per cent to pensioners and 30 per cent to family pensioners*: The successive Pay Commission recommendations (normally appointed every five years) have raised the emolumets of the staff manifold. Employees who retired before the recommendations of the Fifth Pay Commission were getting pensions according to

the last salary drawn by them. This meant that they got in some hard cases just a pittance. Considering the present conditions, the government has now provided that every retired employee should get a minimum of 50 percent of the present scale of his/her post.

It also provides that the family pension payable should be 30 percent of that scale. This shows how the concept of pension has broadened out, covering even the dependents of the retired employees.

2. *Extension of the Scheme of Widow Pass to the cases of Railway Servants who retired prior to 12th March, 1987*: Earlier, this scheme was applicable only to widows of those who retired from service after 12th March, 1987. Now the widows of employees who retired before that date are also given these passes on a one-time lump sum payment of Rs. 250.

3. *Family pension to parents*: Whereas earlier regulations limited the family pension to the wife and children of the employees, the revised regulations entitle parents of such employees who are wholly dependent of 30 percent of basic pay. Divorced sisters are also now included in the list of dependent relative for eligibility for Pass/PTO.

4. First class post-retirement pass holders are now allowed to have a companion with them with the option of travelling II class/SL class.

5. From 1st December, 1997, a medical allowance of Rs.100 per month is allowed to retired employees families living outside the limits of city/town/municipality where Railway Hospitals 1/4 Health Units 1/4 Dispensaries are situated. All medical facilities now available to employees are open to retired employees.

The age of retirement has now been raised from 58 to 60.

The statistics (as on 30th September, 1999) relating to the beneficiaries of the RECHS/RELHS are given below:

RECHS: Retired Employees Contributory Health Scheme (in this scheme 40 per cent of the cost of medical treatment should be provided by the retired employee.

RELHS: Retired Railway Employees Liberal Health Scheme (this is almost free treatment as out patients without payment).

Total number of RELH registration	1236*
Total number of beneficiaries	2952**
Total number of RECHS registrations	3
Total number of RECHS beneficiaries	6
Total number of Railway population in Madurai	55,000
Total number of Railway employees in Madurai	11.000

* includes spouses

** includes children

Conclusion

Yet plans and provisions are pious intentions. Everything depends on the spirit with which they are implemented. Pensioners do not have the clout for negotiated (agitated!) settlements that current employees have. Those who deal with these issues should have the humanity not to use that to their advantage, as a tool for pressurising. The pensioner should not be made to feel an unequal partner in the deal.

The railway and most central government departments normally have a reputation for the quick settlement of such bills. The amount due to a retiree by way of gratuity is paid to him on the evening of his retirement, if he keeps no unsettled bills to the department on his part. The provident fund is also settled very expeditiously, within a week at the latest pension fixation is said to take about a month.

A cheering spectacle in this division is that the retired employees have a union uncontaminated by class, communal feelings. Some of the dedicated and knowledgeable members present themselves everyday near the railway division office to help pensioners prepare their petitions, etc. Their help is most needed in matters like the issue of passes refixation of pensions, etc., and such help is rendered with goodwill.

It is evident that this department, has a very good framework for service to the elders, it is said that most central government departments have it, too.

References

Achenbaum, W.A,1978, *Old Age in the new land,* John Hopkins Press.

Blau, 2.3, 1973, *Old Age in Changing Society* , Franklin Work.

Mlcoy, Peter, 1980, *Towards a strategy for services to the Elderly in Suffolk,* Suffolck County Council.

Nagla, B.K. *Ageing and Health,* pp. 96-117

Thane, P., 1978, *The Muddled History of retirement* at 60 and 65, New society August

Thane, P., 1978, *Contributory vs. Non-Contributory old age pensions 1878-1908 in pat Thaned.* Origins of British Social Policy, Croom Helm, London.

Townsend, P., 1968, in Shanes, E, Townsend, P. Old People in Three Industrial Socities Routledge, London.

The Aged in India, World Assembly on Ageing Vienna 26 July 6 August 1982, Ministry of Social Welfare, Government of India, New Delhi.

List of Contributors

P.K.B. NAYAR is the Chairman, Centre for Gerontological Studies Trivandrum, Kerala.

L. THARA BHAI is Professor in the Department of Sociology, Madurai Kamaraj University, Madurai, Tamil Nadu.

M. THAVAMANI is Reader in the Department of Sociology, Bharathidasan University, Tiruchy, Tamil Nadu.

T. KARUNAKARAN is lecturer in the P.G. Department of Sociology, Madura College, Madurai 11.

D. SELVARAJU is Professor & Head in the Department of Sociology, Annamalai University, Tamil Nadu.

A. MURUGAN is working as a doctoral fellow in the Department of Sociology, Annamalai University, Tamil Nadu.

R. SRIDHARAN is Selection Grade Lecturer in the Dept. of Sociology, P.M.T. College, Usilampatti, Tamil Nadu.

KALARANI RENGASAMY is in the faculty of School of Economics, Madurai Kamaraj University, Madurai, Tamil Nadu.

C.R.W. DAVID is the Director, Unemployed Young People Association, Madurai, Tamil Nadu.

D. SIVAKUMAR is a Research Investigator in the Population Research Centre, University of Kerala, Kerala.

B. SUGUNA is a Lecturer in the Department of Women's Studies, S.P. Mahila Viswa Vidhyalaya, Tirupathi, Andhra Pradesh.

G. SANDHYA RANI is Lecturer in the Department of Women's Studies, S.P. Mahila Viswa Vidhyalaya, Tirupathi, Andhra Pradesh.

R. MOORTHY is a Lecturer in the Department of R.D.S. Arulandur College, Karumathur, Tamil Nadu.

R. SANKAR is Professor & Head in the Department of Sociology, Bharathidasan University, Thiruchirapalli, Tamil Nadu.

PADMA MOHANAN is Associate Professor in the Department of Community Medicine, Kasturiba Medical College, Mangalore, Karnataka.

USHA JOHN is a Selection Grade Lecturer in the Department of Social Work, Loyala College Trivandrum, Kerala.

JONI C. JOSEPH is a Selection Grade Lecturer in the Department of Sociology of the Zamorin's Guruvaurappan College, Calicut.

C. KARUPPIAH is Lecturer in the Department of Sociology, Madurai Kamaraj University, Madurai, Tamil Nadu.

S. IRUDHAYA RAJAN is a faculty member in the Centre for Development Studies, Kerala.

L. PACKIAM is Head, Department of Sociology, Fatima College Madurai, Tamil Nadu.

I. SOBHA is Lecturer in the Department of Women's Studies S.P. Mahila Viswa Vidhyalaya, Tirupathi, Andhra Pradesh.

VIJAYALAKSHMI RAMAMOHAN is a Training Co-ordinator as Rastriya Seva Samithi Tirupathi.

M.S.N. REDDY is working as Professor in the Department of Sociology, Sri Venkateswara University, Thirupathi.

JACOB JOHN KATTAKAYAM is Director Academic Staff College, University of Kerala, Kerala.

ADHINARAYANA is Professor in the Department of Population Studies, Bharadiyar University, Coimbatore.

J. SHEELA is working as a Research Scholar, Department of Population Studies, Bharadiyar University, Coimbatore.

N. KAVITHA is working as a Research Scholar, Department of Population Studies, Bharadiyar University, Coimbatore.

B. DHARMALINGAM is Research Officer, Centre for Women's Studies, Alagappa University, Karaikudi, Tamil Nadu.

K.R. MURUGAN is working as Research Assistant in the Centre for Women's Studies Alagappa University, Karaikkudi.

R. MANGAYARKARASU is a faculty in the Department of Political Science, Madurai Kamaraj University, Madurai, Tamil Nadu.

N. SARASWATHY is Reader in the School of Economics, Madurai Kamaraj University, Madurai, Tamil Nadu.

M.S. KITCHLU is a faculty in the Department of Sociology, Madura College, Madurai, Tamil Nadu.

Subject Index

Name Index